How to Do
Everything

Netbook

Joli Ballew

New York Chicago San Francisco Lisbon
London Madrid Mexico City Milan New Delhi
San Juan Seoul Singapore Sydney Toronto

The McGraw-Hill Companies

Cataloging-in-Publication Data is on file with the Library of Congress

McGraw-Hill books are available at special quantity discounts to use as premiums and sales promotions, or for use in corporate training programs. To contact a representative, please e-mail us at bulksales@mcgraw-hill.com.

How to Do Everything: Netbook

1 2 3 4 5 6 7 8 9 0   WFR WFR   0 1 9

ISBN   978-0-07-163956-9
MHID   0-07-163956-X

Sponsoring Editor Roger Stewart	**Technical Editor** Robin Noelle	**Composition** Glyph International
Editorial Supervisor Patty Mon	**Copy Editor** Andy Saff	**Illustration** Glyph International
Project Manager Vipra Fauzdar, Glyph International	**Proofreader** Julie Searls	**Art Director, Cover** Jeff Weeks
Acquisitions Coordinator Joya Anthony	**Indexer** Ted Laux	**Cover Designer** Jeff Weeks
	Production Supervisor George Anderson	

For Mom, I miss you deeply.

About the Author

Joli Ballew is a technical author, a technology trainer, and web site manager in Dallas, Texas, USA. She holds several certifications, including MCSE, MCTS, and MCDST. In addition to writing, she occasionally teaches computer classes at the local junior college and works as a network administrator and web designer for North Texas Graphics. She has written three dozen plus books, including many in Pearson Education's Brilliant and In Simple Steps series. In her free time, she enjoys golfing, yard work, exercising at the local gym, reading, watching disaster movies on the Science Fiction channel, and teaching her cat, Pico, tricks, as time allows.

Joli welcomes all correspondence and can be contacted at Joli_Ballew@hotmail.com.

About the Technical Editor

Robin Noelle is a professional writer with more than 12 years experience in the fields of marketing and public relations. Having worked for five years at two leading high-technology public relations agencies, Noelle has collaborated with a variety of clients, from fledgling Internet startup companies to market leaders such as Microsoft and IBM/Lotus. She has written for all facets of the technology industry, including technical FAQs, corporate biographies, tips and tricks, press releases, and case studies.

She is an expert user of many current software products, including Adobe Photoshop CS, Microsoft Office, Wordpress, multiplatform IRC programs, gaming systems, and all social networking platforms.

Contents

PART III   Installing and Using Hardware and Software

Acknowledgments

The older I get and the more books I write, the more people there are to thank and acknowledge. I am thankful for many things, including the opportunities offered by McGraw-Hill Education every time there is a new Windows edition, and the awesome team of editors and print setters who work tirelessly to turn my words into pages and those pages into books. These people include Roger Stewart, Joya Anthony, Robin Noelle, Laura Blake, Katy Robinson, and everyone else at McGraw-Hill who helped bring this book to publication.

I am thankful that I have a supportive family, including Jennifer, Andrew, Dad, and Cosmo. I am thankful to my extended family for all playing a role in my daughter's upbringing and success, and for my health, much to the credit of my doctor, Kyle Molen. Between the lot of them, they keep me in check, on track, healthy, and sometimes even sound.

I miss my mother, who passed away in February of 2009, but I am thankful that someday I will be able to see and talk to her again, something she worked hard to make me understand shortly after she passed away.

And finally, I am thankful to my agent, Neil Salkind, who encourages me, is my biggest fan, and who always has my back, no matter what. Everyone should have someone like that in their lives.

Introduction

If you have a netbook, you know how convenient it is to carry it with you, as well as how easy it is to use. Netbooks are especially handy when you need to edit a Word document or Excel spreadsheet, update your Facebook status, upload photos to the Web, collaborate with others online, look up directions, or send and receive e-mail on the go. But, are you getting the most you can from your netbook? Probably not, and that is what this book is all about. As you will learn here, there is much more you can do to work smarter, be safer, and connect with others more easily.

As you are aware, a netbook is a smaller and less powerful version of the larger laptops you are familiar with. The thing that sets apart the netbook the most, of course, is just that—its smaller size. You can carry a netbook with you just about anywhere you want to go, in your purse or a small bag, and with the netbook's built-in Wi-Fi, you can remain connected to the Internet all the time. A netbook is not a laptop, though; netbooks just are not big enough to have 4GB of RAM, and they do not have a CD or DVD drive, so there *are* drawbacks. Because of this, you have to learn to use the resources you do have access to more effectively.

For example, because of its small size, a netbook is more likely to get lost, stolen, or damaged than a larger laptop. Therefore, you really need to get used to using web-based software such as Windows Live Essentials, Live Workspace, or Google Apps. Learning to store important data in online servers will allow you to keep that data safe *and* also allow access from any other computers you use. As a bonus, it also saves space on your hard drive.

Your netbook has limited resources, too—for instance, you may only have 1GB of RAM. You will want to choose your web browser and software wisely to work within those limitations. It is important to learn how to get the most out of the resources you have by limiting what programs run in the background, how many programs you run concurrently, and what you download from the Internet.

You will have to learn a few workarounds too. For instance, if you must install a software program that you can access only from a CD or DVD, and you do not have a CD or DVD drive installed on the netbook, you will have to understand your options. Finally, you will learn how to connect to all kinds of networks, including free Wi-Fi, secured Wi-Fi, Ethernet, and even a stand-alone PC.

What Does This Book Cover?

Chapter 1, "Getting to Know Your Netbook," helps you identify the parts of your netbook, including the available ports, and find out what operating system is installed and how to use the keyboard and touchpad. It is important to know what operating system you are using, because throughout the book, as operating system–specific tasks are introduced, instructions will be included for the various editions of Windows as well as explanations of how to locate the items in Linux.

Chapter 2, "Safety First," shows you how to configure user accounts and apply passwords, configure a password-protected screen saver, delete web browser data such as cookies and passwords, configure a firewall, and install anti-virus software. These actions, when combined, will help protect your personal data should your netbook become lost or stolen.

Chapter 3, "Find and Connect to Public Wireless Networks and Wi-Fi Hotspots," introduces you to free Wi-Fi hotspots and explains how to find them and then how to connect. Once connected, you will learn how to manage the Wi-Fi networks you use often and delete ones you no longer use, and how to set security options when first connecting to a network.

Chapter 4, "Connect to a Wired Ethernet Network," explains how to connect to Ethernet networks. There will be cases where no Wi-Fi is available but Ethernet is, such as in a home or small office. You will also learn how to connect to a workgroup to access data on the local network, if applicable.

Chapter 5, "Make a Direct Connection with a Stand-Alone PC," shows you how to connect to the Internet using a single PC. You may encounter this situation at your parent's house where only one PC exists and connects to the Internet via dial-up or cable modem, or, in a rural area where there is no Wi-Fi available. Once connected to the stand-alone PC, you can also access data on that PC, if desired.

Chapter 6, "Connect with a Satellite Provider," outlines the best possible option for connecting to the Internet via your netbook. By signing up with a satellite provider—such as AT&T, for instance—you can have always-on Internet connectivity. The upside is that you are always connected; the downside is the monthly cost. This chapter shows you how to choose, how to install the USB satellite card, and how to connect once the hardware and software are installed.

Chapter 7, "Surfing the Internet," offers options for browsing the Web. Here, Internet Explorer, Firefox, Safari, Opera, and Google Chrome are introduced. While each company claims its web browser is faster than anyone else's, there is no definitive proof that one is better than the other. The trick is to run the web browser *cleanly*, with as few add-ons as possible. You will learn about that as well as the pros and cons of each browser.

Chapter 8, "Add New Hardware," shows you how to connect additional hardware to your netbook, such as portable printers, USB drives, and backup devices.

Chapter 9, "Install Software," offers various options for installing software onto your netbook. There are lots of options, including locating the software online, copying the files to an external drive, sharing a CD/DVD drive on another computer and connecting to it via a network, and more.

Chapter 10, "Web Cameras and Video Messaging," teaches you how to use your web cam to video conference with others. You will need to download and install a messaging program, configure the camera to work with it, add a contact, and start a video conversation. Although netbooks come with web cams, they do not come with the software you need to hold a video conversation (in most instances).

Chapter 11, "Expand Your Netbook with Accessories," shows you how to use ReadyBoost, a feature available in Windows Vista and Windows 7 that can help your computer run faster by allowing you to use a USB memory stick as RAM, and how to use the same hardware to add hard drive space. You may also choose to purchase an additional battery, add a GPS receiver, use a Wi-Fi finder, get an all-in-one AC adapter, or purchase other accessories.

Chapter 12, "An Introduction to Windows Live Services," introduces you to the free web-based Live programs available from Microsoft. Specifically, you will learn about Live Messenger, Live Mail, Live Photo Gallery, Live Toolbar, and other Live offerings.

Chapter 13, "An Introduction to Office Live Workspace," introduces you to the free web-based workspace programs available from Microsoft. You will learn how to get a Live ID, create a workspace, and share documents on online servers. With this program, you will be able to save data to an online server and access it from any computer or share the space with others for collaboration.

Chapter 14, "An Introduction to Google Apps," introduces you to the free Google Apps, including Google Calendar, Google Docs, and others. As with Microsoft Live and Workspace, you can use the space to store data online or to share it with others.

Chapter 15, "An Introduction to OpenOffice.org," introduces the Open Office programs generally preinstalled on Linux netbooks. Open Office is free for anyone to use, and is a good alternative for those who do not want to pay for Microsoft Office or use web-based applications.

Chapter 16, "Additional Web-Based Applications to Try," shows you a few of the free online and web-based applications available to you, the netbook user. You might enjoy playing games on Kongregate, watching TV on Hulu, using Zimbra Desktop, creating a schedule with Yahoo! Calendar, or storing data online at Box.net, among other applications.

Chapter 17, "An Introduction to Windows 7," teaches you how to get up to speed quickly with Windows 7. You will learn about the new Start menu and Taskbar, how to personalize Windows 7, how to connect to wireless networks, and more. This is a crash course on Windows 7.

PART I

Getting Started

1

Getting to Know Your Netbook

HOW TO...

- Locate and use external components
- Identify your operating system
- Use the keyboard and touchpad
- Maintain the battery
- Locate and turn the wireless LAN on/off switch

Congratulations on your new netbook! You're going to love its size and portability and the ability to go online seamlessly wherever there's free Wi-Fi. You can surf the Web, send and receive e-mail and instant messages, and check out Facebook, Twitter, and YouTube to your heart's content. There's a lot more to your netbook, though; for instance, your netbook has a complete operating system and is just as functional as a full-size laptop. You can personalize it with desktop backgrounds and screen savers, store and share data, watch videos, and listen to music. It offers USB, serial, and media ports, and you can install third-party programs, alternate web browsers, and take advantage of online applications. You can access your private home network, corporate networks, and Wi-Fi networks in coffeehouses, hotels, and libraries too.

Netbooks do have limitations, though. You'll find you need to remain aware of its limited battery life, which is often under three hours, and you'll have to get used to the smaller keyboard. Since there's no CD or DVD drive, you'll have to have a plan in place to install applications from CDs and DVDs, and you'll need to keep the number of applications you run simultaneously to a minimum to conserve RAM. These limitations will not stop you from enjoying your netbook, though, I can guarantee you that! Figure 1-1 shows a netbook.

FIGURE 1-1   Netbooks are small and portable.

Locate and Use External Components

Your netbook has most of the external components you'd expect to see in a laptop. There are always USB ports for connecting digital cameras, printers, external CD/DVD drives, flash drives, and scanners, and there's always a battery bay. There are usually ports for plugging in headphones and speakers, connecting to an Ethernet (wired) network, and, most of the time, a media card slot (reader) and a web cam. Sometimes you'll even find a FireWire port or an option to connect to an external monitor, such as a projector.

USB Ports

USB ports let you connect USB devices. The most common devices you'll connect are digital cameras, printers, thumb or flash drives, and external CD/DVD drives. To locate your USB ports and connect USB devices:

1. Place your netbook on a desk or table.
2. Look for USB ports at the front, back, and sides of the netbook.
3. Use the USB cable to connect the device to the port.

If you connect a device that has not previously been installed, you may have to install the device driver or other software before the device can be used. This poses a problem because the required software for most devices is often on a CD or DVD, and netbooks don't come with CD or DVD drives. If this happens, refer to Chapter 10, "Install an Application Stored on a CD or DVD."

Power Button

All netbooks come with a Power button. For the most part, the Power button is accessible only after you open the netbook's lid. Your netbook's Power button may work differently from the one on your PC, Mac, or laptop, though.

In most cases, a netbook's Power button is preconfigured to shut the netbook down safely. Sometimes, pressing the Power button may put the netbook to "sleep," place it on "standby," or cause it to "hibernate," though, so you'll want to read your netbook's user's guide to be sure. Whatever the case, you'll press the Power button to turn the netbook on.

 Although you have to use the Power button to turn the netbook on, you can often simply shut the lid of the netbook to shut it down or have it stand by.

 Read the manual that came with your netbook to find out what the Power button does by default when you press it.

Depending on the netbook manufacturer and operating system, there is an assortment of options regarding what happens when you press the Power button while the computer is on (or close the netbook's lid while the computer is on). You can access these options from the Power options on your netbook. As shown in Figure 1-2, you may see one or more of the following:

- Do nothing
- Ask me what to do
- Stand by
- Hibernate
- Sleep
- Shut down

 Figure 1-2 shows the Power Options Properties dialog box for a netbook running Windows XP. Your netbook may be running Windows Vista, Windows 7, or Linux.

 It's difficult to state exactly what Hibernate, Sleep, and Stand By mean for your specific netbook, because these terms are often used fairly loosely by computer manufacturers. For the most part, though, Stand By allows a computer to awaken faster than Hibernate or Sleep.

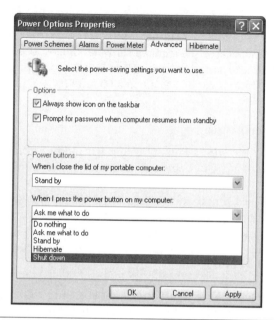

FIGURE 1-2 You can configure what happens when you press the Power button or close the netbook's lid.

Speakers, Headphones, and Microphone Ports

Most netbooks come with ports that allow you to connect speakers, a microphone, or headphones, although in most instances these features are built into the netbook, making attaching additional devices unnecessary. These additional ports can be pink or green, but are occasionally other colors. You should see icons next to each that offer an explanation of what type of port it is. Here's an example. You may want to use these ports to connect a headset for clearer audio during a web cam conversation.

Tip Most of the time, you can plug speakers into the headphone port (or vice versa), and they'll work just fine.

To see what sound ports are available on your netbook:

1. Place the netbook on a desk or table.
2. Look for sound ports on the sides, back, and front of the netbook.
3. If applicable, plug in a microphone, speakers, or headphones.

Note Generally, speakers, headphones, and microphones install automatically.

Media Card Reader

A media card reader is a slot that allows you to insert a media card. These media cards are the same ones you use in your digital camera. To use the slot, simply insert the card, and when prompted, choose what you'd like to do.

To locate and use your media card reader:

1. Locate your media card reader. It is a small slot on the outside of the netbook.
2. Insert your memory card.

The memory card may insert all the way or only partially. Do not force the card farther than it should go.

3. When prompted, select an option. (See Figure 1-3.)

The options you see when you insert a media card will differ depending on what operating system is installed on your netbook.

Additional Ports and Features

You'll find additional ports and features on the outside of your netbook. These include but are not limited to Ethernet, the battery bay, and FireWire. You may also see a button that allows you to turn Wi-Fi off and on without opening the netbook's lid.

FIGURE 1-3   In all Windows-based netbooks, you'll see options for viewing what's on your memory card.

Turn On and Off Wireless LAN Functionality

When your netbook's Wi-Fi capabilities are enabled, the netbook is constantly searching for available networks. If you don't need to be online or connected to a network, you can turn off Wi-Fi to save battery power.

Look for these features:

- **Ethernet** An Ethernet port allows you to connect your netbook physically to a network using an Ethernet cable. An Ethernet port is the same shape as a telephone outlet, but is slightly larger. When you insert the cable, it snaps into place.
- **Battery Bay** The battery bay is generally on the bottom or the back of the netbook, and there are often instructions on inserting or connected the battery there too. You'll need to install the battery when you first get your netbook, and plug it into a wall outlet to charge it.
- **FireWire** A FireWire port is a small port you can use to connect FireWire devices such as digital video (DV) cameras. FireWire is much faster than USB and should be used when available.
- **Wi-Fi** A Wi-Fi button allows you to turn the netbook's Wi-Fi capabilities on or off. Turn off Wi-Fi when you do not need to connect to a wireless network or the Internet to save battery power. You may also have to turn off Wi-Fi when you're in an airplane. You'll be informed of the airline's policies before takeoff. As shown in Figure 1-4, you'll be informed (at least in Windows XP and Vista) when you are connected to a wireless network.

Tip You won't be informed of, receive pop-ups about, or be able to connect to wireless networks if the Wi-Fi button is in its off position.

FIGURE 1-4 A prompt like this shows that Wi-Fi is enabled and that you are connected to a wireless network.

Identify Your Operating System

Depending on your netbook's make, model, and manufacturer, you will have one of several operating systems. The most common are Microsoft Windows XP, Microsoft Windows Vista, Microsoft Windows 7, and various Linux editions (Ubuntu versions are very popular). If you aren't sure what operating system you have, work through the following steps to find out.

1. If you're running an earlier version of Windows, click the Start button. Then:
   a. Right-click My Computer, shown in Figure 1-5.
   b. Click Properties.
   c. Under System, you'll see what version of Windows XP is installed.
2. If your netbook has a round button with the Windows logo on it, click it. Then:
   a. Right-click Computer, shown in Figure 1-6.
   b. Click Properties.
   c. Read the information presented to see what version of Windows Vista or Windows 7 you have.

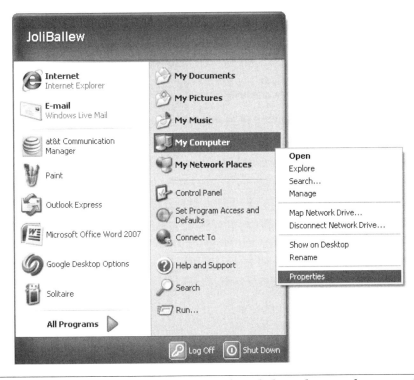

FIGURE 1-5   If you see something like this after clicking the Start button and right-clicking My Computer, you're running a version of Windows XP.

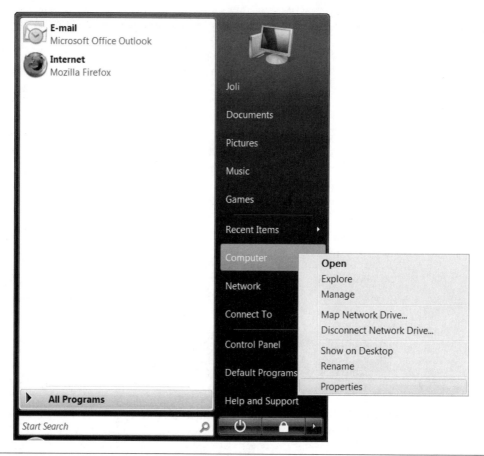

FIGURE 1-6 If your Start menu looks something like this, then you're running a version of Windows Vista or Windows 7.

3. If your netbook has tabs, offers a toolbar across the top or bottom of the desktop, or has a Start menu that does not resemble Figures 1-5 or 1-6, it's most likely some form of Linux. Look for Computer, System, System Information, or something similar for more information (see Figure 1-7).

 Linux comes in lots of versions, and thus Linux desktops differ depending on the manufacturer and version of Linux installed.

Explore Microsoft Windows XP

Microsoft Windows XP is an older, stable operating system and is often preferred over Windows Vista for netbooks because of its lower system requirements. You can explore Windows XP by clicking the Start button. The Windows XP Start button and menu were shown earlier in Figure 1-5.

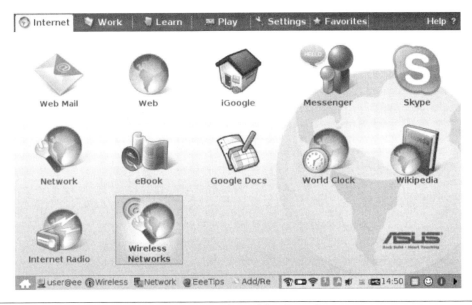

FIGURE 1-7   If your screen looks something like this, then you're running a version of Linux.

To get started with Windows XP, click and explore the following Start menu options:

- **Internet**   Click Internet to open Internet Explorer. Internet Explorer is a web browser you can use to surf the Internet.
- **E-mail**   Click E-mail to open Outlook Express. Outlook Express is the default program for working with e-mail in Windows XP.
- **All Programs**   Click All Programs to view and access the programs and accessories installed on your Windows XP netbook.
- **My Documents and My Pictures**   Click either to open your personal Documents and Pictures folders.
- **My Computer**   Click My Computer to view information about your computer, including installed hard drives, user files, devices with removable storage, scanners and cameras, and more.
- **My Network Places**   Click to see network resources, including shared files, and to add a network place, view network connections, set up a network, view workgroup computers, and more.
- **Connect To**   Click to connect to available networks, including wireless networks.
- **Control Panel**   Click Control Panel to personalize your netbook, add hardware, add or remove software, set folder options, configure Internet options, change power options, access the Security Center, and more.
- **Help and Support**   Click to get help on anything about Windows XP.
- **Search**   Click Search to look for files, programs, and more.

Explore Microsoft Windows Vista

Microsoft Windows Vista is also an operating system. Windows Vista is newer than Windows XP and older than Windows 7. Netbooks that have sufficient resources can run Windows Vista, but for the most part, Windows Vista is not installed on netbooks because of its demanding system requirements. You can explore Windows Vista by clicking the Start button and selecting any item on it (see Figure 1-8).

To get started with Windows Vista, click and explore the following Start menu options:

- **Start Search**   Click inside the Start Search window, and then type the name of any file, folder, or word in an e-mail to see the results. Start Search is not included in Windows Vista. (In Figure 1-9, you can see what happens when I type **Joli** into the Start Search window.)
- **Internet**   Click Internet to open Internet Explorer. Internet Explorer is a web browser you can use to surf the Internet.

FIGURE 1-8   Click the Start button in Windows Vista to access installed programs, Games, Network, Control Panel, and Help and Support.

FIGURE 1-9   The Start Search window lets you search for any data type quickly and easily.

- **E-mail**   Click E-mail to open Windows Mail. Mail is the default program for working with e-mail in Windows Vista.
- **All Programs**   Click All Programs to view and access the programs and accessories installed on your Windows Vista netbook.
- **Documents, Pictures, Music**   Click to open your personal Documents, Pictures, and Music folders.
- **Games**   Click to open the games that come with Windows Vista plus any installed by the netbook manufacturer.
- **Computer**   Click Computer to view information about your computer, including installed hard drives, user files, devices with removable storage, scanners and cameras, and more.
- **Network**   Click to see the computers on the network, access the Network and Sharing Center, add a wireless device, and more.
- **Connect To**   Click to connect to available networks including wireless networks.
- **Control Panel**   Click Control Panel to personalize your netbook, add hardware, add or remove software, set folder options, configure Internet options, change power options, access the Security Center, and more.
- **Help and Support**   Click to get help on anything about Windows Vista.

Explore Microsoft Windows 7

Microsoft Windows 7 is also an operating system. Windows 7 is the newest Microsoft operating system (see Figure 1-10). Because Windows 7 utilizes resources better than Windows Vista, it's becoming a popular option for netbook manufacturers. You can explore Windows 7 by clicking the Start button and selecting any item on it.

To get started with Windows 7, click and explore the following Start menu options:

- **Search Programs and Files** Click inside the Search Programs and Files window and then type the name of any file, folder, or word in an e-mail to see the results. Start Search is not included in Windows XP.
- **All Programs** Click All Programs to view and access the programs and accessories installed on your Windows 7 netbook.
- **Documents, Pictures, Music** Click to open your personal Documents, Pictures, and Music folders.
- **Games** Click to open the games that come with Windows 7 plus any installed by the netbook manufacturer.
- **Computer** Click Computer to view information about your computer, including installed hard drives, user files, devices with removable storage, scanners and cameras, and more.

FIGURE 1-10 As with Windows XP and Windows Vista, Windows 7 offers familiar options, including Shut Down, Log Off, and Restart.

- **Connect To**   Click to connect to available networks, including wireless networks.
- **Control Panel**   Click Control Panel to personalize your netbook, add hardware, add or remove software, set folder options, configure Internet options, change power options, access the Security Center, and more.
- **Help and Support**   Click to get help on anything about Windows 7.

 The options on the left side of the Start menu change based on how often you use them. The most recently used and most often used programs are listed.

Explore Linux

The edition of Linux installed on your netbook is one of many available versions. Linux comes in many flavors including but not limited to Ubuntu and Gnome, with both of those having myriad editions of their own. For instance, Ubuntu offers Ubuntu Ultimate, Ubuntu Brown, and even Ubuntu Christian Edition, to name only a few. Exploring Linux, then, mostly requires you click tabs, menus, and desktop icons to see what's available, as there's often not a traditional "Start menu" like the one you see in Microsoft XP, Vista, and Windows 7. Figure 1-11 shows a popular Linux desktop configuration.

For the most part, the tabs, menus, icons, and other Linux features are self-explanatory:

- **Internet**   An Internet option usually offers a place to access web mail, go online, use Skype, access networks, and listen to Internet radio.
- **Work**   The Work tab offers access to applications such as Open Office, the Documents folder, File Managers, and other work-related tools.

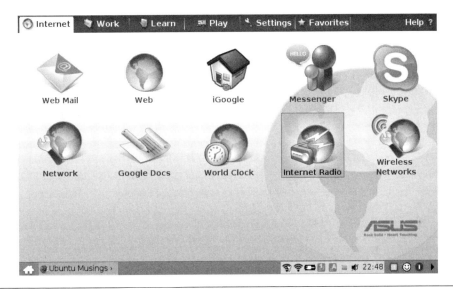

FIGURE 1-11   Linux editions often have tabs you click instead of a traditional Start button.

- **Learn**   The Learn tab offers access to dictionaries, a thesaurus, an encyclopedia, links to web sites such as BrightHub or Wikipedia, and other resources.
- **Play**   The Play tab offers games, of course.

 Manufacturers almost always add their own touches. The Learn or Play options on your netbook may not match the Learn or Play options on another. (In fact, another Linux netbook may not even have Learn or Play tabs!)

- **Settings, Favorites, and others**   The Settings tab lets you change how your version of Linux looks, how files are handled, and what happens when you close the lid or press the Power button, while the Favorites option lets you manage your favorite network places. As noted, Linux versions and netbooks differ greatly, and what you see here may not look like what you see on your netbook.

 At the time this book was published, Apple had yet to produce a netbook. The MacBook Air, while thin, is not technically a netbook. For that reason, the Macintosh operating system (OS) is not covered here.

Learn More

There are lots of ways to learn more about your netbook's operating system. You can:

- Access Help and Support from the XP, Vista, or Windows 7 Start menu. Figure 1-12 shows the Windows Vista Help and Support Center.

FIGURE 1-12   The Help and Support Center in Windows Vista offers options for getting help and support.

- Purchase books online or in bookstores.
- Visit web sites such as Microsoft.com, Linux.org, BrightHub.com, or Support .Microsoft.com.
- Ask a friend, child, or grandchild.

Use the Keyboard and Touchpad

Your netbook has a keyboard and some type of pointing device. Most of the time, the pointing device is a touchpad, although you can connect a USB mouse if you prefer. Your netbook has specialty keys too. One of those is the FN key, which allows you to perform functions by pressing a key combination (such as changing volume or brightness). To get the most from your netbook, you need to be aware of these features and any additional features outlined in your user guide.

FN

The FN key lets you access secondary or alternate key functions. A key has an alternate function if it has a letter, symbol, or number in one color and an additional icon, word, or letter in another. Figure 1-13 shows an example. Pressing the F2 key in this instance will perform a specific function on its own; it may be a shortcut to a command such as Rename, Copy, or Paste, for instance. But when the key also has a second icon and you hold down the FN key and press this key together, you can access the secondary function. In this instance, holding down FN and pressing F2 will open a window that shows the status of the battery and open the Power Options dialog box.

 Tip   You can often hold down the FN key and press the UP ARROW button to increase the volume, or, hold down the FN key and press the DOWN ARROW button to decrease it.

To use the FN key to perform a function:

1. Locate the FN key on the keyboard. Note its color.
2. Press and hold the FN key.
3. Locate the UP ARROW key, DOWN ARROW key, or F1, F2, F3, or similar key that contains an alternate function.
4. While still holding the FN key, press the alternate function key. Your netbook will perform the function.

FIGURE 1-13   This key has a secondary function that can be accessed only by holding down the FN key while pressing this one.

Double-Tap and Left- and Right-Click

The touchpad on your netbook is a pointing device, like a mouse. You move the on-screen mouse pointer by dragging your finger across the touchpad in the direction you want the mouse pointer to move. You can also single-tap and double-tap the touchpad to highlight or select items. You can use the left and right buttons included with the touchpad to left- and right-click.

Most netbooks offer additional touchpad features. For instance, placing your first finger and thumb in the center of the touchpad and moving them outward in a stretching motion (while keeping both fingers on the touchpad) often zooms in on what you're viewing. Doing the reverse zooms out.

In addition to these basic touchpad techniques, you can often:

- Hold down the left button to select a window and move your finger across the touchpad to move the selected window.
- Press the right button to access contextual menus.
- Press the left button quickly two times to execute a command.
- Press the left button in a document, spreadsheet, or other data sheet and move your finger across the touchpad to copy data.
- Right-click to paste copied data.

Keyboard Shortcuts

As with desktop keyboards and laptops, there are keyboard shortcuts. Pressing the Windows key in combination with other keys allows you to perform various tasks, including opening the Start menu or Control Panel or even minimizing all windows.

 Refer to your user's manual for more information about keyboard shortcuts.

You may also have hotkeys. A list of these is included in your user guide or on the manufacturer's web site. You may want to try these key combinations to see what happens:

- FN + F1   This key combination often opens help for the open application, but may also open the netbook's user guide.
- FN + <**arrow keys**>   This key combination often changes the display brightness or the volume up or down.
- FN + <**a specific function key**>   Combining the FN key with various function keys such as F2, F3, and F4 often toggles computer functions on and off such as the speaker or display, or are shortcuts for putting the computer to sleep or disabling and enabling Wi-Fi functionality.

 For more information about key combinations, how to use the touchpad, or keyboard shortcuts, click Start and Search and type **User Guide.** This guide will help you get the most from your new netbook.

Maintain the Battery

It's important to take care of your battery to prolong its life. There are several things you can do to lengthen the life of your netbook's battery:

- Allow the battery to discharge (drain) completely three or four times a year, but avoid consistent and frequent full discharges, as this puts a strain on the battery.
- Don't leave the netbook plugged into an electrical outlet for long periods of time (days or weeks). This will keep the battery in a constant state of "charging up" and will wear out the battery faster.
- Understand that the battery can be charged only a specific number of times. Therefore, use each charge wisely. You may want to remove the battery when you plan to leave the netbook plugged in for a long time.
- Keep your netbook safe from high temperatures or extremely low ones. Avoid leaving your netbook in a hot car, for instance.
- When removing a battery, store the battery at 40 percent charge in a cool, dry place.
- Avoid purchasing spare batteries, unless you're sure you'll use them. Batteries do have a manufacturing date, and those dates will pass.

Turn the Wireless LAN Feature On or Off

When your netbook's wireless LAN feature is enabled, it is constantly searching for available wireless networks. This uses battery power, so if you aren't looking to join a wireless network you can turn off this feature. There are other reasons to turn off the wireless LAN capability:

- To stop pop-up notification about available wireless networks.
- To use your netbook on an airplane without interfering with the navigational system (once it's OK to use electronic devices).
- To lessen how often you have to plug in your netbook to recharge the battery, which in turn will lengthen the life of the battery.
- To know you will not be automatically connected to familiar wireless networks once in range.

Because netbooks are created by many different computer manufacturers, it's difficult to say how you will turn off your netbook's wireless capabilities. However, you'll likely find a switch or button on the outside of the netbook, and/or a keyboard key or key combination inside the netbook. You may have a function key (F1, F2, F3) that serves this purpose, or, you may have to press a specialized key on the keyboard. If you can't find it, refer to your user's manual.

2

Safety First

You'll want to keep your new netbook safe to protect your investment, your data, and your personal information. There are lots of ways to do this, including but not limited to registering the components, configuring a user account and password, deleting sensitive data, configuring a firewall, and using anti-virus software. When combined, these precautions can go a long way toward keeping your netbook safe.

Activate and Register Components

If you've chosen a netbook that runs a Microsoft operating system such as Windows XP, Windows Vista, or Windows 7, the first thing you will want to do after turning on your netbook is activate it. Activation is a mandatory part of owning a Microsoft product and proves to Microsoft that you own a valid copy of the operating system. (Activation also holds true for Apple products, although at the time this book was written, Apple had not yet released a netbook of its own.) Linux also requires activation of a sort, which involves agreeing to some terms and conditions.

You may also choose to register your netbook or its components with the companies involved in creating those components. This may mean registering the operating system, an office suite, or even the netbook itself. Don't be surprised if you're prompted to register with Acer, ASUS, Dell, Hewlett-Packard, or another computer manufacturer along with software components such as Microsoft Office or Adobe.

In general, activation is mandatory while registration is not.

To activate a Microsoft product:

1. During setup, choose Activate Now if it is presented. Often, this will happen the first time you use the computer.

If you are connected to the Internet, activation will be automatic.

2. If you are not connected to the Internet, a phone number may be provided during setup. Call this number if you do not have a connection to the Internet or do not plan to connect within 30 days.
3. If you delay activating a product, you will be prompted each time you use it. Alternatively, locate and use an activation button as shown in Figure 2-1. In this example, Microsoft Office is being activated.

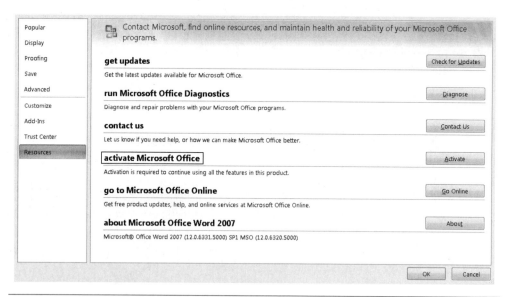

FIGURE 2-1   Activation is almost always mandatory.

OS Activation Is Mandatory

If you do not activate a Windows operating system such as Windows XP, Windows Vista, or Windows 7 within 30 days, the operating system will not let you do anything until you complete the activation process.

Registration is generally part of any activation process, but it is not mandatory (see Figure 2-2). If you'd like to receive software updates, receive e-mails regarding the product, or enable its warranty, you'll want to register it. Be advised, though, that registration may result in spam from the company or manufacturer and is generally not required for warranty purposes (no matter what the larger print says).

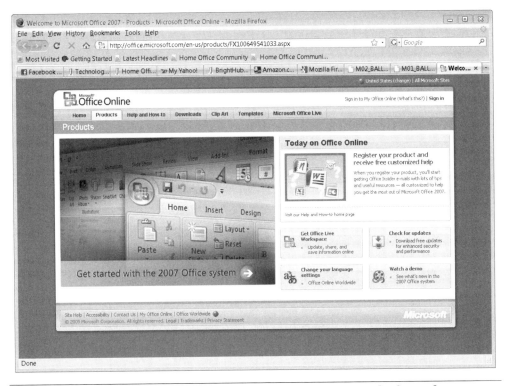

FIGURE 2-2   Register a product to receive updates, e-mail, and other information about the product regularly.

Using the Guest Account

The Guest account is part of all Windows operating systems. Turn on the Guest account when someone needs to use your computer for a short time. Log off, and then let the guest log on using the Guest account. Turn off the Guest account when it is no longer needed.

Configure a User Account

It's important to create a user account (and apply a password) for yourself and anyone else who uses the netbook. When user accounts are in place, each user logs on and logs off when he or she needs access to the netbook instead of sharing a single logon account. With accounts, each user then has his or her own settings, his or her own data folders, and his or her own preferences. Figure 2-3 shows a Windows XP netbook with a single account, JoliBallew, and a default Guest account that is turned off. Notice there's an option to create a new account under Pick a task....

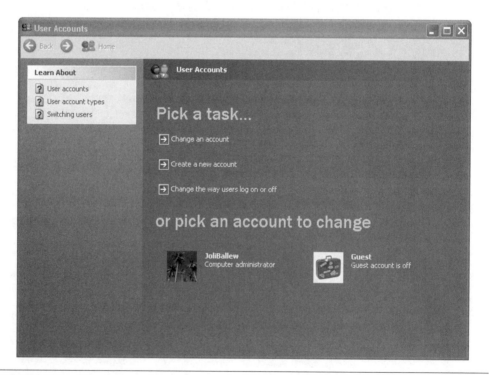

FIGURE 2-3   User accounts can be created in Control Panel in Windows XP.

Why Create a Password?

Password-protected accounts can help secure your netbook if it is ever stolen or if an unwanted guest, coworker, or family member tries to use it. Anyone who tries to access the computer will have to log in, which means he or she will have to know your password!

You, as an "administrator," can also define what other users can and can't do, such as installing programs, accessing personal or shared data, and making changes to the computer that affect all users on it. This helps protect a user from unintentionally causing the computer harm. To do this, create a "standard" or "limited" account for a user you want to have access. You should have the only "administrator" account.

The process of creating an account is different for each operating system. In all Windows products, you use Control Panel. In Linux, it's often achieved from the System tab, the System menu, or an Administration option. For the sake of reaching as many readers as possible, here's how to create a user account in Windows Vista:

1. Click Start, then click Control Panel.
2. Click User Accounts and Family Safety (see Figure 2-4).

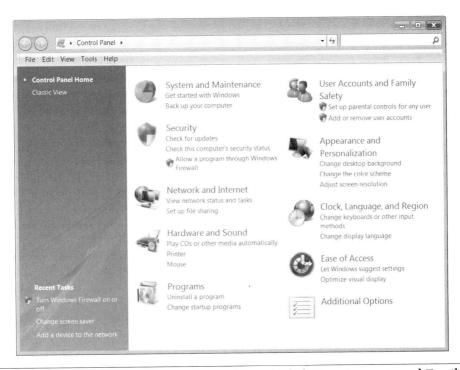

FIGURE 2-4   In Windows Vista, in Control Panel, click User Accounts and Family Safety.

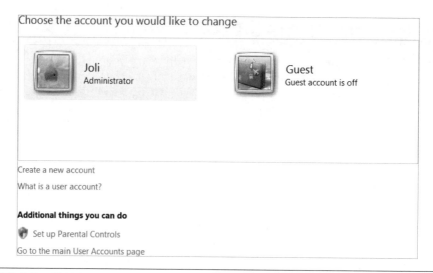

Choose the account you would like to change

Joli
Administrator

Guest
Guest account is off

Create a new account

What is a user account?

Additional things you can do

Set up Parental Controls

Go to the main User Accounts page

FIGURE 2-5 Create a new user account. Note that the existing account is an Administrator account.

3. Click Add or remove user accounts.
4. Click Create a new account (see Figure 2-5).
5. Type the new account name, select Standard user, and click Create Account (see Figure 2-6).

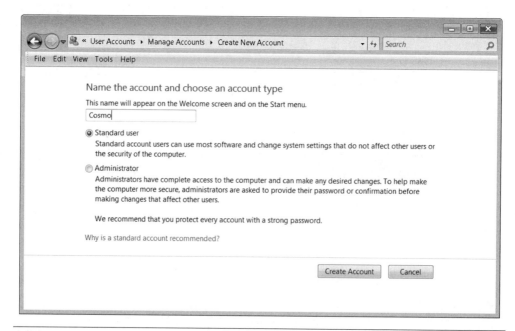

« User Accounts ▸ Manage Accounts ▸ Create New Account

File   Edit   View   Tools   Help

Name the account and choose an account type

This name will appear on the Welcome screen and on the Start menu.

Cosmo

⦿ Standard user
Standard account users can use most software and change system settings that do not affect other users or the security of the computer.

◯ Administrator
Administrators have complete access to the computer and can make any desired changes. To help make the computer more secure, administrators are asked to provide their password or confirmation before making changes that affect other users.

We recommend that you protect every account with a strong password.

Why is a standard account recommended?

Create Account   Cancel

FIGURE 2-6 Create a standard user for all secondary accounts so you can remain the only administrator of the netbook.

By default, no password is created during account creation. Refer to the next section to apply a password to each account on the netbook, especially your own.

Set a Strong Password

It doesn't do any good to create a user account if you do not assign a password to it and to all the other accounts on the netbook. Here's why. Say you create a standard user account for your daughter, assign her a password, and set parental controls allowing her to log on between 5 p.m. and 7 p.m., but you do not assign a password to your own administrator account. She can easily log on to your account any time she wants and do whatever she wants, because your account is not password-protected (and it's an administrator account). Therefore, it's important to assign a password to every account on the netbook and leave the Guest account turned off until needed.

 Avoid passwords that people you know might be able to figure out. These include pet names, birthdays, or your children's names. In fact, it's best to include upper- and lowercase letters and a couple of numbers in your passwords for the best security.

 Parental controls are part of Windows Vista and Windows 7, but are not built into Windows XP or Linux systems.

 Always log off of your account when you are finished using the computer. If you don't log off, anyone can use your user account to access your data and the netbook.

To create a password for an account in Windows XP (and steps are similar in Vista and Windows 7):

1. Click Start, then click Control Panel.
2. Click User Accounts (see Figure 2-7).
3. Click Change an account and select the account to which you want to assign a password.
4. Click Create a password. The screen shown in Figure 2-8 appears.

 A "strong" password is one that contains uppercase and lowercase letters, numbers, and symbols.

5. Type a new password, confirm it, and type a password hint.

 Don't forget your password; you won't be able to log in without it.

6. Click Create Password.

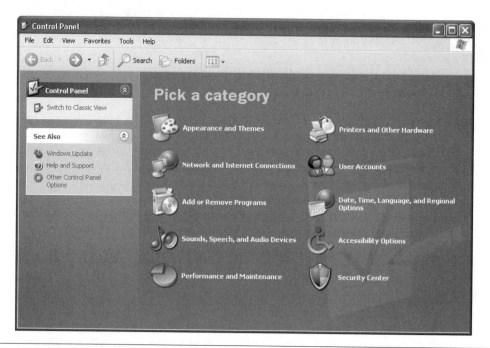

FIGURE 2-7   Click User Accounts to access the accounts on the netbook.

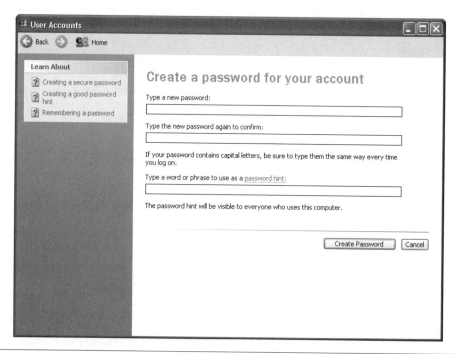

FIGURE 2-8   Create a password in Windows XP for your account or any Standard account.

Apply a Password-Protected Screen Saver

A screen saver is a moving animation or a set of images that appears after a period of inactivity that you set. The screen saver disappears when you move the mouse or press a key on the keyboard. It used to be that a screen saver prevented monitor "burn-in" of the image on the desktop, but that is no longer the case. Now screen savers are used aesthetically, but also to secure the computer by hiding the data on the desktop and/or requiring a password when the screen saver is disabled and the computer is brought out of screen saver mode.

Screen savers are applied through "properties," "appearance," "personalization," "preferences," or "customization" options. If you're running a version of Linux, you'll have to look through these kinds of tabs and menus to find the settings. An example is shown in Figure 2-9.

Windows screen savers can be applied under Display Properties in Windows XP and Appearance and Personalization options in Windows Vista and Windows 7 (see Figures 2-10 and 2-11). You can access all of this and more from Control Panel.

To apply a password-protected screen saver in Windows Vista:

1. Click Start, then click Control Panel.
2. Click Appearance and Personalization.
3. Click Change screen saver.

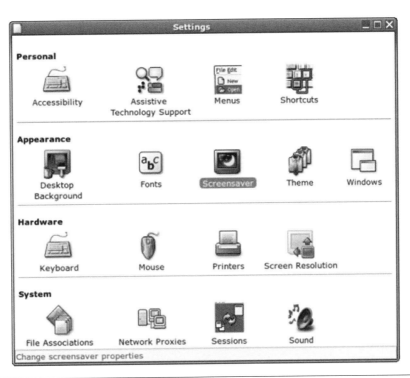

FIGURE 2-9   Linux screen savers may be applied through appearance settings.

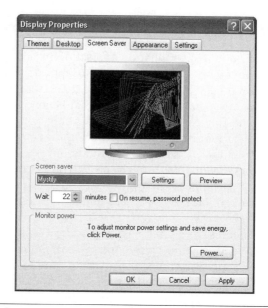

FIGURE 2-10   Windows XP screen savers are applied through Display Properties.

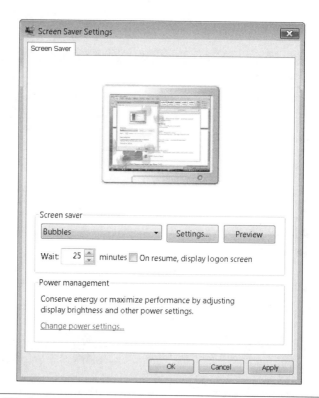

FIGURE 2-11   Windows Vista screen savers are applied through Control Panel,
Appearance and Personalization, and Screen Saver Settings.

FIGURE 2-12   Select On resume, display logon on screen to apply a password-protected screen saver.

4. Select a screen saver from the drop-down list.
5. Type the amount of idle time before the screen saver is applied.
6. Select On resume, display logon screen (see Figure 2-12).

 You must have a password applied to your account to make this a secure screen saver and to require a password on wake up.

Delete Internet Explorer Data

When you surf the Internet, no matter what web browser you use, you leave "footprints" (traces) of where you've been and what you've done on the Internet. This data can include the names and URLs of the web sites you visited, the types of data you viewed, login information (including usernames and passwords), and data you typed into online forms (including but not limited to your address, phone number,

What Are Cookies?

Cookies are small text files that contain information that defines who you are and what products you prefer when you visit a web site. For instance, it's what allows www.amazon.com to know to put "Hi, Joli!" at the top of each Amazon web page. (For more information on what types of files web browsers save, refer to the next "Did You Know?" box.)

and zip code). Internet Explorer and other web browsers keep this information so that web pages you've previously visited will load faster the next time you visit them, so that you don't have to keep typing in the same information into web forms, and to improve your web experience by personalizing web pages you visit.

Most of the time, this is acceptable, especially if you do not share the computer, you have a password-protected account, and you strive to keep the computer physically safe. Unfortunately, netbooks are easier to lose (or have stolen) than desktop computers, and if your online data is not protected adequately, it can become a security risk. To reduce this risk, you may opt to delete the data that Internet Explorer saves. I suggest deleting Internet Explorer data before traveling, anytime you will share the netbook without logging off of it, or any other instance where the netbook will be out of your physical proximity for a length of time. To delete Internet Explorer data:

1. If the Tools menu is not available, press the ALT key on the keyboard.
2. Click Tools, and click Delete Browsing History (see Figure 2-13).
3. Click each option as desired to delete the associated files (see Figure 2-14).
4. Click Close when finished.

FIGURE 2-13 The Tools menu in Internet Explorer offers the option to delete your browsing history.

FIGURE 2-14 You control what types of data to delete in Internet Explorer 7 and 8.

Delete Firefox Data

Firefox is a web browser similar to Internet Explorer. As with Internet Explorer and other browsers, Firefox keeps records of where you've been and what you've done on the Internet. The data saved can include URLs of the web sites you visited, images, login information, and form data. Firefox keeps this information so that web pages you've previously visited will load faster the next time you visit them, so that you don't have to keep typing in the same information into web forms, and to improve your web experience by personalizing web pages you visit.

Most of the time, this is acceptable, especially if you do not share the computer, you have a password-protected account, and you strive to keep the computer physically safe. Unfortunately, netbooks are easier to lose (or have stolen) than desktop computers, and if your online data is not protected adequately, it can become a security risk. Firefox can make you especially vulnerable, because it offers the option to remember passwords, and thus you can log in automatically to any web site you've logged in to before, if you select this option. This means that if someone steals your computer, you use Firefox, and you've told it to save your passwords, the thief has immediate access to your online accounts. (Internet Explorer makes you type in the password, even if you choose to save passwords.) As with Internet Explorer,

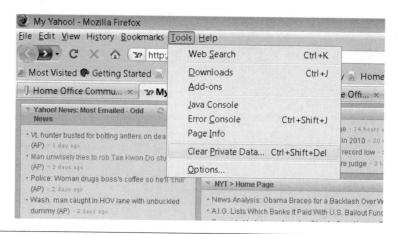

FIGURE 2-15   Firefox offers a Tools option to clear your private data.

you should delete this data before traveling or when you feel your netbook is at risk of unauthorized access:

1. Click Tools, then click Clear Private Data (see Figure 2-15).
2. Select the items to clear, then click Clear Private Data Now (see Figure 2-16).

 Other web browsers such as Google's Chrome, Apple's Safari, and Opera offer similar features.

FIGURE 2-16   Clear private data in Firefox to protect your online identity.

What Is Browsing History?

Browsing History is a list of web sites you've previously visited; Download History is a list of files you've downloaded; Saved Form and Search History is a list of phrases you have entered in text fields, used in web searches, and typed in name and address fields; Cache consists of temporary files such as web pages and images; Cookies are files created by web sites that store your preferences for the site; Offline Website Data is information web sites have stored on your computer for use without an Internet connection; Saved Passwords are usernames and passwords you have told Firefox to remember; Authenticated Sessions keep you logged in to secure web sites when you have already used the password manager when logging in to them.

Configure a Firewall

Most netbooks come with some sort of a firewall, as the operating system generally has one built in. Firewalls monitor incoming and outgoing data and decide whether it is good data or bad. A firewall will block harmful data from entering or leaving the computer, and will let good data pass without incident.

All Windows operating systems have a firewall, and it's turned on by default. You can turn it off or tweak it if you desire. Linux (Ubuntu) comes with a firewall too (called iptables), although it's difficult to configure and to learn to use. If you want to learn more about Linux firewalls and you'd like to play around with iptables, consider Firestarter or Firewall Builder. These are programs that can help you configure a firewall on Linux more easily.

If you purchased a Linux netbook, you may be rethinking that decision. Microsoft products are easier to use, have more features, and require less technical expertise to configure. If you desire a Microsoft netbook, consider selling your Linux netbook on eBay and replacing it with one running a Microsoft operating system.

View XP's Firewall Settings

To view and configure the firewall in Windows XP:

1. Click Start, then click Control Panel.
2. In Control Panel, click Security Center.
3. In Security Center, under Manage security settings for:, click Windows Firewall (see Figure 2-17).
4. Verify the firewall is on, and if it is not, select On (see Figure 2-18).
5. Click OK.

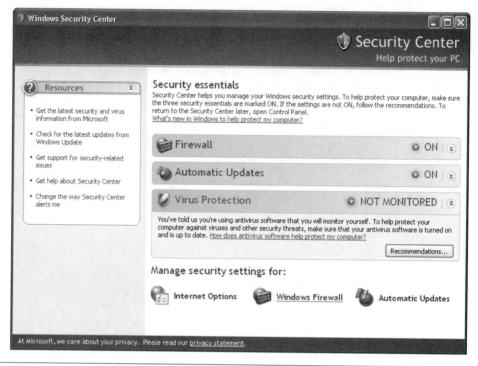

FIGURE 2-17   The Security Center in Windows XP lets you access the firewall settings.

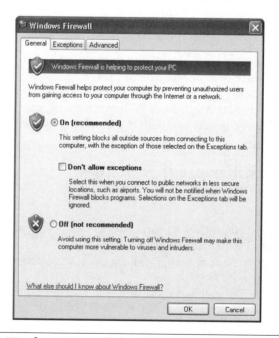

FIGURE 2-18   The Windows Firewall should be turned on.

Click the Exceptions tab and the Advanced tab to see additional settings for the firewall. You should not need to configure anything here, as it will be changed automatically at your request when you try to access these kinds of data.

View the Firewall Settings for Windows Vista and Windows 7

Both Windows Vista and Windows 7 offer a firewall, and both can be accessed from Control Panel, just as in Windows XP. However, the interface for Vista and 7 differ greatly from that of Windows XP, although the end result is the same. To view firewall settings for Windows Vista or Windows 7:

1. Click Start, then click Control Panel.
2. Click Security in Vista or System and Security in Windows 7 (see Figure 2-19).
3. In Windows 7, click Windows Firewall.
4. Click Turn Windows Firewall on or off.
5. Make the desired changes as shown in Figure 2-20.
6. Click OK.

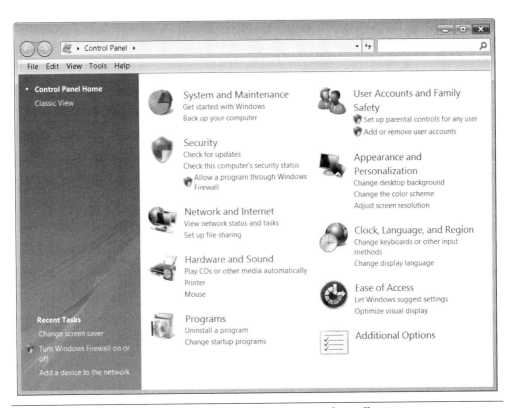

FIGURE 2-19   Click Security in Windows Vista to access firewall settings.

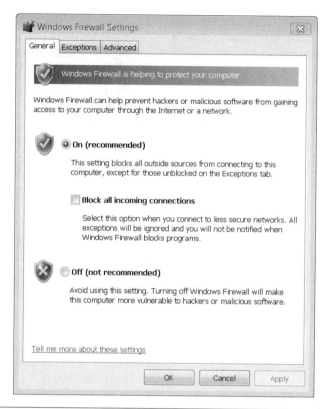

FIGURE 2-20   The Windows 7 firewall offers these choices; Vista's firewall looks like XP's and is shown in Figure 2-18.

Use Anti-Virus Software

Windows, Linux, and Apple products do not come with built-in anti-virus software. Most come with some sort of firewall, and Windows offers Windows Defender (for malware), but none comes with its own anti-virus program. It's up to you to purchase and install anti-virus software yourself.

There are lots of anti-virus options you can pay for, including subscription services such as Windows Live OneCare, Symantec's Norton, and McAfee's Internet Security, but there are several good free options too. One is AVG Free, available at http://free.avg.com. Whatever you decide, you'll need to download the product or order a CD, install the product, and configure the settings.

The general consensus on Linux computers is that you don't need anti-virus software. However, I believe all computers, no matter what operating systems they use, should have anti-virus software.

Download and Install the Product

It's becoming more and more common to download anti-virus software from the Internet instead of going to a store and purchasing the software you need on a CD or DVD (or purchasing from Amazon or a similar eStore). This is especially true for netbook users, because netbooks don't come with a CD or DVD player for installing that kind of media. If you purchase anti-virus software on a CD, you'll have to install it from a shared network drive, which adds another couple of steps to the process. That said, it's best to choose an anti-virus software package you can download from a reliable Internet web site, pay for it if necessary, and install it without a CD or DVD drive.

 In the following example, I'll download and install AVG Free, a very popular (and free) anti-virus program.

To download and install AVG Free Anti-Virus:

1. Open your web browser and go to http://free.avg.com/ as shown in Figure 2-21.

 Make sure to download the "free" edition! Other editions are available.

2. Locate the Download Now, Get It Now, or Download button for AVG Anti-Virus Free Edition. (The actual button name can change over time.)

FIGURE 2-21 Choose the edition you want to install—in this case, the free edition—and click Download Now.

3. If applicable, select the free edition and/or click Download. Note that you may have to click Download Now on another page if prompted to do so.

 On almost every page you'll encounter, you'll be prompted to "upgrade," download additional software, purchase additional features, and more. If you want to download the free edition and nothing else, be careful!

4. Click Save File in Firefox, shown in Figure 2-22, or click Save in Internet Explorer, shown in Figure 2-23. (In Internet Explorer, you'll have to click Save one more time, in the Save As dialog box.)

 If you're using Opera on Linux, choose AVG Free Linux and follow the prompts in Opera to download and install the product.

5. In Firefox, double-click the file in the file list to start the installation; in Internet Explorer, click Run, then click Run again.
6. Click Next as prompted to install the product. Note that the default options are generally fine, and installation is only a matter of working through the required installation pages.

Configure the Product

Once you've downloaded and installed AVG Free—or any other anti-virus program, for that matter—you'll need to configure it. Configuration tasks differ depending on the application, but for the most part, all you have to do is work through a group of configuration pages and choose the settings you want. The default settings are often fine, but you should still work through the pages carefully.

Here are a few things you can and should configure:

- **Daily scanning** Enable daily scanning to keep your computer free from viruses and other Internet threats. When configuring this feature, choose a time when the computer will be on but you will not be using it.
- **Information sharing** If prompted to share information about threats detected on your machine, do so. This will help make the application stronger and better in future editions. No personally identifiable information will be obtained from you.

FIGURE 2-22   Save the file to your hard drive using Firefox.

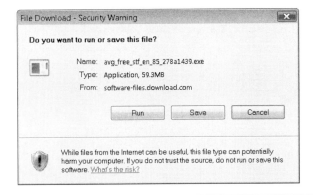

FIGURE 2-23   Save the file to your hard drive using Internet Explorer.

- **Check for updates to the software**   Agree to have the anti-virus program check for program updates as often as suggested.
- **Register**   You may need to register to receive technical support for free editions of anti-virus software. If prompted to register, read the fine print carefully and register the product if desired.
- **Check for virus definitions**   If prompted, agree to let the program check daily or weekly for updated virus definitions.
- **Double-check settings weekly**   Open the program at least once a week to verify everything is properly configured and that you are protected (see Figure 2-24).

FIGURE 2-24   Open the anti-virus program to verify you are protected.

PART II

Connecting to the Internet

3

Find and Connect to Public Wireless Networks and Wi-Fi Hotspots

HOW TO...

- Find a free Wi-Fi hotspot
- View available wireless networks and connect to them manually
- Connect to a public network automatically
- Change the order of listed wireless networks
- Manage the wireless network list
- Know what network types to trust

By far, connecting to the Internet for free, from anywhere, without having to lug around a huge laptop, is the best part of having a netbook. Just bring your netbook with you into a coffee shop, library, hotel lobby, or café, open the lid, and get connected. Almost all of these places have free Wi-Fi and you can easily take advantage of it. In this chapter, you'll learn how to connect to free hotspots, how to manage those connections, and how to stay safe while on public and private networks.

Find a Free Wi-Fi Hotspot

Although there are several ways to find a free Wi-Fi hotspot, by far the easiest is to go to a web site that offers a Wi-Fi search function, such as www.jiwire.com/. At sites like these, you can select a state or input a zip code and use the results to find the hotspot closest to you. Figure 3-1 shows the results after searching Seattle, Washington.

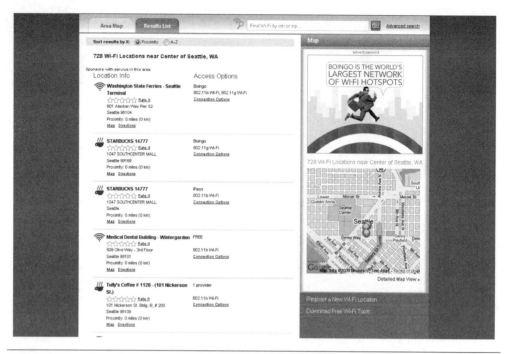

FIGURE 3-1   Search for free Wi-Fi hotspots on the Internet at sites such as jiwire.

Here are some other ways to find free Wi-Fi:

- Call City Hall to find hotspots in libraries and other public places.
- Purchase a Wi-Fi finder, a device that detects wireless networks. If a network is detected and you're in a public place, you can open your netbook and log on (if it's a free, public Wi-Fi hotspot).
- Install a Wi-Fi finder application on your phone. There are several applications available.
- Visit a place known for free Wi-Fi, such as Starbucks or a local library, then open your netbook and see if you can log on. If you're prompted for a key or passcode, ask an employee. Common keys include 1234567890 and 0123456789.

View Available Wireless Networks and Connect to Them Manually

You can view available wireless networks in any operating system, be it Windows XP, Windows Vista, Windows 7, or Linux. Most of the time, you'll find the list of available wireless networks in Network, Network Connections, Wireless Networks, or a similar folder. Figure 3-2 shows the Wireless Networks folder on a Linux netbook.

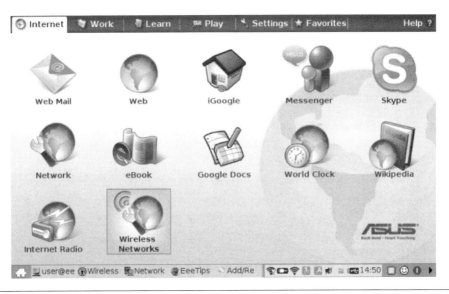

FIGURE 3-2   On a Linux netbook, look for a Wireless Networks option.

Once you have access to the list of available wireless networks, it is easy to connect to them, provided you have the proper credentials. For the most part, you simply click the network you want to connect to and click Connect.

Windows XP

To view a list of available wireless networks in Windows XP and connect to one, you can use the Network Connections option, available from Control Panel (this is one of many ways to access Network Connections). When you open the Network Connections window, you'll see an icon for a wireless connection. A connection may or may not be configured. Figure 3-3 shows a wireless network connection that is connected and configured and the result of right-clicking that icon. Note the option to view available wireless networks.

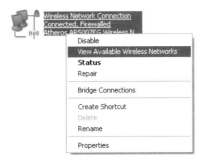

FIGURE 3-3   Right-click the wireless network connection icon in the Network Connections window in Windows XP to view available wireless networks.

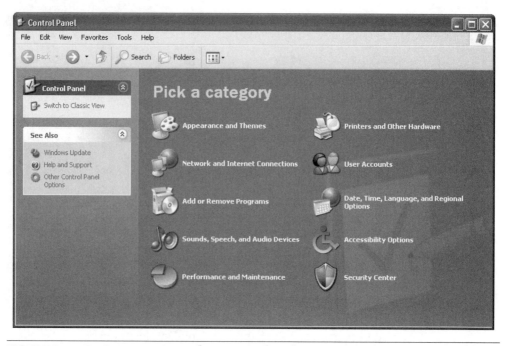

FIGURE 3-4　In Category view, select Network and Internet Connections. (In Classic View, click Network Connections.)

To view available wireless networks in Windows XP and connect to one manually:

1. Click Start, then click Control Panel.
2. Click Network and Internet Connections, shown in Figure 3-4. You'll have to click Network Connections in the resulting window.
3. Right-click the Wireless Network Connection icon (it may say Connected, Firewalled, Disabled, or something else). Click View Available Wireless Networks. (This is shown earlier in Figure 3-3.) You can also right-click the network icon on the Taskbar, as shown in Figure 3-5.
4. Figure 3-6 shows an example of what you might see in the results list. Click any network, then click Connect. If prompted, input credentials.

FIGURE 3-5　You can right-click the wireless network icon on the Taskbar to access available wireless networks.

Did You Know? **Your Netbook Will Remember the Network**

Once you've logged on once to a wireless network, Windows XP will remember the network key the next time you're within range and connect automatically.

Note In this example, I am connected to a wireless network, but there are others in the area. All of the networks here are security-enabled, and thus require authentication to log on.

Windows Vista

As with Windows XP, you can view and connect to a wireless network from the Taskbar. Specifically, it's the Taskbar's Notification Area where you access this icon, located on the right side of Windows Vista's Taskbar. If your netbook is not connected to a wireless network, the icon will have an *X* through it, as shown in Figure 3-7. You can hover the mouse over the icon to see the notification that wireless networks are available (or not available).

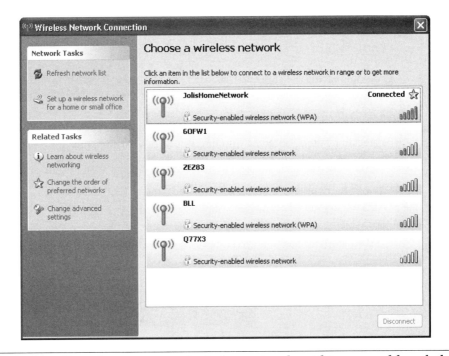

FIGURE 3-6 Here there are several wireless networks within range, although they all require authentication. These are all security-enabled wireless networks.

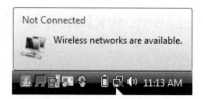

FIGURE 3-7   Here, no connection to a wireless network has been made, but wireless networks are available.

If the netbook is connected to a wireless network, the icon will not have an *X* through it. Such an icon is shown in Figure 3-8. You can hover the mouse over the icon to view the signal strength and see the status of the connection.

 Always verify that wireless LAN is enabled. For Vista netbooks, look for a switch on the outside of the netbook or a key on the keyboard (try FN + F2).

To view available wireless networks and connect to one, you'll need to access the network icon noted in Figures 3-7 and 3-8:

1. Right-click the network icon in the Notification area of the Taskbar. A pop-up will appear.
2. Select Connect to a network to view available networks.
3. Select the network to connect to, then click Connect, as shown in Figure 3-9. If prompted, input the required credentials.

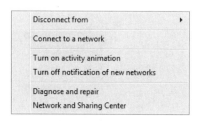

 Public places that offer free Wi-Fi may require you to input credentials. This is especially true of hotels. If prompted, call or visit the front desk to acquire the proper password, network key, or other credential.

 If your netbook has Windows 7 installed, follow the instructions for Windows Vista. The steps are virtually the same.

FIGURE 3-8   If connected, you can hover the mouse over the icon to see the connection status.

FIGURE 3-9   Choose the network to connect to and click Connect. Input credentials as required.

Linux (General)

There are multiple versions of Linux, and what's on your Linux netbook is likely different from what's on mine. Because of the sheer number of editions, it's impossible to state how you can view wireless networks on your specific netbook and connect to one. However, there are some guidelines you can use:

- Look for a network icon and click it. You might find one across the top bar of the screen (see Figure 3-10). (You may also have an icon for Wireless Networks, as shown earlier in Figure 3-2.)
- Look under each of the menus if they exist. Specifically look for Administration, Network, Wireless, or similar options.
- Open the Wireless Networks folder, Networks folder, Administration, or System folders to look for wireless settings and network lists.
- Click the desired network to connect to, and input credentials if required.

FIGURE 3-10   Some Linux editions offer a network icon (this one looks like two netbooks) that you can click to access a list of wireless networks.

If you think you are in range of a wireless network but can't see it or any others, verify that wireless local area network (LAN) hardware is enabled. Sometimes there's a switch on the outside, and other times there's a key combination you need to press, such as FN + F2.

Connect to a Public Network Automatically

Connecting to a public network requires that you first get within range of it. This may mean entering a coffee shop or hotel lobby or sitting in a specific part of a public library. Once you're within range, you should receive a pop-up box in the bottom-right corner of the Taskbar that announces the available network. (If no pop-up appears, refer to the previous section, "View Available Wireless Networks and Connect to Them Manually." If a pop-up does appear, simply click it to connect.)

You won't see any wireless networks if your netbook's wireless LAN hardware is disabled. Most netbooks have an external switch that you can use to enable or disable wireless capability, and it can be switched off inadvertently.

Connect Using Windows Vista or Windows 7

To connect to a public network on a Windows Vista or Windows 7 netbook:

1. Click the notification that states that wireless networks are available (see Figure 3-11).
2. Click the icon. If this is the first time you are connecting to the network, you may be prompted by Windows to choose what kind of network it is (see Figure 3-12).
3. Choose Public network as shown in Figure 3-12.
4. Click Close. Note the pop-up that says you're connected, as shown in Figure 3-13.

FIGURE 3-11   By default, when you are in range of a wireless network, and wireless LAN is enabled, a pop-up will appear notifying you of the network.

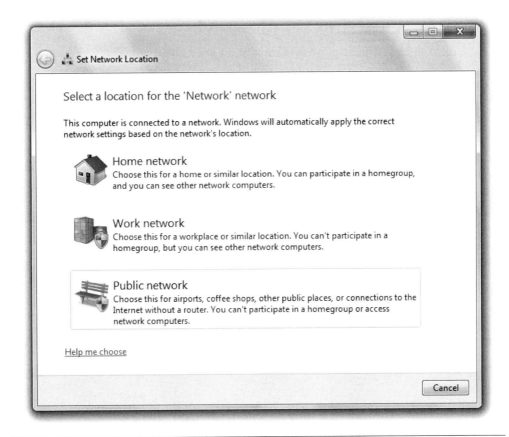

FIGURE 3-12   To create a secure connection, choose Public network if you are in a public place.

FIGURE 3-13   After you click Close, a pop-up notifies you that you are connected to a network.

Connect Using Windows XP

To connect to a public network on a Windows XP netbook:

1. Click the prompt that states that wireless networks are detected. It will look similar to what was shown in Figure 3-11 earlier.
2. Select the network to connect to; in Figure 3-14, that's Gold's Gym Garland.
3. Click Connect.
4. If the network is unsecured, click Connect Anyway when prompted.
5. Click the *X* in the top-right corner of the Wireless Network Connection window to close it.

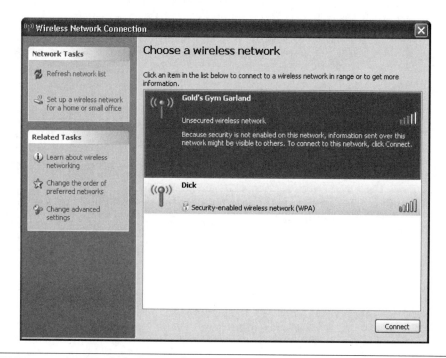

FIGURE 3-14   In XP, click the wireless network connection you want to connect to, then click Connect.

Connect Using Linux

To connect to a public network on a Linux netbook:

1. Get within range of the wireless network.
2. Look for a wireless network icon and click it. It may be under a tab named Internet, on the menu bar that runs across the top or bottom of the screen, or under a System or Network menu or tab.
3. Select the wireless network you want to connect to and click Connect.
4. A pop-up will likely appear to notify you that you are connected to the network.

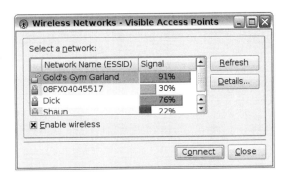

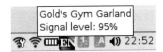

 Some netbooks support only two kinds of wireless networks: WEP and WPA. If your home network is not one of these types, you won't be able to connect. If this happens, consider reconfiguring your wireless network.

Manage the Wireless Networks List

You may want to change the order of your listed wireless networks. For example, you may want to put the network you use most often at the top of the list and the one you use least at the bottom. You may also want to delete wireless networks you've used but no longer need or even add a new network manually. In Windows, you do all of these things from your list of wireless networks.

Look back at Figure 3-6. That figure contains a list of the wireless networks that have been used in the past on a Windows XP netbook. Note that there is an option to change the order of the preferred network. Clicking that opens the dialog box shown in Figure 3-15. Here you can delete networks you've logged on to before or move them up or down the list. You can also configure advanced properties, add a new network manually, or learn more about wireless network configuration.

Windows Vista and Windows 7 have a different interface. With these editions, you open the Network and Sharing Center, then click Manage wireless networks. You then have access to the wireless networks in a window where you can add, remove, move up and down, and even configure adapter properties (see Figure 3-16).

Linux also offers wireless network management, often through an option named Wireless or Network. Because Linux editions differ greatly, you'll have to look for the settings using the available menus and folders.

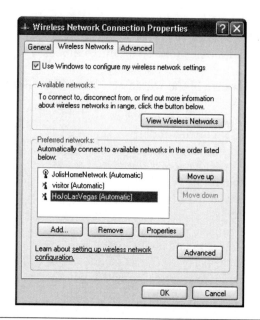

FIGURE 3-15 In Windows XP, you manage preferred networks in the Wireless Network Connection Properties dialog box.

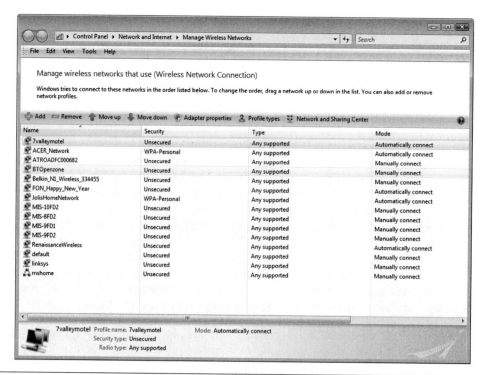

FIGURE 3-16 Windows Vista and Windows 7 offer a different interface for managing wireless networks.

It's best to keep your wireless network list in order, for the following reasons:

- Windows tries to connect to wireless networks in the order in which they are listed. If the network you connect to the most is at the bottom of the list, your netbook has to use battery power and other resources to search through those networks to find the one you want.
- By removing networks you no longer need, you can reduce the number of networks that Windows will search through for a signal.
- You won't accidently connect to a network that you know to be "unsecured," where others may be able to view your transmissions.

Know What Network Types to Trust

As shown earlier in Figure 3-12, when you connect to a new network on a Windows-based netbook, you're prompted to choose Home, Work, or Public. When you connect to a network in a public place, you should always choose Public if prompted. This is because free Wi-Fi networks are not secured and thus have no protection in place to protect who (or what) accesses that network. (The fact that it's not secure is what allows you to access the network without a password, passcode, network key, or other credential.) The other options, Home and Work, should be reserved for networks you trust, such as the one in your home or office or the network at a relative's home.

Here's a little more information on these network types:

- **Public**   In any Windows edition, choose Public when connecting to a network in a public place, like a hotel, cafe, airport, or library. Network discovery is turned off so that others on the network cannot see your netbook and you cannot see theirs. This helps keep you safer on the network by hiding your netbook from others. This setting also enables higher security to protect you against malware and other Internet or network threats.
- **Home or Work**   Choose either of these locations when connecting to a home or small office network you trust, such as the one on your home or office. With this setting enabled, network discovery will be enabled, which allows you to see other computers and devices on a network and allows other network users to see your computer. If you have the proper permissions, you will also be able to access these resources.
- **Private**   You'll see this option when reconfiguring a network in Vista's Network and Sharing Center. Choose Private to configure a private network. In Figure 3-17, note that a private network allows you to see computers and devices while also making your computer discoverable by others on the network. Only choose Private when the network is one you manage or trust.

In my experience, no option for public or private is offered on Linux-based netbooks. However, when joining a wireless home network, you will be prompted to input the type of security that's currently in place. You will not be able to connect to

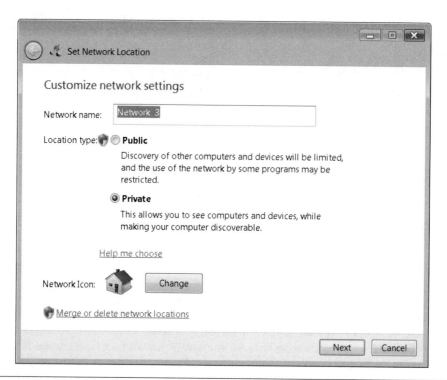

FIGURE 3-17   Private will be an option in the Network and Sharing Center.

the network without the proper credentials and without compatible security settings. When prompted to connect to a network in a place you trust, such as your home or office, choose Home or Work.

For the most part, if you log on to a network that is "secured" and you enter a network key, passcode, or other credential, the network is probably safe. If you log on to a network that is "unsecured," be careful. Anyone and everyone can access this network, and you want to protect yourself by choosing Public when offered.

4

Connect to a Wired Ethernet Network

Make the Physical Connection

Most of the time, you'll connect to wireless networks with your netbook. However, on rare occasions, perhaps when you are at your own home, a friend's or relative's, or staying in a hotel that offers only wired access to the Internet, you'll have to connect physically. You will physically connect using an Ethernet cable, shown in Figure 4-1.

You'll find the corresponding port on the outside of your netbook. There will be only one Ethernet port, and only one port that will accept an Ethernet cable. The cable will snap into the port and click when the connection is properly made.

In a hotel or public place, the other end of the Ethernet cable will already be connected to a router (or another piece of equipment like a hub or switch). These types of hardware allow you to connect your netbook to the local network. In a home environment, you will likely have to make the connection yourself. That said, you'll need to locate the router, hub, or switch (see Figure 4-2); find an empty port; and connect the Ethernet cable to it.

To connect your netbook physically to a wired Ethernet network:

1. Turn on your netbook and log in if necessary.
2. Connect the Ethernet cable to the Ethernet port on the netbook. It should snap into place.

FIGURE 4-1   Use an Ethernet cable to connect your netbook to a wired Ethernet network.

3. Connect the other end of the Ethernet cable to an available port on the router, switch, or hub. It should snap into place.
4. Wait one minute while the network initializes the connection.
5. In Windows XP, you may see a network icon in the Notification Area, but you can verify your connection in the Network Connections window (see Figure 4-3).

If you don't see a network icon in the Notification Area of a Windows XP netbook, right-click the connection, choose Properties, and from the General tab, select Show icon in notification area when connected, and click OK.

6. In Windows Vista or Windows 7, you may see a network icon in the Notification Area, but you can verify your connection in the Network and Sharing Center (see Figure 4-4).
7. In Linux, look for a network icon or tab. Locate the local area connection and verify that the connection is enabled (see Figure 4-5).

FIGURE 4-2   Locate the router and plug in the other end of your Ethernet cable.

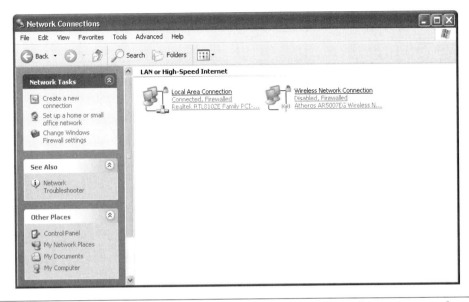

FIGURE 4-3   To verify that your connection is enabled in Windows XP, open the Network Connections window.

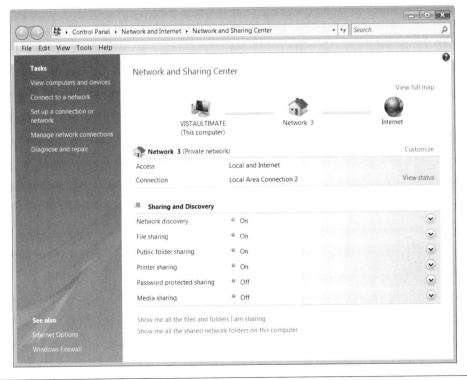

FIGURE 4-4   To verify your connection is enabled in Windows Vista or Windows 7, open the Network and Sharing Center.

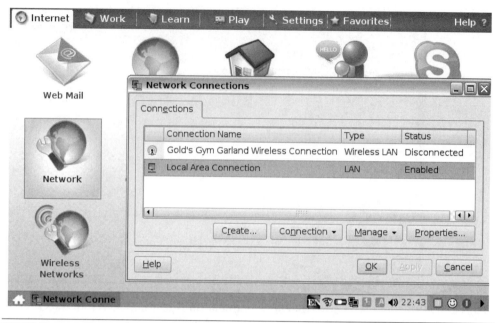

FIGURE 4-5 To verify your connection is enabled in Linux, open the Network or Internet tab, locate an icon representing the network, and click it.

Troubleshoot Connection Problems

Sometimes a proper connection isn't made automatically when you physically connect to the network. If that happens, your first step is to reboot the netbook. In almost all cases, rebooting causes the proper connection to be made. If for some reason a connection is not made after restarting the netbook, you'll need to create a connection manually.

How you create a connection manually depends on what operating system you have. The steps here are for Windows XP. Vista and Windows 7 require similar steps, though, and I've added additional information here to help you adapt these steps to suit your needs, if it's required.

Vista and Windows 7 connect more easily to networks than XP does. It's more likely you'll have problems with an XP netbook than one running another operating system, that's why I've chosen to use XP as an example here.

Before continuing, reboot your netbook to see if a network is created automatically.

To set up a connection manually in Windows XP:

1. Click Start and click My Network Places. (In Vista or Windows 7, open the Network and Sharing Center.)
2. Under Network Tasks, click View network connections (see Figure 4-6).

Just because you can see computers in the My Network Connections window doesn't mean you've successfully connected to a network. On a Windows XP netbook, you may see computers that were available from a previous network connection but that are now inaccessible.

3. If you see a Local Area Connection icon and the connection is disabled:
   a. Right-click the icon.
   b. Choose Enable as shown in Figure 4-7.
4. If you do not see a Local Area Connection icon, click Create a new connection.
   a. Click Next to start the New Connection Wizard.
   b. Click Connect to the Internet. Then click Next. See Figure 4-8.

If you are attempting to set up a new network and not connecting to an existing network, select Set up a home or small office network. Because you are connecting to an existing network via your netbook, it's highly unlikely you'll want to make this choice, though.

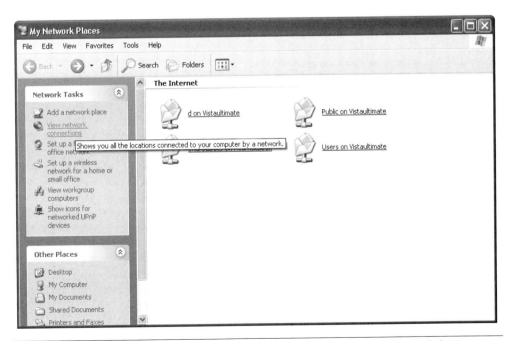

FIGURE 4-6   To view or create a network connection in Windows XP, click View network connections from the My Network Places window.

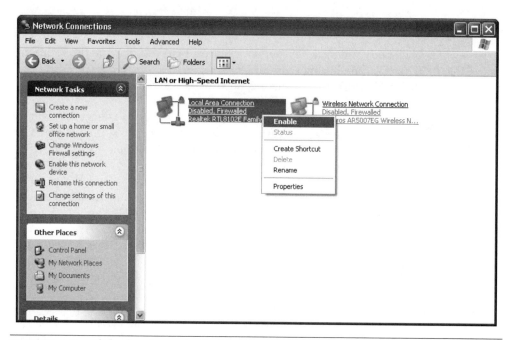

FIGURE 4-7   If the local area is disabled, enable it.

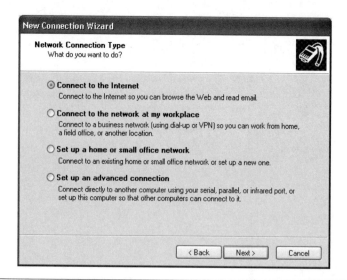

FIGURE 4-8   Although there are other options, click Connect to the Internet to create a basic local area network connection.

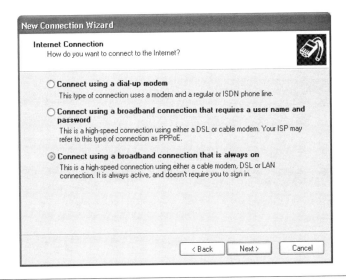

FIGURE 4-9   Select the type of Internet connection to use.

   c. Click Set up my connection manually. Click Next.

   d. Make the proper selection from the resulting list. Most likely, it's Connect using a broadband connection that is always on (see Figure 4-9). Click Next.

   e. Click Finish.

You will have to enter additional information if you make a choice other than Connect using a broadband connection that is always on.

Connect to the Internet

Once you're physically connected to a local area network, you can probably access the Internet without any additional configuration. Hotels and other public places are already set up to share their Internet connections, as are home networks that are already in place. For the most part, you simply open your favorite web browser. Firefox on Linux Ubuntu is shown in Figure 4-10; Internet Explorer is shown in Figure 4-11.

If you have any problems connecting to the Internet and you're sure the local area connection is enabled, the problem is likely with the local area network settings. An Internet connection that was created on another computer must be shared for you to access it, or a private or public network has to have been created. When you set up a network using Vista or Windows 7, this is done for you. When you create a network with Windows XP, depending on the Internet connection type, you may have to specify that you want to share the connection from the Local Area Connection Properties dialog box.

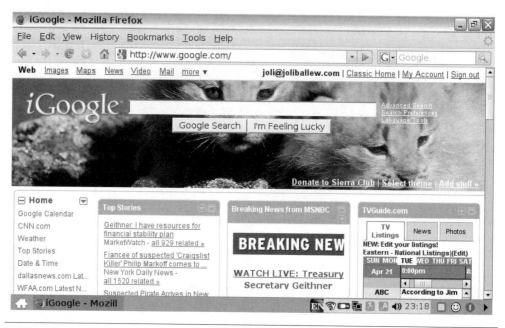

FIGURE 4-10 Open your favorite web browser, such as Firefox, once connected to the local area network.

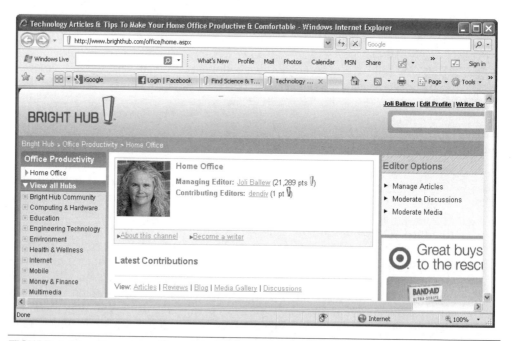

FIGURE 4-11 Open your favorite web browser, such as Internet Explorer, to access the Internet.

Access a Local Area Network

Although you should be able to access the Internet from a local area Ethernet network, you may not be able to access the local resources on it. If you're in a hotel, for instance, you can access the Internet, but you probably can't access the computer at the front desk or the file server in the basement. However, you may be able to access a shared printer (if you're a registered guest) for printing boarding passes and receipts. The network administrator decides who can access what on a local network, and only those with the proper credentials (username and password) can access protected files and hardware.

 If you created your home network, you're the network administrator.

On a home or personal network, you can almost always access "public" or "shared" files and folders on the local network, and generally a printer as well. Public and Shared folders are created by default to share data among users who have local area access. Depending on how these public and shared folders were set up, you may or may not have to input a username and password. Most of the time, these folders don't require such input.

The best way to see if you have access to Public or Shared folders is to try to access them. Although there are several ways to do this, using Windows Explorer on a Windows netbook is often the most straightforward:

| Open |
| Explore |
| Snaglt |
| Groove Folder Synchronization |
| Scan with AVG Free |
| Properties |
| Open All Users |
| Explore All Users |

1. Make sure you are physically connected to the network and that the network is enabled. This was detailed earlier in this chapter.
2. Right-click the Start menu.
3. Click Explore All Users.

 When you right-click the Start menu in Windows 7, you have to select Open Windows Explorer. Explore All Users is no longer an option. Look for the Public folders.

4. In Windows XP, locate the Shared Documents folder. Inside that folder are subfolders for Shared Music, Shared Pictures, and more.
5. In Windows Vista or Windows 7, locate the Public folder (see Figure 4-12). Inside that folder are subfolders for Public Pictures, Public Videos, Public Music, and more.
6. Double-click any folder to access what's inside the folder. Note that you may be prompted to input a username and password.

 To disconnect from a network, disconnect the Ethernet cable or right-click the connection in the appropriate network window and choose Disable.

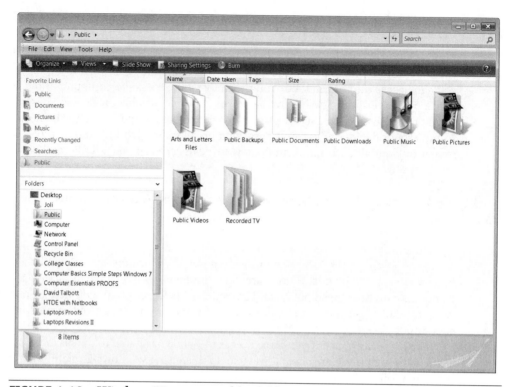

FIGURE 4-12 Windows Vista uses Public folders, whereas Windows XP uses Shared folders.

5

Make a Direct Connection with a Stand-Alone PC

HOW TO...

- Share an Internet connection on the stand-alone PC
- Physically connect the two PCs with a crossover cable
- Access the Internet
- Access shared data

If you have a single-PC household with a wired or wireless connection to the Internet, no existing home network, and no unsecured, wireless network to connect to, getting online is going to take a bit of finagling. When this is the case, the only way to connect to the Internet is to configure the stand-alone PC to share its Internet connection and then connect to the Internet through it. If you don't mind running a cable from your netbook to the PC, making the connection is relatively easy to do, and that's what you'll learn to do here. If you want to set up an ad hoc wireless network between the two PCs, that's a bit more complicated, and you'll need to know quite a bit more about networking than what is offered here.

Set Up the Stand-Alone PC

If you need to connect to the Internet through another PC's Internet connection, that connection has to be shared. Once shared, a simple direct connection with the proper cable is all you need to access the Internet.

Share an Internet Connection on Windows XP

To share an Internet connection on a Windows XP stand-alone PC, you'll need to access the Network Connections window. As with other areas of XP, there are many ways to access this window. One way is to locate it in the Control Panel:

1. Click Start, then click Control Panel. The screen shown in Figure 5-1 appears.

 Tip If you don't see what is shown in Figure 5-1, click Switch to Category View in the Tasks pane on the left side of the Control Panel window.

2. In Control Panel, click Network and Internet Connections.
3. Click Network Connections.
4. Right-click the connection to the Internet and click Properties. As shown in Figure 5-2, there may be more than one connection. (You should be connected to the Internet.)
5. From the Advanced tab, click Allow other network users to connect through this computer's Internet connection. If you desire, click Allow other network users to control or disable the shared Internet connection (see Figure 5-3).
6. Click OK.

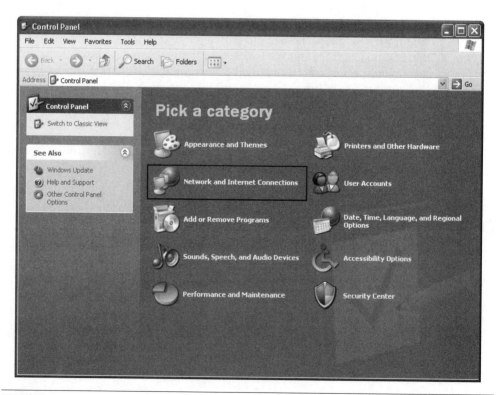

FIGURE 5-1 Locate network and Internet connections.

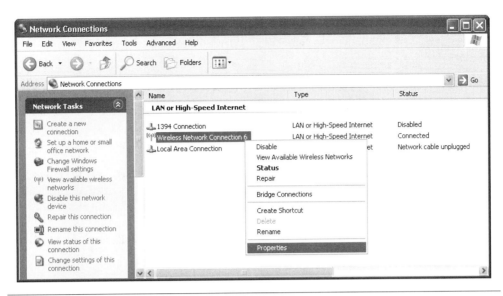

FIGURE 5-2   Click Properties to share the connection.

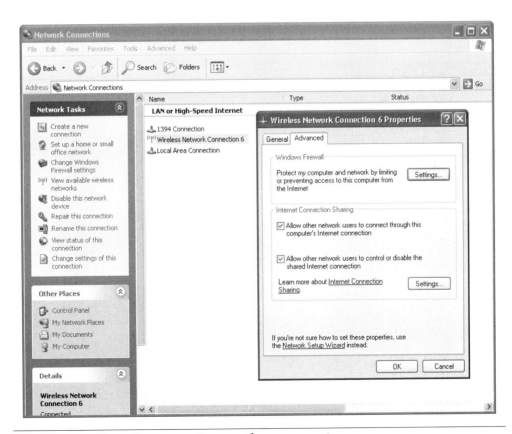

FIGURE 5-3   Share the connection so others can use it.

The stand-alone PC has to be turned on for others to access the Internet through it.

Share an Internet Connection on Windows Vista

To share an Internet connection on a Windows Vista stand-alone PC, you'll need to access the Network and Sharing Center. As with other areas of Vista, there are many ways to access this. One way is to open it from the Start menu:

1. Click Start, and in the Start Search box, type **Network and Sharing**.
2. From the results, click Network and Sharing Center. The screen shown in Figure 5-4 appears.
3. Click Manage network connections.
4. Right-click the connection to the Internet and click Properties. As shown in Figure 5-5, there may be more than one connection.
5. From the Sharing tab (see Figure 5-6), click Allow other network users to connect through this computer's Internet connection. If you desire, click Allow other network users to control or disable the shared Internet connection.

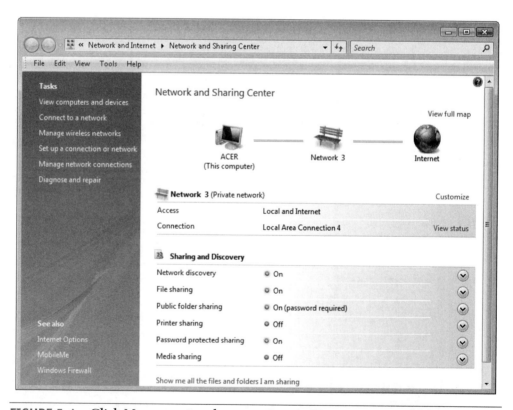

FIGURE 5-4   Click Manage network connections in Vista to view available connections.

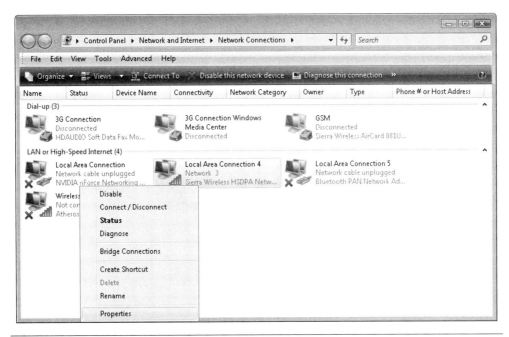

FIGURE 5-5   Select the connection to share; there may be one or several.

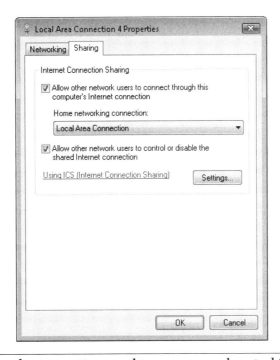

FIGURE 5-6   Share the connection so others can use and control it.

6. Under Home networking connection, use the drop-down list to choose the connection you'll use to connect the netbook.
7. Click OK.

 The stand-alone PC has to be turned on for others to access the Internet through it.

Connect Using a Crossover Cable

After sharing the stand-alone PC's connection to the Internet, you can now physically connect them. You'll need a crossover cable, also called a null-modem cable, or an Easy Transfer cable, which looks just like a regular Ethernet cable (but isn't).

To connect using a crossover cable:

1. Purchase the required cable.
2. Connect one end of the cable to the Ethernet port of the stand-alone PC.
3. Connect the other end of the cable to the Ethernet port of the netbook.
4. After a few seconds, you should automatically be connected and have access to the Internet. If not, restart the netbook.
5. Once connected, you'll see a new network listed under Internet Gateway in Network connections on a Windows XP machine, as shown in Figure 5-7. On Windows Vista, you can view the connection in the Network and Sharing Center, and in Network Connections, shown in Figure 5-8.
6. To access the Internet, simply open a web browser.

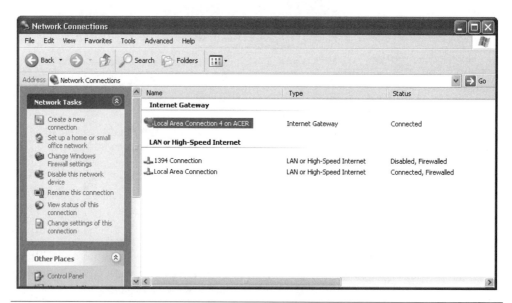

FIGURE 5-7   In XP, you'll see the connection in Network Connections.

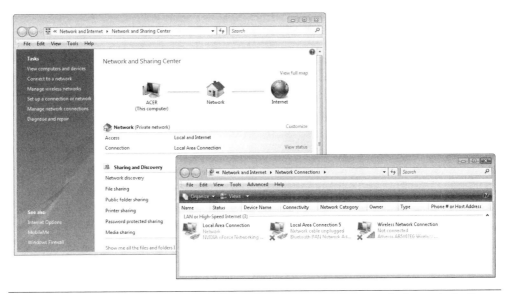

FIGURE 5-8   In Windows Vista, you'll see the connection in several places, including the Network and Sharing Center.

Access the Internet and Shared Data on XP or Vista

Almost all of the time, to access the Internet after making the physical connection with a crossover cable, you need only open a web browser. In rare instances, you'll need to reboot the PC. Once connected to the local network, you can access any shared data too. Although there are several ways to access shared data, one way is to open Computer, then click Network (or My Network Places).

To access the Internet and shared data:

1. Click Start, then click Computer.
2. In Windows XP, click My Network Places, and then click Show workgroup computers.
3. In Windows Vista, click Network.
4. To access shared data on the stand-alone PC (or vice-versa), double-click the computer that holds the shared data. If it is required, type a username and password. Figure 5-9 shows what you might see on a Windows XP netbook.
5. The window that opens will contain a list of folders that have been manually shared or those that are automatically shared by the operating system. Figure 5-10 shows what you might see on a Vista (or Windows 7) netbook.

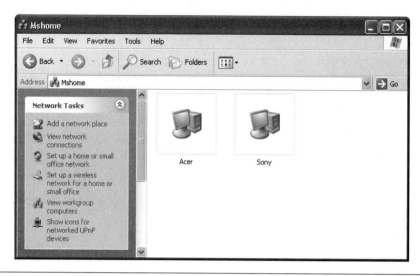

FIGURE 5-9   One way to access shared data is to access the workgroup computers.

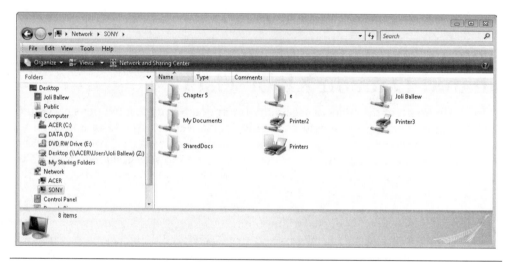

FIGURE 5-10   Shared data is offered after you access a shared computer.

Access the Internet and Shared Data on Linux

Linux netbooks connect just as seamlessly as Windows netbooks. Almost all of the time, accessing the Internet after making the physical connection with a crossover cable only requires you open a web browser. In rare instances, you may need to reboot the netbook, although I've never experienced this. If for any reason you are not automatically connected to the stand-alone PC, you can open network settings and connect manually:

1. Locate a Network icon or menu option. In Figure 5-11, the Network icon is shown on the left. Clicking it opens the Network Connections window shown on the right.

 Note Because of the number of Linux operating systems available, what you see and what's shown here will likely differ. However, the concept is the same: Locate the network settings, locate the network to connect to, and click Connect.

2. Locate the local area network.
3. Click it and select Connect.
4. Once connected, you can then easily connect to the Internet.

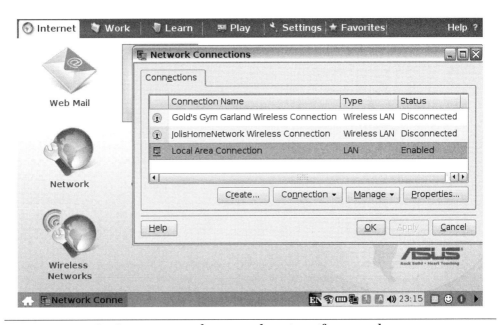

FIGURE 5-11 On Linux, access the network options if you need to connect manually to a network. Chances are you won't.

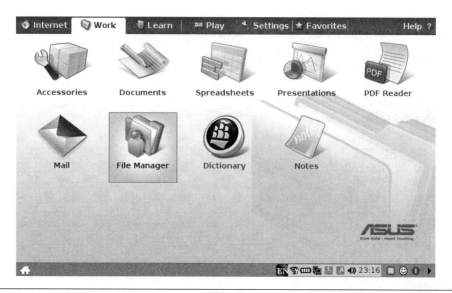

FIGURE 5-12   In Linux, generally the File Manager or some form of it will allow you to access the network shares.

Once connected to the stand-alone PC, you can access any shared data too. On Linux, there are several ways to access shared data. Here is one way:

1. Locate a File Manager and open it (see Figure 5-12).
2. Expand any necessary folders to access the shared data. In Figure 5-13, Windows Network, Mshome (the workgroup name), and Sony are expanded.

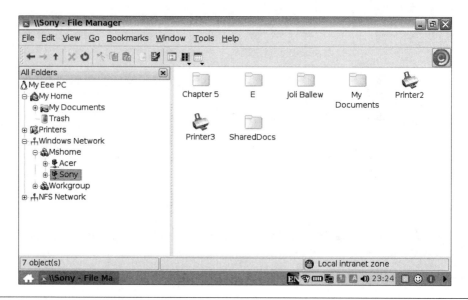

FIGURE 5-13   In Linux, shares are often accessed using a File Manager like this one.

6

Connect with a Satellite Provider

HOW TO...

- Choose a satellite option
- Install the hardware and software
- Connect to the Internet

As you know, your netbook came preinstalled with a Wi-Fi adapter. With it, you can connect to free Wi-Fi hotspots and wireless home networks. But what happens when you can't locate a wireless network (and aren't in close proximity to a wired one)? In these cases, you'll need a Wi-Fi subscription or pay-as-you-go service to gain Internet access (see Figure 6-1).

Choose a Satellite Option

To have access to the Internet at all times, even when you're not in range of free Wi-Fi hotspots or wireless networks, you'll need a subscription to a satellite (wireless) service provider. There are many ways to go about this:

- You can buy a netbook that comes preinstalled with built-in wireless network capabilities and a built-in subscription. Not long ago, Radio Shack offered the Acer Aspire One for $99, provided you signed up for Internet Access through AT&T for two years (at a cost of around $65 a month).
- You can purchase and install a USB device from a provider such as AT&T or Verizon and pay a monthly service fee for unlimited Internet service. These devices, sometimes called USB dongles or USB modems, are often free provided you sign a two-year contract with the company.

 Much of the hardware that cell phone companies offer isn't compatible with Linux netbooks. If you have a Linux netbook, make sure you tell the provider that and make sure that what you're buying is Linux-friendly.

FIGURE 6-1 Many times, no wireless network is available.

- You can connect (tether) your cell phone to your netbook using a USB cable to gain Internet access through the phone's Internet connection. Sometimes, it's a "hack" and can be achieved without incurring additional charges. However, most cell phone providers have data plans especially for this purpose, although they often impose limits and additional charges for this feature. Also, you may be able to wirelessly connect your netbook/laptop to many phones through a Bluetooth connection if both the phone and computer are Bluetooth-enabled.
- Sign up with a company such as Boingo that offers a low-cost way to access Wi-Fi hotspots across the United States (or globally). At this time, for $9.95 a month, you can connect as often and for as long as you like at thousands of hotspots in the United States. These hotspots are provided by AT&T, Wayport, iBahn, T-Mobile, BT Openzone, Orange France, Livedoor, Singtel, Telmex, Pronto, HubTelecom, Vex, Attingo, Bell Mobility, Net Near U, StayOnline, Kubi Wireless, Telenet, Internet Solutions, and many more. If you travel a lot, this might work for you.
- There may be pay-as-you-go or even free wireless options available in your area. Recently, Seattle, Washington, unveiled a citywide free Wi-Fi pilot program (see Figure 6-2). If you are within certain city boundaries, you can access the Internet for free. In the future, look for more of these options.

FIGURE 6-2 See if your metropolitan area offers any free Wi-Fi services.

Whatever the Wi-Fi plan claims to cost per month, to be safe, add another 10 percent onto that. There are fees and taxes you aren't told about during the sign-up process. A subscription that is $59.99 a month will probably cost about $65–70.

Install the Hardware and Software

The most popular way to keep your netbook connected is to purchase and install a USB modem or USB satellite device and pay a monthly service fee. For the most part, you obtain these devices and the service from a cell phone company such as AT&T, T-Mobile, or Verizon. The USB device generally comes with the required software preinstalled on it so you don't have to worry about connecting a CD drive to your netbook for a related CD. The first time you plug the device into your netbook, the installation process starts.

Here's an example of how such an installation might go:

1. Plug the device into an available USB port on your netbook.
2. Click Start, Next, or Continue to begin the installation. In most cases, an installation program begins when you connect the USB modem or USB connect card.
3. Wait while the installation process completes and answer any questions posed.
4. Complete the installation and reboot the PC if needed.

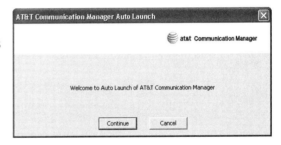

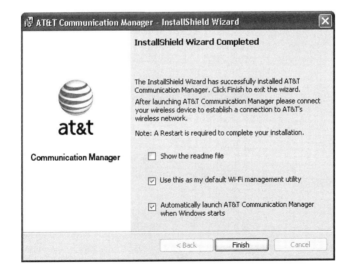

FIGURE 6-3   Locate the program icon and click Connect.

Connect to the Internet

After installing the hardware and software, it's easy to connect to the Internet. You first have to connect to the satellite provider using the hardware and software and then open a web browser. As an example:

1. Locate the program icon. It is likely on the desktop, but if it isn't, click the Start menu and check the All Programs submenu. Double-click the icon.
2. Click Connect, shown in Figure 6-3. Once connected, note the bars on the interface or in the Notification Area of the Taskbar. They indicate the status of the connection (see Figure 6-4).
3. Open any web browser to get online (see Figure 6-5).

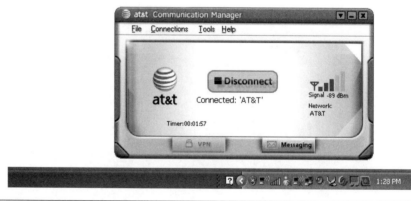

FIGURE 6-4   Once connected, you can see the status of the connection on the program and in the Notification area of the Taskbar.

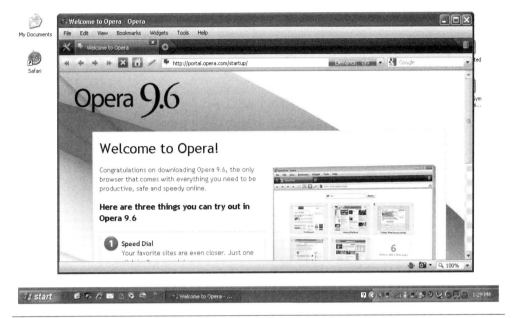

FIGURE 6-5   Once connected, use the web browser of your choice.

7

Surfing the Internet

HOW TO...

- Use Internet Explorer to set a home page and explore tabbed browsing
- Delete unwanted files in Internet Explorer
- Disable unwanted toolbars in Internet Explorer
- Disable unwanted add-ons in Internet Explorer
- Find out if you should upgrade Internet Explorer
- Download and install Internet Explorer 8
- Download and install a third-party web browser
- Explore Mozilla Firefox
- Explore Apple's Safari
- Explore Opera
- Explore Google Chrome

A web browser is what allows you to access the Internet efficiently, move from web site to web site, search for information, download programs, and use social networking web sites to keep in touch with friends and acquaintances. You can use the web browser that came with your Windows-based netbook, Internet Explorer, or you can choose from a variety of others. Linux netbooks most often come with Firefox, another option for any netbook user.

Although there's no consensus regarding which of the available web browsers offers the best web performance (they all claim to be the fastest), suffice it to say that how you use and configure your web browser plays a large role in how well your browser performs. If you run the available web browsers side by side with no add-ons, for instance, it's likely you won't be able to discern a performance difference between any of them. With that in mind, you should choose a web browser that you like, not one you've heard is faster or better; do not simply opt for the latest fad in browsers.

In this chapter, you'll learn about Internet Explorer (which will likely suit you fine), as well as others, including Firefox, Safari, Opera, and Chrome. You may want to read this chapter before you decide on a browser to use, or at least look at the screen shots throughout.

Many people will claim that one browser is faster than another, but there is simply no conclusive test that has proven this. Most of the time, a new browser is faster than an old one because it's "clean" and has no add-ons, toolbars, or other features to slow it down (while the old web browser does).

Use Internet Explorer

Because Internet Explorer comes with your Windows-based netbook, you should consider it first. (If you're using Linux, try Firefox first.) Internet Explorer integrates easily (using the Windows Live Toolbar) with other Microsoft programs you might add later, such as Windows Live Mail, Windows Live Photo Gallery, Windows Live Writer, and Windows Live Messenger. This integration allows you to access everything you need from a single toolbar and a single interface.

As noted, add-ons such as toolbars can slow down browser performance. Choose your add-ons wisely and keep them to a minimum.

To get started with Internet Explorer (IE) and configure a home page:

To get started with Firefox, skip to the appropriate section of this chapter.

1. Locate the blue *e*. It may be in the Quick Launch area of the Taskbar on the Desktop, but you'll always find it at the top of the Start menu (see Figure 7-1).

In Windows 7, Internet Explorer is pinned to the Taskbar.

2. Notice the parts of Internet Explorer, including the Address Bar where you type in the web address to visit, the Tools menu, and the tabs (see Figure 7-2).
3. Type any web address in the Address Bar and press Enter on the keyboard to visit the site.
4. To add a page as a home page, click the arrow next to the Home button and click Add or Change Home Page (see Figure 7-3).

A home page opens every time you open Internet Explorer. You can have multiple home pages.

5. To take advantage of Internet Explorer's tab feature, when prompted, select Add this Webpage to your home page tabs.
6. To open a new tab, click the tab and type in a web address or right-click any link and choose Open in New Tab (see Figure 7-4).

FIGURE 7-1   Locate the blue *e* to open Internet Explorer.

FIGURE 7-2   The Internet Explorer interface offers many features.

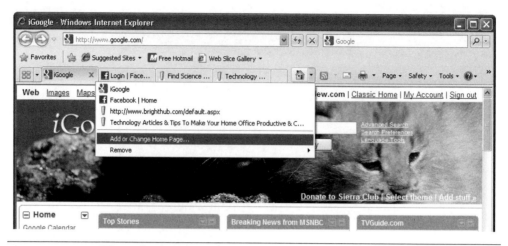

FIGURE 7-3   Add a web page as a home page and it will open every time you open
Internet Explorer.

FIGURE 7-4   Open a link in a new tab.

Toolbars and Add-Ons

Toolbars and add-ons can be saved and applied to your computer without your explicit knowledge. These may be added when you agree to a web site's terms of service, download a new product, or access a web page and choose Yes to run an ActiveX control, among other things.

The screen shots here are from Internet Explorer 8 (IE8). If you purchased a netbook that runs Windows XP, it may have an earlier version, Internet Explorer 7 (IE7). Learn how to upgrade later in this chapter.

Keep Internet Explorer Running Smoothly and Quickly

You'll want to perform some maintenance tasks once a month or so to keep Internet Explorer running smoothly. You may want to delete your browsing history (or at least delete temporary Internet files), review and disable unwanted toolbars, and disable unwanted add-ons.

To delete temporary Internet files and/or delete your browsing history:

1. Click Safety, and click Delete Browsing History (see Figure 7-5). If you don't see the Safety option, you're likely running Internet Explorer 7. In that case, click Tools and then click Delete Browsing History.
2. Click any item to delete unwanted contents. The options include the following (which are shown in Figure 7-6):
   a. **Temporary Internet Files**   These are copies of web pages, images, and media saved by Internet Explorer. IE saves this information to help pages load faster, but a folder that's too large can actually hamper performance.

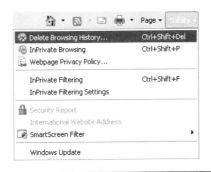

FIGURE 7-5   To delete unwanted files, choose Delete Browsing History.

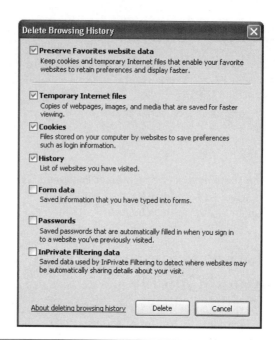

FIGURE 7-6 Delete IE data frequently, especially temporary Internet files, form data, and passwords.

b. **Cookies** These are small text files that web sites place on your computer to enhance your Internet experience. This is what allows you to go to, say, Amazon.com and be greeted by "Hello, Joli." Many people never delete any cookies, because their size is so small.

c. **History** This contains a list of web sites you've visited. You can delete this list if you don't want anyone to log on to your PC and see what web sites you frequent.

d. **Form Data** This contains data you've saved that you've typed into web sites. I think it's best to delete the information in here often, because if your netbook is stolen, the thief will have access to this data as well.

e. **Passwords** This contains passwords you've chosen to save. As with Form Data, with a netbook, it's best to delete this often in case your netbook is stolen.

f. **InPrivate Filtering Data** This contains information relevant to IE8's InPrivate feature, which protects you from web sites that may be automatically sharing information you leave behind regarding your visit. You can leave this information intact.

Internet Explorer and some web pages require specific add-ons to function properly. If you disable an add-on that is required by IE, web pages may not open properly (if at all). Disable only add-ons you recognize from programs you installed yourself, and do not disable add-ons you do not recognize or those that have not caused error messages.

To disable unwanted toolbars and add-ons:

1. Click Tools, click Toolbars, and click Manage Add-ons (see Figure 7-7). (In IE7 you'll see a pop-out list and active toolbars will have a check beside them. Click any active toolbar to disable it.)
2. In the Manage Add-ons window, click Toolbars and Extensions.
3. Select the toolbar to disable.
4. Click Disable (see Figure 7-8).
5. Click Search Providers.
6. Select the search provider to disable.
7. Click Remove.
8. Click Accelerators, then click the accelerator to disable, then click Disable.
9. Click Close.

 You can also delete search providers, accelerators, and other add-ons here.

 To disable unwanted add-ons in IE7, click Tools, Manage Add-ons, and Enable or Disable Add-ons. Do not disable anything you did not install yourself.

FIGURE 7-7   Locate the Manage Add-ons option to open the Manage Add-ons window.

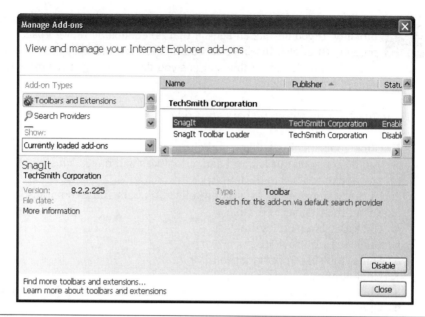

FIGURE 7-8   Select any toolbar to disable.

More About Internet Explorer 8 (and How to Get It)

If you purchased a netbook running Windows XP, you probably have Internet Explorer 7 installed. If you purchased a netbook running Windows Vista or Windows 7, you have Internet Explorer 8. By the time you purchase this book, though, there may even be a newer version, Internet Explorer 9. If you have Internet Explorer 7, it's time to upgrade.

To find out what version of Internet Explorer you're running and to decide whether you need to upgrade:

1. Locate the Help menu. If you don't see it, click the ALT key on the keyboard to make the menu appear.
2. Click Help, and click About Internet Explorer, as shown in Figure 7-9.

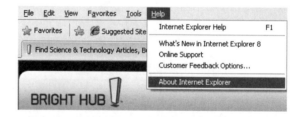

FIGURE 7-9   Click the ALT key to show the Menu bar (if it's not showing), and then click Help.

3. In the About Internet Explorer window, view the version number.

If you're not running Internet Explorer 8, note that it offers some excellent new features not included in previous versions:

- **Accelerators**   To access an Accelerator, highlight any text on any web page and click the Accelerator icon. From there, you can map a route, send the text in an email, and more. An accelerator icon, accelerator options, and resulting map are shown in Figure 7-10.
- **Compatibility View**   If a web page is not yet optimized for IE8, clicking the Compatibility View icon will correct display problems.
- **Favorites bar**   Earlier versions of IE featured a Favorites menu. You can now save favorite web sites to a toolbar that allows one-click access.
- **Web slices**   Web slices let you "subscribe" to ever-changing information offered on a web page, such as the weather, traffic reports, or sports scores. When the RSS/Web Slices icon turns green, web slices are available for that page (see Figure 7-11).

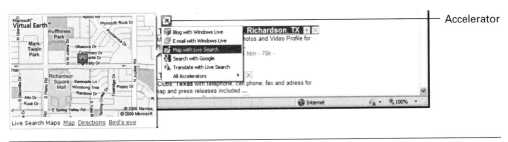

FIGURE 7-10   The Accelerator icon is a blue square with an arrow in it. Click it to view options for working with selected text.

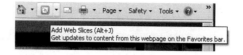

FIGURE 7-11 Web slices let you get updated content easily.

To download and install Internet Explorer 8:

1. Go to www.microsoft.com and search for Download Internet Explorer 8.
2. Click the Download now link.
3. If necessary, click Download Now again.
4. When prompted, click Run. Click Run again when or if you are prompted.
5. Answer any questions and wait for the download and installation to complete (see Figure 7-12).
6. Restart your netbook, if prompted.

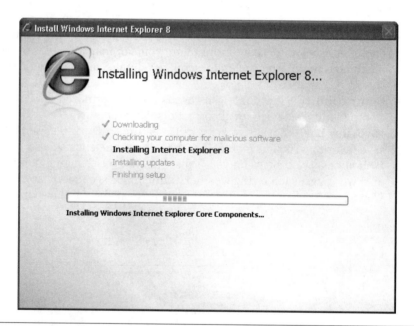

FIGURE 7-12 Installation of IE8 is almost completely automatic.

Download and Install
a Third-Party Web Browser

If you decide, after browsing the rest of this chapter (or at least looking at the screen shots) that you'd like to use something other than Internet Explorer for surfing the Internet, you'll have to download and install that browser yourself. Internet Explorer is the only browser preinstalled on your Windows-based netbook, and if you want something else, it's up to you to obtain it.

 All of the web browsers mentioned here are free.

To download a third-party web browser, navigate to the web site of the company that offers it:

- **Mozilla Firefox (www.mozilla.com)**   A download link for Firefox is available on the home page.
- **Apple's Safari (www.apple.com/downloads/)**   A link to download Safari is available from the Downloads page on Apple's web site.
- **Opera (www.opera.com)**   A link to download is on Opera's home page.
- **Google Chrome (www.google.com/chrome)**   A link to download Google Chrome is available from the Chrome page at Google.

To download any third-party browser:

1. Visit the web page that contains a link to the download.
2. Click the Download or Download Now button.

 You may have to run an add-on to download and install the browser. If prompted, click Run, and click Download Now again.

3. Read and accept the Terms of Service and/or Licensing Agreement pages.
4. Click Run and work through the installation process to complete the installation. You will have to click Run again if prompted.

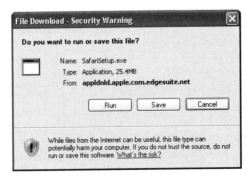

It's best to allow the automatic installation of browser updates if prompted.

5. When you first start your new browser, you'll be prompted to make it your default browser. If you choose Yes, the new browser name will appear on your Start menu where Internet Explorer was, and will open automatically when you click a web page link in an e-mail, document, or other media.

Explore Third-Party Web Browsers

Almost all web browsers offer similar features: the ability to surf the Web, save favorites, set home pages, configure security options, block pop-up ads, set preferences, and search from a search window. However, each web browser has a very different interface. And, while some browsers claim to use less memory, use resources more effectively, or even run faster than other browsers, what really matters is that the browser does what you want it to do at a speed you're happy with.

If you do decide to install and use a third-party browser because you've heard it's faster than another one, you have to appreciate that (for the most part) it's your connection to the Internet that determines how fast a web site loads; using Firefox on a dial-up connection isn't going to let you surf at the speed of light, and using Internet Explorer 8 on a fiber-optic connection isn't going to provide a noticeable slowdown. Additionally, it's important to note that when you install a brand-new, never-before-used-on-your-computer web browser, it has no add-ons, no toolbars, and no browsing history to slow it down. New browsers almost always perform better initially over existing browsers, but all have the same tendency to slow down after a few months, and for the most part, the speed issue evens out in the long run.

If you decide to install and use a third-party browser because you've heard it's more secure than other browsers, you're probably right; third-party web browsers are less prone to Internet attacks than Internet Explorer. When hackers want to create viruses and code to attack computers, they want to attack as many as possible. Hackers write their viruses to attack IE, not Firefox, Safari, Opera, or Google Chrome, because IE is the most popular browser available and is used by more people than any other. So, hackers do spend more time focusing on compromising those users rather than any others.

In the end, though, your choice will ultimately be a matter of preference. While I find Firefox a nice change from Internet Explorer, I don't like Google Chrome. That isn't to say you won't like it, though, or that it won't grow to be more popular than IE. It's just my personal preference. Therefore, in the following sections, I'll list some of the best features of each browser and supply a screen shot. You can review this information to find out which browser will suit your needs the best and which one catches your eye the quickest.

 Your web browsing speed is determined by the type of connection you have to the Internet. Dial-up is slow, whereas satellite, cable, and DSL are faster and the most popular, and fiber-optic lines are the fastest.

Explore Mozilla Firefox

Firefox almost always comes preinstalled on Linux netbooks (see Figure 7-13). The browser integrates nicely with Linux, allowing for easier file downloads and familiar-looking menus and options. With Firefox, you can easily pause and restart downloads with the Download Manager and watch the file download process.

Some other Firefox features you may like include:

- A built-in spell checker that can be used when typing blog posts, writing inside web pages, and when using web-based e-mail.
- The session restore feature that lets you pick up where you left off should Firefox quit unexpectedly (or if your netbook quits unexpectedly). Even if you were in the middle of typing a web-based e-mail, you can quickly and easily regain your place on the Web.
- Improved zooming lets you zoom in on any web page without losing the page elements.
- An option to forgo image loading. If you have a slow connection to the Internet, you can save time and bandwidth by choosing to load the site without images.
- Over 5,000 ways to customize the browser to suit your exact needs.
- An add-ons manager that lets you easily see and manage the add-ons you've selected. You can disable add-ons with a single click for better performance.
- A password manager that can be configured to remember passwords for all of the web sites you visit. Note, however, that this behavior is not a safe one with a netbook. If you lose your netbook, whoever gets it can gain access to your personal data.

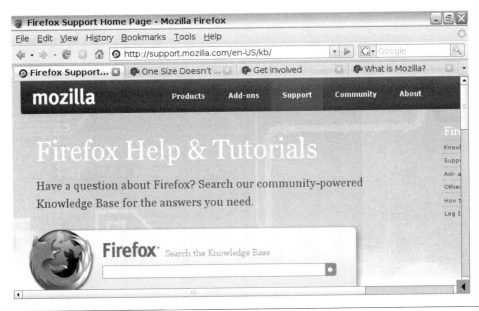

FIGURE 7-13   Firefox offers tabbed browsing and its interface will look familiar to Linux users.

As with other browsers, Firefox offers the ability to customize security settings, clear private data, use tabbed browsing, incorporate anti-virus software, get automatic updates, use an included pop-up blocker, and more.

Explore Apple's Safari

You'll get everything with Safari you'd expect, including the ability to manage bookmarked pages, integrated RSS, search, security, and spectacular graphics. What you may not expect is the streamlined interface, the ability to add your own "folders" to the Bookmark Bar, and the ability to set many different preferences.

Some other features you may enjoy include:

- The ability to navigate the Web easily without a mouse or touchpad, using keyboard features such as Tab and Enter.
- An option to change the font size for a web page so you can read the text more easily.
- Plug-in support for all kinds of technologies, such as Flash, Shockwave, and QuickTime, all of which help animate the Web.
- Bookmark folders built in that hold links to your favorite web sites. Bookmark folders appear on the Bookmark Bar (see Figure 7-14).
- Drag-and-drop bookmark organization and the ability to import bookmarks from another browser.
- The option to reopen the windows from your last Safari session. As with Firefox, you can simply pick up where you left off.

FIGURE 7-14   The Bookmark Bar is a nice feature in Safari.

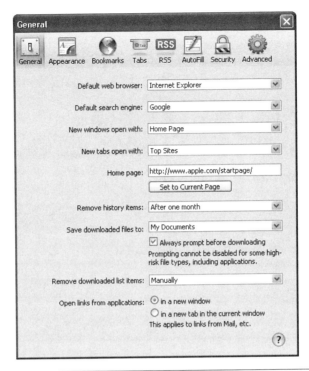

FIGURE 7-15 Safari preferences let you be in charge of the browser.

- Auto-remove History items removes history that is over a month old.
- An amazing number of preferences you can configure to personalize Safari (see Figure 7-15).

Explore Opera

As with other third-party web browsers, Opera claims to be better than all the rest (see Figure 7-16). And as you would expect, you can surf the Web easily, bookmark pages, set home pages, and set security options. Here are a few reasons why you might choose Opera over other browsers:

- Opera Link lets you synchronize data from different computers and devices. You can sync things like custom searches, bookmarks, history, and even notes between multiple computers (like the one at home and the one at work).
- Quick Find is a feature that remembers content on a page, so if you ever forget where you saw something on the Internet, this feature can help you find it again.
- Search quickly from various search engines such as Google, eBay, Amazon, and more.
- Opera Mail lets you manage your e-mail while staying integrated with Opera. This may help you work faster and better, or at least be more efficient.
- Mouse gestures let you navigate the Web with touchpad movements like a flick left or right, or up or down.

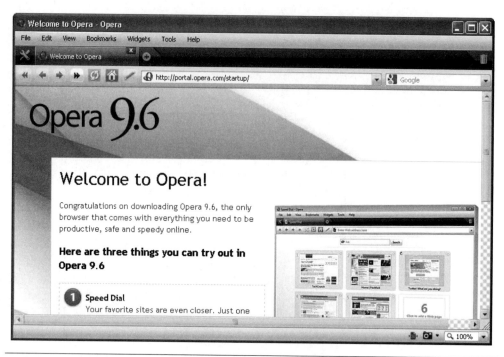

FIGURE 7-16 Opera may look quite a bit different from other browsers, but it offers quite a few features you've never seen before.

- Widgets let you add small web applications such as news feeds and games to your desktop.
- Speed Dial offers a set of visual bookmarks to help you access your favorite pages more quickly.

Explore Google Chrome

Google Chrome was created by Google, so it has to be great, right? Featuring a sleek, clean interface (see Figure 7-17), the Google search engine has outperformed other search engines for years. With Google Chrome, you get the power of Google built right in. Chrome offers some features other web browsers do not:

- The Task Manager for web sites lets you view all web sites currently open in the browser (see Figure 7-18). Just press SHIFT + ESC. Using the Task Manager, you can see how much memory is being used by those web pages and close them if desired.
- You can launch web sites from the Start menu or the Quick Launch bar.
- Upgraded tabs let you expand tab functionality. Clicking New Tab opens a page that features your most-visited web sites, making bookmarking those sites simple.
- Incognito browsing lets you browse the Web and have all aspects of that session erased after you close Chrome. This lets you surf where you want without fear of others finding out.

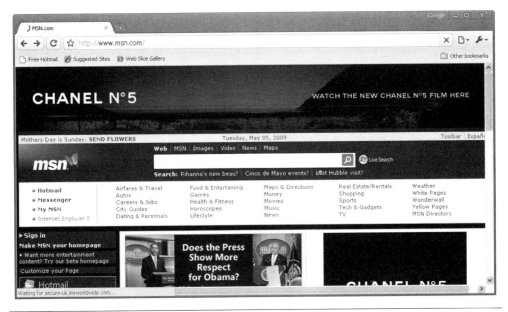

FIGURE 7-17   Chrome's interface is sleek and clean.

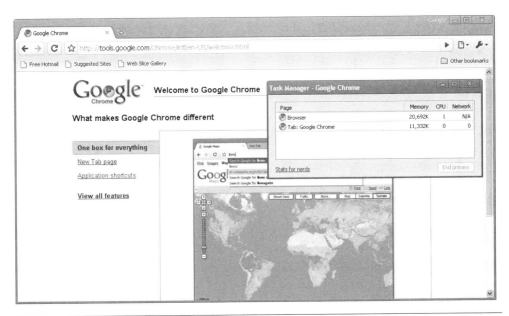

FIGURE 7-18   Task Manager lets you see how open web sites are affecting memory usage.

PART III

Installing and Using Hardware and Software

8

Add New Hardware

HOW TO...

- Insert and read from a memory card
- Connect and install a digital camera
- Connect and install a mini-printer, card reader, or scanner
- Connect and install unrecognized, new hardware
- Connect and install a Bluetooth device
- Connect a backup device
- Connect, install, and sync a cell phone

Your netbook probably didn't come with additional external hardware like a Bluetooth mouse or a backup device, but you may well be interested in obtaining and installing such devices after using your netbook for a while. You may already own hardware you want to install too, like a digital camera or cell phone, or you may be thinking about purchasing equipment like a larger keyboard you can pack in your suitcase or a small printer or backup device you can use while on the go. Whatever circumstance you find yourself in, installing hardware is a common task for netbook users.

In most instances, installing a device involves connecting it with a USB cable, turning it on, waiting for Windows to install it, and then learning to use it. However, sometimes a piece of hardware won't install or isn't recognized, and when that happens, you'll have to find another way to install the device. This may involve downloading and installing a driver, or installing the driver and software from a CD or DVD included with the device.

In this chapter, you'll learn how to install most hardware devices; in the next chapter, you'll learn how to install devices that aren't recognized, require an installation disk, and/or require you to locate a device driver on your own.

Insert and Read from a Memory Card

Most netbooks come with a media card reader. This is a small, rectangular slot in the side, back, or front of the netbook that accepts media cards from digital cameras and cell phones, as shown in Figure 8-1. Because media card readers are so user-friendly, you may find that removing the digital card from your camera and inserting it into the card reader is more convenient than physically connecting the camera to your netbook with a USB cable.

There are other uses for media cards, though. You can use a media card the same way you used to use a floppy disk: You can copy data on to the media card from a desktop PC, and then transfer the data to the netbook via the netbook's card reader. This is a handy alternative when a network isn't available, when you don't have your netbook available, or when you need to transfer data quickly. (Of course, you can do the same with a USB flash drive, but it's always good to have alternatives. Figure 8-2 shows another alternative.)

To use the reader you simply remove the card from your digital camera, phone, or other device and insert it into the proper slot:

1. Insert the media card into the card reader. Most of the time, the printed side of the card faces upward.
2. When prompted, select the option you prefer (see Figure 8-3). You may want to open the folder to view the files, if they are documents or other data. If they are pictures, you may choose to view pictures with a program such as Windows Live Photo Gallery, import the pictures using a program such as Windows Live Photo Gallery or the Microsoft Scanner and Camera Wizard, or view a slideshow of the images. Most often you'll want to import the data and save it to your netbook's hard drive.

The options you'll see after inserting a memory card depend on your operating system, installed programs, and AutoPlay preferences.

3. Depending on your selection, you can view, edit, or manage the data as desired (see Figure 8-4).

Card Reader

FIGURE 8-1   Most netbooks have a built-in media card reader. Some have more than one reader, as shown here.

FIGURE 8-2   If your netbook doesn't have a media card reader, there are options, such as this external USB card reader.

Did You Know? **Erasing Your Media Card**

When you import pictures from a digital media card, they are saved to your netbook. They are not erased from your media card unless you specifically tell the importing application to delete them after importing.

FIGURE 8-3   You will be prompted to view, import, or print any pictures on your media card after inserting the card.

FIGURE 8-4   After importing pictures using Windows Live Photo Gallery, the images are ready to access.

Connect and Install a Digital Camera

Digital cameras come with all kinds of additional hardware, including cables for connecting the camera to the computer. Some cameras come with a cable for transferring photos and another cable for transferring video. Before you can connect your camera to your netbook, you'll have to know what cable to use and how to connect it. After you know how to physically connect the camera, you also need to know the setting to use once the camera is connected. Some cameras simply need to be powered on, but others need to be configured to a "playback" or "computer" setting. You can find this information and more in your camera's user manual.

With the camera connected to the computer and the camera properly enabled, to connect and install a digital camera:

1. Wait while the camera is installed. Most of the time, installation will be automatic.

2. After the installation has completed, you can choose what to do with the photos on the camera. On a Windows XP netbook, the Microsoft Scanner and Camera Wizard will often automatically import the picture.

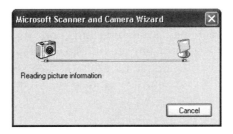

 Almost every netbook comes with a card reader. You don't have to install your camera if the camera uses a compatible memory card. Just take it out of the camera and insert it into the netbook.

What you see when you plug in a digital camera on a Windows Vista or Windows 7 machine differs from what you'll see on Windows XP. Depending on what else is installed, you'll see a window like what is shown in Figure 8-5.

If you are running Linux on your netbook, good luck. Unless your camera is specifically built to be Linux-compatible, it probably won't install. You can try third-party applications such as libgphoto2, but you'll have to locate it, download, and install it first.

FIGURE 8-5   On a Windows Vista or Windows 7 netbook, you'll see something like this when connecting a camera.

Connect and Install a Mini-Printer, Card Reader, or Scanner

You install additional hardware devices—such as printers, keyboards, scanners, and the like—by connecting the device and turning it on. Most of the time, the device will plug directly into a USB port or connect via a USB cable. Rarely, a device will require a FireWire port and, on occasion, an Ethernet port. As with a digital camera, you generally connect the device, plug it in, and/or turn it on.

To connect such a hardware device:

1. Read the instructions that came with the device. The instructions may require that you install a driver before connecting the device, but this is not the norm.
2. Connect the device and turn it on per the manufacturer's instructions.
3. Wait while the device is installed. If the device does not install properly, refer to Chapter 9. In most cases, hardware installs automatically.

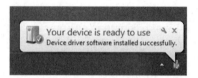

4. If the device contains photos, the photos may begin to import automatically, especially on a netbook running Windows XP. If the device connects via USB and already contains pictures (such as a card reader with a card inserted), the pictures may also begin to import automatically. This is shown in Figure 8-6.
5. If the device does not contain photos, you may see a message that the device has installed successfully and is ready to use.

The generic instructions in this section can be applied to the installation of USB speakers, USB flash drives, headphones, microphones, and other plug-and-play hardware.

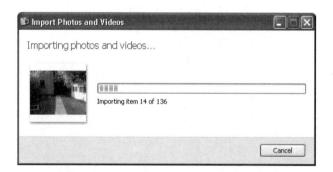

FIGURE 8-6   If the device connects via USB and already contains pictures (like a card reader with a card inserted), the pictures may begin to import automatically.

Connect and Install Unrecognized New Hardware

Devices that aren't plug-and-play or that require configuration during the installation process may cause the operating system to bring up the Found New Hardware Wizard on XP or the Add Hardware Wizard on Windows Vista. Windows 7 may prompt you to visit the manufacturer's web site, run Windows Update, or wait for Windows to find a solution (see Figure 8-7).

If you're prompted to work through a wizard in Windows XP, follow the prompts:

1. When prompted, choose the recommended options, clicking Next to work through the wizard (see Figure 8-8). If this doesn't work, you can try a different approach later.

If hardware doesn't install automatically in Windows Vista or Windows 7, you won't work through any kind of wizard. You'll simply follow the directions offered for locating and installing the proper driver for the device.

2. If the hardware does not install properly, click Back to try another option.
3. Because netbooks do not have CD or DVD drives, when prompted, select Don't search, I will choose the driver to install (or something similar), as shown in Figure 8-9. Click Next.

Wizard screens differ depending on the operating system installed.

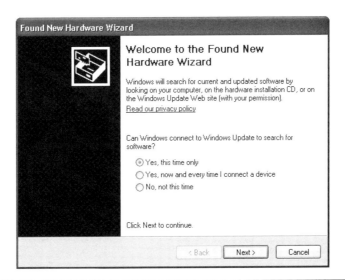

FIGURE 8-7   If a device isn't recognized in Windows XP, you'll be prompted to work through a wizard.

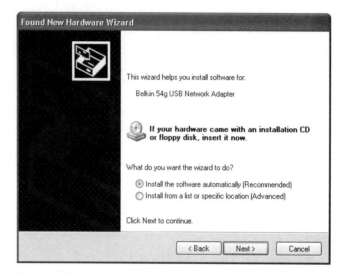

FIGURE 8-8 Select the recommended options to install an unrecognized device.

4. Choose your device from the list of devices offered (see Figure 8-10). Click Next.
5. Continue through the wizard to complete the installation. If installation is not successful and you are prompted to install from a disk, refer to Chapter 9.

Sometimes, simply rebooting and attempting to reinstall works. Try that before moving to other options.

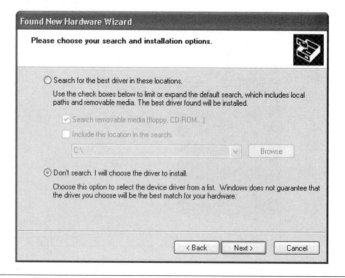

FIGURE 8-9 Select Don't search to choose the hardware from a list.

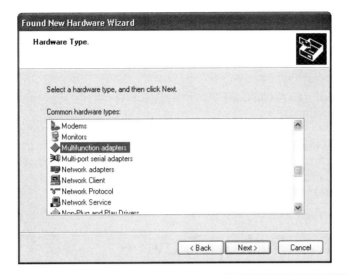

FIGURE 8-10   Select your device type from the list offered.

Connect and Install a Bluetooth Device

Bluetooth devices allow you to connect hardware wirelessly. Generally, a Bluetooth device has two parts: The first part is a USB "dongle" that plugs into a USB port, and the second is the Bluetooth device itself (see Figure 8-11). The first time you use the device, you "pair" it with its USB dongle. This pairing allows the device to send and

FIGURE 8-11   A Bluetooth mouse and USB dongle make a great addition to any netbook.

receive information to and from the notebook and keeps it from interfering with other Bluetooth devices you've connected. Bluetooth devices you'll use with your netbook may include headphones, speakers, or mice, or perhaps even a keyboard.

To connect a Bluetooth device:

1. Read the instructions that came with the device. Specifically, look for how to pair the device.
2. Plug the USB dongle into an available USB port. Wait while the hardware is installed.
3. Perform the tasks to pair the dongle and device. Most of the time, you'll need to hold down a button on the dongle for a few seconds and then hold down a button on the device for a few seconds.

Connect a Backup Device

Because netbooks come with a media card reader, in a pinch you can save data to any media card. Additionally, netbooks come with several USB ports, which readily accept USB thumb drives and flash drives. Connecting these devices is simply plug-and-play. Once connected, you can see the device in the Computer or My Computer window.

There are several physical backup options:

- USB flash drive or thumb drive
- External hard drive
- Cell phone with data storage capabilities
- Portable music player (iPod, Zune)
- External CD/DVD burner

To connect a backup device, simply plug it in. Click the Start button and Computer (or Start and My Computer in Windows XP) to view the device (see Figure 8-12). You can drag files to the device to copy them and thus create a backup.

Backup Options

There are lots of virtual places to back up data. If you download and install Windows Live Essentials and get a free Windows Live ID, you can backup data on the Internet using SkyDrive (see Figure 8-13). You can also take advantage of Microsoft Office Live and create your own workspace, where you can share and store files. You'll learn more about both of these in Chapter 12.

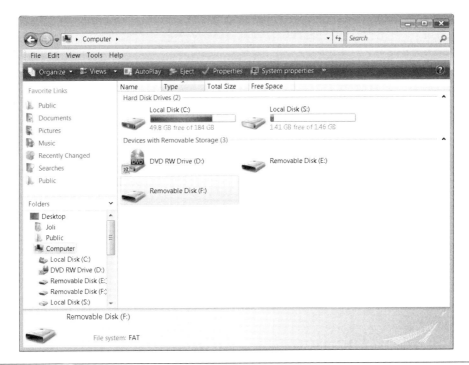

FIGURE 8-12   Thumb drives, external hard drives, flash drives, and other USB storage devices appear in Computer (or My Computer).

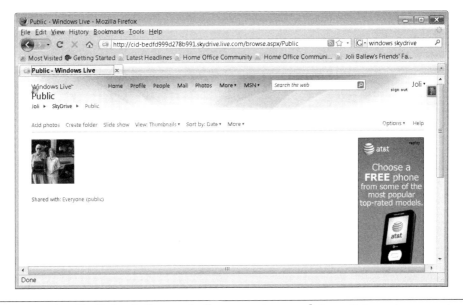

FIGURE 8-13   SkyDrive is free and allows you to save data on Internet servers to back up your netbook while on the go.

About Installing Phones

You can connect an iPhone to any Windows netbook and import the pictures from it, but you can't purchase and download music or video without iTunes. A Blackberry requires specialized Blackberry software, too, and Blackberry App World to download applications, music, and video. The same is true of most phones: You are required to install software specific to the phone before you can sync the phone with your computer.

Connect, Install, and Sync a Cell Phone

To connect and install a cell phone, you need to have the proper cables, a phone that is recognized by Windows, and possibly additional software. You can get information about your specific cell phone and how to install it from the phone manufacturer's web site. As with other devices, though, Windows is pretty good about installing a driver to communicate with the phone, but you may need additional software to interact with it.

Obtain the Required Software

Before trying to sync your phone, download music or applications, or otherwise interact with the phone via the computer, visit the phone manufacturer's web site. Download and install the required software. There will be specific instructions on the manufacturer's web site. In Figure 8-14, iTunes is being installed. iTunes

FIGURE 8-14 The first step in connecting and installing a cell phone is to download and install the required software. For the iPhone, it's iTunes.

is required for obtaining music and video online and syncing the phone with the computer. Other phones require similar applications.

Once the software is installed, you may be prompted to register or perform an initial sync with the computer. Carefully read the instructions and configure the settings during this installation.

Sync the Phone

With the software installed, you're ready to begin synchronizing the phone with your netbook. What you can sync depends on the phone and the capabilities of the software and hardware, but for the most part, you can sync contacts, music, calendar data, pictures, videos, web browser bookmarks, and e-mail accounts. You'll use the software to configure how to sync these items.

Your phone will appear in the Computer window, as shown in Figure 8-15. Double-click the icon to see items stored on the phone, if the phone allows this. You might be able to pull photos from the phone using this method.

FIGURE 8-15   Look in Computer for your phone.

9

Install Software

It's highly unlikely that your netbook came with a CD or DVD drive. There are many reasons for this, but it's mainly due to the size of the netbook: There just isn't enough room for a drive. Also, it takes a lot of battery power to run a spinning CD/DVD drive, and with limited battery resources, allowing a CD or DVD drive to run would drain battery power really quickly.

So what do you do when you want to install a software program? If there's no CD or DVD drive, you have to have another option. Luckily, there are several. You can connect an external CD/DVD drive, share and then connect to a network drive, install the program from the Internet, or even copy the installation files to a network share, among others.

Choose an Installation Option

It's important to know your options for installing an application from a CD or DVD so that you can choose the best method for your situation. Once you've decided on an option, simply skip to the appropriate part of the chapter. Here are your options in a nutshell:

- **Use the Internet**   If the program you want to install is available from the Internet, this is the easiest option. Try this option for anti-virus or anti-malware applications, web-based applications such as Windows Live Mail or Windows Live Photo Gallery, and web browsers such as Firefox and Google Chrome.
- **Connect an external CD/DVD drive**   If you own or can borrow an external CD/DVD drive that connects using a USB cable, this is the second best option. CD and DVD drives are plug-and-play, so installation should be a breeze. Once connected, you can use the drive as if it were an internal drive and actually part of the netbook. Figure 9-1 shows a set of DVDs.
- **Browse to a shared network CD/DVD drive**   If you have a home network with a desktop PC, it's easy to share the PC's CD/DVD drive. Once shared, insert the CD, browse to it from the netbook, and run the installation program.
- **Copy the CD to a network share**   If you have a home network, you can copy the CD to a network share (that's a shared folder) and then browse to the network share to access the installation files.

FIGURE 9-1   CDs and DVDs are common installation mediums for applications and software.

Locate, Download, and Install the Software Using the Internet

Many companies sell their software on the Internet as a download. Anti-virus software is a common application available for download, as are web-based programs such as Windows Live Essentials. If you can obtain the software from the Internet, this is the best option because you won't have to connect any hardware or copy any installation files. To find out if the software you want is available for download, visit the manufacturer's web site.

If you find the program online, you will need to follow the directions on the web site for downloading and installing it. This generally involves clicking Download a few times, clicking Run, and working through a set of prompts. It's pretty easy.

If you are downloading a "free" version of something, beware. First, you'll be prompted at every turn to get the "full" version (you'll have to pay for that version), and second, unless you know that the software is offered by a reputable company, you could infect your computer with malware or spyware.

Although all download processes differ a little, for the most part you simply follow the prompts carefully. In this example, we'll download AVG Free Anti-Virus Software from AVG Technologies, formerly Grisoft. This is a great program to have, especially if you don't have any anti-virus protection currently.

AVG is a reputable company. Its software is trusted by more than 80 million users.

To download and install a program from the Internet:

1. Locate the program online.
2. Locate the Download, Get It Now, or a similar link or button for the product you want (see Figure 9-2).
3. Continue through additional web pages to select the program to install (see Figure 9-3).
4. When prompted, click Save File as shown in Figure 9-4.
5. Double-click the executable file to start the installation.

An executable file ends in .exe and begins the installation process.

6. Click Next to work through the installation process. Most of the time, a standard installation is the best option when prompted, as shown in Figure 9-5.
7. Click Finish and reboot the netbook if necessary.

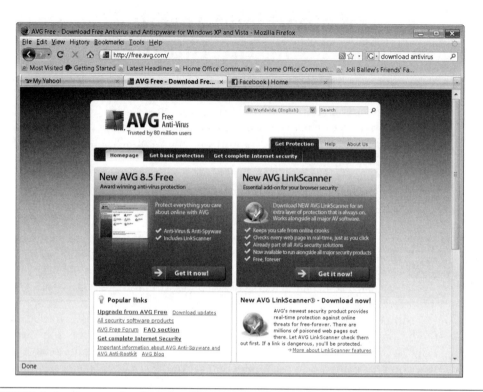

FIGURE 9-2 Locate the download button for the product you want to install.

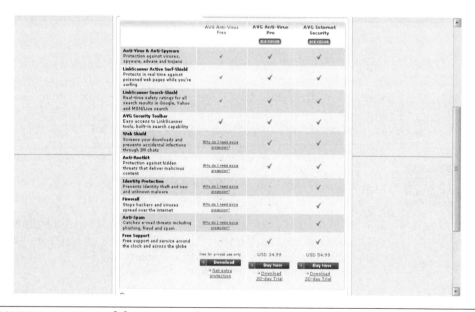

FIGURE 9-3 Most of the time you have several options and program selections.

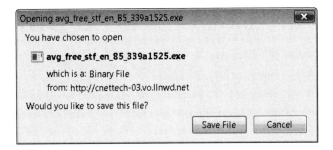

FIGURE 9-4 Choose Save File and save the file to your hard drive. You can then copy the installation files to a network share, a shared CD or DVD drive, or a USB flash drive if you want to make a backup copy of the software.

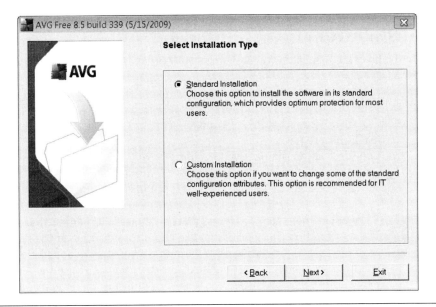

FIGURE 9-5 Work through the installation wizard to install the program.

Use an External CD or DVD Drive

Desktop PCs come with a CD/DVD drive built into the tower. Netbooks don't, because they are too small to incorporate that size hardware and because a spinning drive would sap the power from the battery very quickly. However, netbooks do have USB ports, and if you have an external CD/DVD drive, it's simple to connect. Once connected, installing from the drive is just like installing from one that's built in.

Connect and Install the Drive

To connect an external drive to your netbook:

1. Plug the drive into an electrical outlet, using the supplied hardware.
2. Connect the drive to the netbook using its USB cable.
3. You should not have to turn the drive on, but if you don't hear a whirring noise, go ahead and look for an on/off switch.
4. Wait while the drive installs (see Figure 9-6).

Install from the External Drive

With the drive installed, you can access the drive as if it were part of the netbook. To install a CD or DVD:

1. Insert the CD or DVD into the external drive.
2. If an installation dialog box appears, work through the installation wizard to install the program.
3. If an installation dialog box does not appear:
   a. Click Start, click Computer (or My Computer).
   b. Right-click the drive letter, and choose to install the program (see Figure 9-7).

 Some applications look to the installation CD or DVD the first time the program is run or the first time something like clip art is accessed. If the data is or was acquired from a non-native drive during installation, the application may prevent you from accessing it, offering a message that you can't use the program across a network. In these instances, you'll need to uninstall the program, copy the entire CD/DVD disk to the netbook, and reinstall from the netbook files. You might be able to reinstall using the Full Install option, but that still won't always work.

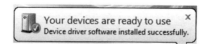

FIGURE 9-6   CD/DVD drives are almost always plug-and-play and will install automatically.

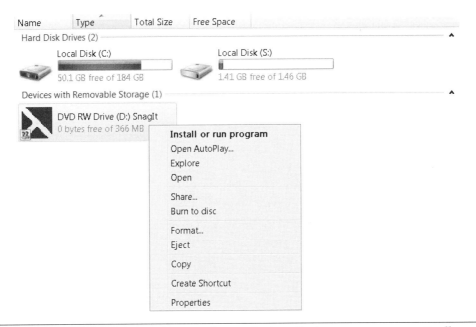

FIGURE 9-7   If the program does not begin the installation process automatically, right-click the icon for the external drive to see the installation options.

Access a Networked CD or DVD Drive

Another way to install a program from a CD or DVD is to share a CD/DVD drive already installed on a networked computer and then access that drive from the netbook. The network can be wired or wireless; you only need to be able to access the drive from your netbook. Using this method requires that you first share the drive on the networked PC and then that you browse to that drive from your netbook.

Share the Network Drive

On a networked desktop PC or laptop computer, share the CD/DVD drive:

1. Click Start, and click Computer (or My Computer).
2. Right-click the CD/DVD drive and click Share, Sharing, or Sharing and Security (whichever is offered). See Figure 9-8.
3. Locate the option to share the drive. If you don't see an option, click Advanced Sharing, as shown in Figure 9-9. Choose the option to share the drive.
4. Click OK, Close, or the appropriate options to apply the changes.

Note   Once shared, the drive icon will have an icon on it that shows it's shared.

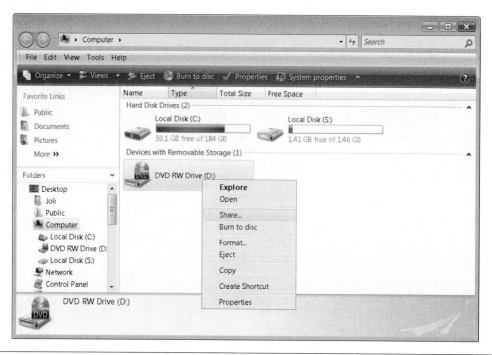

FIGURE 9-8 Right-click the drive to share and click Share, Sharing, or Sharing and Security.

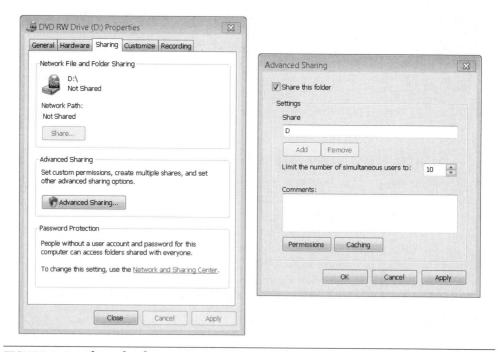

FIGURE 9-9 Share the drive so you can access it from your netbook over the network.

Install Software from a Shared Network CD or DVD Drive

To install software from a shared network CD/DVD drive, insert the disk into the drive and close any installation windows on the desktop PC or laptop computer. (You want to install the program on your netbook, not this PC.) Then, on the netbook, browse to the location of the drive to access the installation files:

1. Verify the netbook is able to access the network. You may want to access the Network window in Windows XP or the Network and Sharing Center in Windows Vista and Windows 7. You should be able to view other networked computers (see Figure 9-10).

   Alert: Just because you can access the Internet using the network doesn't mean you have access to the local network. To have local access, you should be part of the same workgroup or homegroup and have the required permissions and privileges.

2. Browse to the shared drive. There are several ways to do this, including using Explorer:
   a. Right-click Start and choose Explore or Open Windows Explorer.
   b. Click Network.
   c. Double-click the icon for the computer that contains the shared drive.
   d. Double-click the icon for the drive (see Figure 9-11).
3. Locate the executable file to start the installation.

Often the executable file that begins installation is represented by a colorful icon with the name or logo of the software on it.

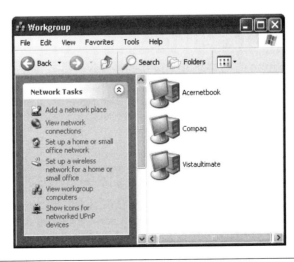

FIGURE 9-10   If you can view other networked computers, you're part of the local area network.

FIGURE 9-11 Locate the shared CD/DVD drive. It's often called D:.

Use a Network Share

You can copy the CD's installation files to any networked computer. Once you've copied them, you can access the shared data using any type of network connection. There are a few steps: You have to copy the files into a folder others will have access to, you have to copy the files, and you have to be able to access the files from your netbook.

Choose a Shared or Public Folder

To make the installation files available from a network share (a shared folder on a networked computer), you must either create a shared folder to hold the files or know how to use the Public or Shared folders that come with all Windows PCs. The easiest way to share data is to save the data to the already created and available Shared or Public folders. Access to these folders is made available automatically to those who have access to the network and your PC.

In Windows XP, there is a set of folders called Shared folders. They include Shared Documents, Shared Pictures, and Shared Music. To locate these shared folders, right-click the Start button, click Explore all users, and locate Shared Documents.

In Windows Vista and Windows 7, the name of these shared folders was changed to Public. Public folders include Public Documents, Public Pictures, and Public Music, among others. The best way to navigate to these folders is to access C:\Users\Public (see Figure 9-12).

Copy the CD to a Network Drive

Although there are many options for copying the contents of a CD/DVD to a network share, in this example, we'll simply browse to the files on the CD or DVD and drag and drop those files to the shared folder.

Using a desktop PC or a laptop computer:

1. Insert the CD into the CD/DVD drive. Close any installation windows that appear.
2. Click Start, and click Computer (or My Computer).
3. Locate the icon for the CD/DVD drive.
4. Browse to the Shared or Public folders.
5. Position the two windows so you can see both.
6. Right-click the icon for the installation CD, shown in Figure 9-14 in the top window, and drag the icon to the icon for the Public folder, also shown in Figure 9-13.

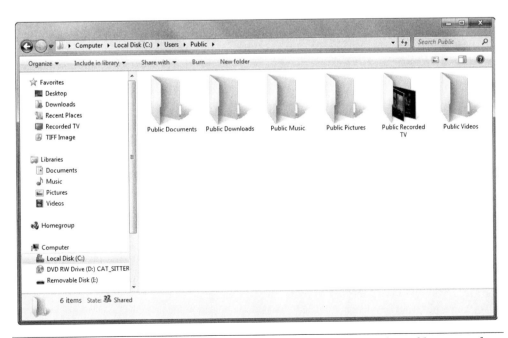

FIGURE 9-12   In Windows Vista and Windows 7, it's easiest to share files using the Public folders.

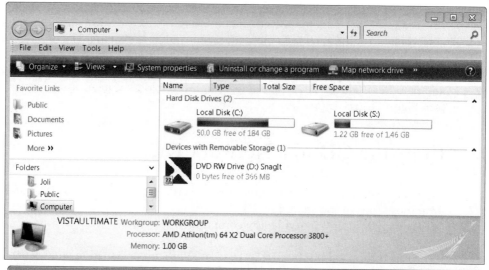

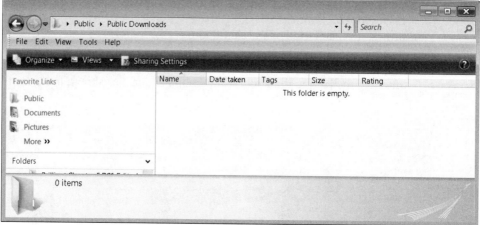

FIGURE 9-13   Position the windows so you can see both, and so that you can drag
and drop the files to copy them.

7. You'll see a new icon appear as you drag, shown in Figure 9-14. Drop the icon
   into the desired window.
8. Choose Copy Here.

 This process works no matter what window you are dragging from or what window
you are dragging to.

FIGURE 9-14   Drag and drop to copy the files from the Computer window to the Public folder.

Install Software from the Network Drive

Once the entire CD has been copied to the network share, browse to the share to access the executable files, as shown in Figure 9-15:

1. From the netbook, connect to the network and browse to the location of the shared folder.
2. Open the folder to locate the executable file.

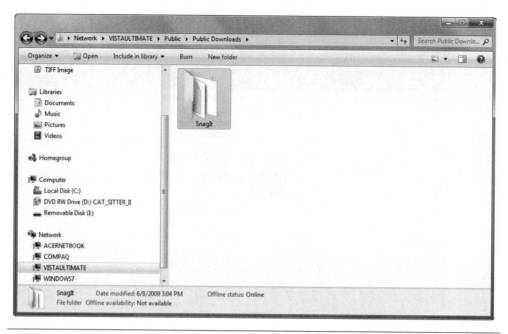

FIGURE 9-15 Locate the shared folder that contains the copied files.

10

Web Cameras and Video Messaging

HOW TO...

- Find out if you have a built-in web cam
- Test the camera for voice and video
- Install a third-party web cam
- Choose a video messaging program
- Download and install a messaging program
- Obtain a messaging ID
- Configure the messaging application
- Add a contact
- Send your web cam
- Receive web cam video from others
- Be safe while using a web cam

Every netbook I've ever seen comes with a built-in web cam. Sometimes the web cam comes with its own software for holding a video chat, but more often than not you'll opt to download and install an instant messaging program such as Yahoo!, Windows Live Messenger, AIM, or Trillian. These programs are all well known and more than functional and allow you to voice and video chat with others easily.

In this chapter, you'll first discover whether you have a web cam and install one if you don't, and learn what your options are for conferencing with others. You'll also learn how to add contacts and buddies, how to set up the program you choose, and, finally, how to use your web cam (and built-in microphone) to video and voice chat with others.

Discover Your Web Cam

A web cam is a piece of computer hardware, like a keyboard or mouse. A web cam lets you send live video of yourself to others you choose to video chat with. Video messaging, as it's often referred to, has become more and more popular over the last few years, allowing people to keep in touch with sons and daughters overseas, grandkids in different states, and even parents while they're on business trips. Your netbook probably came with a built-in web cam and microphone; most netbooks do.

Find Out If You Have a Built-In Web Cam

You may already know that you have a built-in web cam, and if that's the case, you can skip this section completely. However, if you aren't sure, there are several ways to find out:

- Read the documentation that came with your netbook. If your netbook has a web cam built in, it'll say so on the box or user's guide.
- Look for a very small camera above the computer screen. Generally the camera lens is a small, round lens located on the top of the monitor, in the middle.
- In Control Panel, browse through the hardware options. Your camera should be listed there.
- Open Computer (or My Computer in Windows XP) and look for the camera in the appropriate section of the window, as shown in Figure 10-1.

Test the Camera for Voice and Video

Once you're sure you have a built-in web camera, it's best to test it to make sure it's installed and working properly. For the most part, this only involves locating the icon for the camera and double-clicking it. In Figure 10-1, you'd double-click the camera icon in the My Computer window, but you can also locate the camera from the

Did You Know? Look for Proprietary Software

Some netbooks have their own applications that sit right on the desktop. Acer has one called Launch Manager. You may be able to locate and open the camera from there.

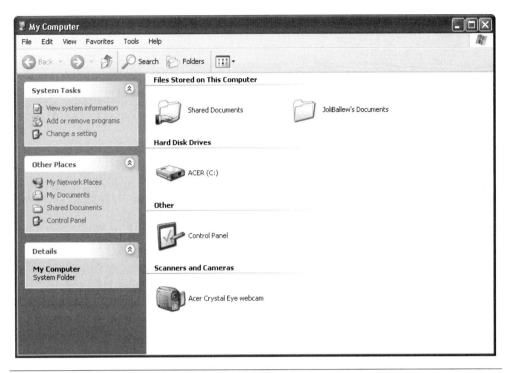

FIGURE 10-1   You'll see the web cam listed in the Computer or My Computer window.

Camera and Scanners window (among other places). To start the camera (and these are generic instructions):

1. In Windows, click Start, then click Control Panel. In Linux, look under the tabs or related icons.
2. Look for one of the following:
   a. Printers and Other Hardware (Windows XP).
   b. Scanners and Cameras (Windows XP).
   c. Hardware and Sound (Windows Vista and Windows 7).
   d. Scanners and Cameras (Windows Vista and Windows 7).
   e. Webcam, Web Cam, or Camera (Linux) (see Figure 10-2).
   f. A keyboard key with a picture of a camera on it. Press the key to start the web cam.

 If you have a manufacturer-specific application on your desktop, look for an icon named Messaging, Camera, or Web Cam. You can often click this icon to start the camera.

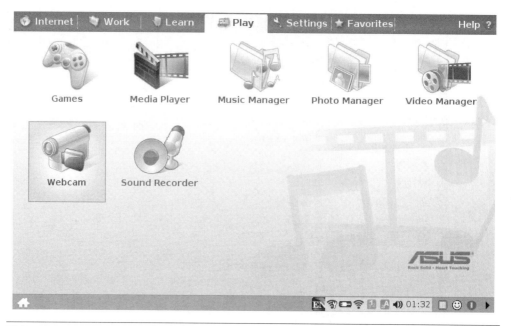

FIGURE 10-2 In Linux, look for a web cam option.

3. Double-click the icon for the camera.
4. Depending on the make and model of your netbook, third-party applications, and the operating system that's installed, you may be prompted to set up the camera. It's more likely it'll begin working automatically, as shown in Figure 10-3.

 If you're prompted to set up the camera, follow the prompts as required.

5. Click the X in the top-right window to close the window and the web cam. You're going to want to use the camera with a messaging program, not through this window.

 If your web cam doesn't start automatically, it may not be installed properly. If that's the case, refer to the next section, "Troubleshoot a Built-In Web Cam," for more information.

Troubleshoot a Built-In Web Cam

If you know a web cam is built in but you haven't been able to activate it, it may not be properly installed. The web cam may also require software to run that you inadvertently uninstalled during the process of cleaning up your netbook, perhaps

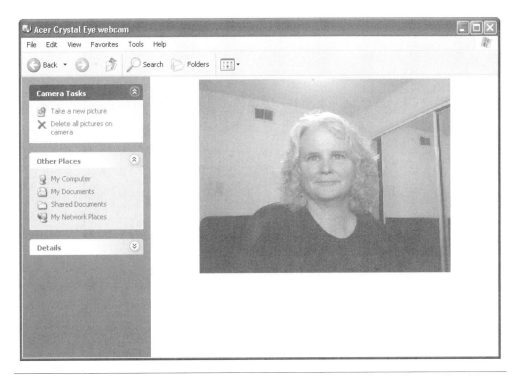

FIGURE 10-3   Double-click the camera icon anywhere and the web cam should start automatically.

when you first purchased it. If you're having trouble accessing your web cam, check Device Manager to see if the computer detects a problem. If a problem exists, you can reinstall the web cam device driver; if no problem is detected, it's possible you need only install a messaging program and configure it to resolve the problem.

To check Device Manager on a Windows netbook:

1. Click Start, and right-click Computer (or My Computer).
2. Click Properties.
3. On Vista or Windows 7, click Device Manager. On Windows XP, click the Hardware tab first, and then click Device Manager (see Figure 10-4).
4. Locate the web cam in the list. It may be under Imaging Devices. If there's a red *X* or yellow exclamation point, double-click the entry to open the hardware dialog box.
5. Click the Driver tab and click Update Driver (see Figure 10-5).

If this process does not resolve the problem, visit the manufacturer's web site, locate the driver, then download and install it. Refer to Chapter 9 for more information.

FIGURE 10-4 Locate Device Manager to troubleshoot any hardware issue.

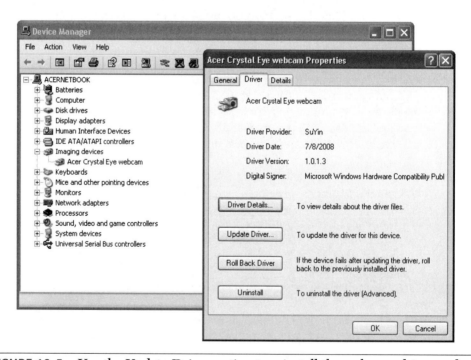

FIGURE 10-5 Use the Update Driver option to reinstall the web cam driver and resolve a problem.

Install a Third-Party Web Cam

If your netbook didn't come with a web cam, you can install one. First, read the directions that came with the web cam you purchased and follow the directions for installation. If the instructions call for the installation of an accompanying CD, first try to install the camera as detailed here. If that doesn't work, refer to Chapter 9. If you don't have instructions, follow the directions here.

To install a web cam:

1. Plug the web cam into the appropriate port on the computer. Generally this is a USB port.
2. Wait to see if the hardware installs automatically.
3. If you see a prompt like the one shown in Figure 10-6, click Locate and install driver software (recommended).
4. If installation completes successfully, you'll see something similar to what is shown in Figure 10-7. If the camera does not install correctly, you'll have to install it from the CD or download and install the driver from the Internet. In either case, refer to Chapter 9.

FIGURE 10-6   If prompted, let Windows locate and install the driver.

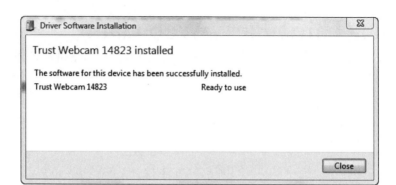

FIGURE 10-7 You'll be informed if the installation was a success.

Obtain a Messaging Application

Although your netbook may have come with its own web cam application, you'll still need to download and install a universal messaging program. With a messaging program, you'll be able to video and voice chat with people around the world. There are several options, including applications from Yahoo! and Microsoft, both of which would be good choices for you and your netbook.

While Yahoo! Messenger and Windows Live Messenger seem to be the most popular, there are many other applications available. One application, called Trillian, lets you log in with multiple messaging identities at the same time and offers features that other programs don't. Trillian lets you communicate with AIM, ICQ, MSN, Yahoo! Messenger, and IRC, all of which are in use around the world as chat clients, without any problem. Trillian also supports multiple simultaneous connections, encrypted messaging, and file transfers. Note that you may have to upgrade to a paid version to have access to the most popular features. Skype is also an option, and is included and preinstalled with some netbooks.

Did You Know? **How Instant Messaging Evolved**

When instant messaging first became popular, instant messaging programs were often proprietary. This meant that if you used AOL's messaging program, the person you wanted to communicate with also had to have that program and be using it. Yahoo! was the same way too, along with others. This caused users to have multiple messaging programs, and you'd have to open the program you wanted to use depending on the person you wanted to communicate with. Now, things are much better, and larger universal programs let you communicate with just about anyone using just about any messaging program.

Choose a Video Messaging Program

The application you choose is really dependent on your preferences, but I suggest you stick with a popular program such as Yahoo! Messenger or Windows Live Messenger. This way, you can be sure that the program you choose allows you to communicate with the people you want to talk to most and that the program is compatible with your computer system. By selecting a popular and well-known program, it's also easy to have your relatives, friends, or colleagues download the same program, which reduces compatibility problems that tend to occur with web cam communications. Ask your friends, colleagues, and family what they use, too, and consider opting for a program they suggest and enjoy using.

 I prefer and suggest Windows Live Messenger over other mainstream messaging applications. If you're not sure what to choose, try this one.

Most of the more popular programs support audio and video conferencing, file sharing, and the ability to send messages to mobile phones, even if you have to install add-ins to obtain the feature. Most also allow you to save your instant messaging conversations. Generally, they enable you to receive a message someone has sent while you were offline, by saving that message and sending it to you once you're online again. Finally, these applications are free.

 I really like the Windows Live Essentials application suite, and have dedicated an entire chapter to it. Windows Live Messenger is part of that suite and thus is incorporated into all of the Live applications, including Live Mail and Live Toolbar.

Download and Install a Messaging Program

Once you've decided on a program to use as your messaging client, you'll need to download and install it. Your first task is to locate the program on the Internet.

To download and install a messaging client:

1. Browse to the location of the application on the Internet. Figure 10-8 shows the Trillian download page.
2. Click the Download button or link. (Note that you may have to click Download again if a new page appears.)
3. Click Run (see Figure 10-9). You may have to click Run again.

 If you're running Firefox, choose Save File, and then double-click the file to run the installation program.

4. If prompted to choose additional features, install additional programs, or select a paid version of the program, read the information carefully and choose wisely.

FIGURE 10-8   Locate the download page for the program you wish to obtain.

 When working through the installation process, install only what you need and nothing more. Don't install toolbars, add-ons, or other applications you don't need or won't use.

5. When the program has completed the installation process, sign in with your messaging ID. If you don't have an ID yet, you'll have to get one.

FIGURE 10-9   Click Run to download and install the application.

Obtain a Messaging ID

Messaging programs require you to have a messaging ID to sign in with. It's how you're identified when you are online. Some programs let you use your own e-mail address as an ID, while others require (or highly suggest) you obtain one from them. Microsoft's Windows Live Messenger lets you do either, but you can incorporate Windows Live services only if you create a Windows Live ID.

Whatever the case, when you first try to log in to your newly installed messaging program, you'll be prompted to log in with an ID. If you don't already have one, you'll have to create one. Figure 10-10 shows the Create your Windows Live ID page from Microsoft.

When creating an ID, you'll be asked to input the following:

- Your e-mail address or the ID you'd prefer to create
- A password of a specific length and meeting specific requirements
- Your first and last name
- Your country
- Your state, zip code, and related information
- Your gender
- Your birth year or birth date
- An alternate e-mail address

You should never be asked for or supply:

- Your social security number.
- A credit card number.
- Passwords for your e-mail account or other online accounts.
- Money.

FIGURE 10-10   To log in to your new messaging program, you'll need to create an ID.

Note If you choose to use your own e-mail account instead of an account native to the application (@Live.com or @Hotmail.com for Windows Live Messenger, @yahoo.com for Yahoo! Messenger, and so on), you may have to complete additional steps, such as verifying your address or adding the address to your preferences for that program.

Configure the Messaging Application

Once signed into your messaging application, it's likely you won't have any contacts or buddies, and you won't see any toolbars or configuration options. Figure 10-11 shows Windows Live Messenger on the left and Yahoo! Messenger on the right. You'll want to explorer any areas of the interface named Settings, Tools, Actions, or Options to see what's available.

FIGURE 10-11 Most messaging programs hide their menus and configuration options.

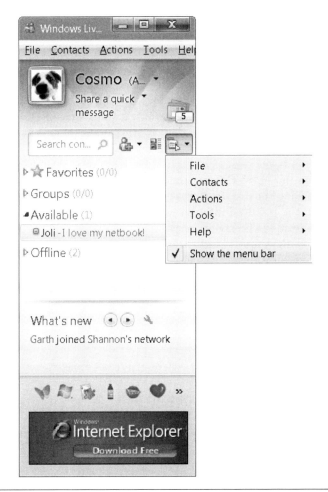

FIGURE 10-12   Show the menu bar in Windows Live Messenger to have easier
access to tools and features.

 In some instances, Windows Live Messenger won't let you log in unless Internet
Explorer is also running and is online. If you're getting an error message stating
that the service is unavailable, try opening Internet Explorer.

If you've decided on Windows Live Messenger, accessing the options is a bit
tricky. In Figure 10-12, you'll see the option to show the menu bar; select it and you'll
make finding the features you need much easier. Then choose Tools, then Options to
personalize the interface.

Add a Contact

To instant message or video and voice chat with someone, you have to add them as a contact. To add a contact, you'll need to click the Add Contact button or link. Most of the time, this is an icon with a plus sign (+) on it. You can see Yahoo!'s option (+ Add a Contact) in Figure 10-11 and Windows Live Messenger's (a silhouette of a person's head with a plus sign on it) in Figure 10-12. Click this and then add a contact using the person's e-mail address, mobile device number, or instant messaging ID.

To add a contact:

1. Locate the Add a Contact, Add, or Add Buddy button or link and click it. If necessary click Add a Contact.
2. Input the required information (see Figure 10-13).
3. A request will be sent when you click Next. You must wait for the contact to receive the request and accept your invitation to connect. Once that is done, you'll see his or her name in your contact list.

 Most programs offer the ability to log in to your e-mail and search your contacts. This is a common feature and is not a security risk or breach.

FIGURE 10-13   Enter your contact's information.

Introduce Your Web Cam

The real meat of any video and voice application is your web cam. Because all programs are different, detailing how to introduce your web cam in all applications isn't feasible. So, I suggest that you look through the program options for something that resembles what's shown in Figure 10-14 for Windows Live Messenger. Here, buried in the Tools menu, is the Audio and video setup wizard. Click this to run the setup wizard and configure your camera.

You'll want to configure your web cam for best performance, which may involve configuring brightness, hue, and other options. Figure 10-15 shows some of these options.

Although instant messaging applications often claim compatibility with others, if you want to share your web cam with someone and see their web cam as well, it's best if you both use the same program.

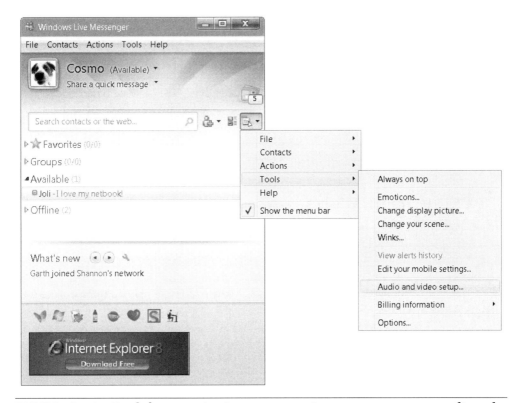

FIGURE 10-14   Look for an option in your messaging program to set up audio and video.

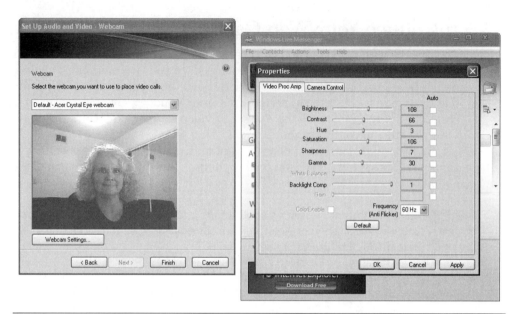

FIGURE 10-15 Configure your web cam for best performance.

Have a Video and Voice Chat

Even though it's not a requirement, it's always best to have web cam video conversations with people who use the same program you're using. That is, if you want to quickly, easily, and reliably connect with someone via video chat on a regular basis, it's ultimately best if you both choose to use the same video messaging application. When two people use the same program, there's much less room for problems to occur.

Send Your Web Cam

As with configuring options for varying messaging programs, starting and holding a video conversation differs from application to application. Additionally, there's usually more than one way to start a video conversation. In Windows Live Messenger, for instance, you can start a video conversation by initiating an instant messaging conversation first, and then opt to send your web cam. Alternately, you can choose Actions, Video, then Start a Video Call.

To start a video call in Windows Live Messenger:

1. After logging in to Windows Live Messenger, click Actions, Video, and Start a Video Call (see Figure 10-16). (If you don't see the Actions menu, click the ALT key on the keyboard; the menu will appear.)
2. Select a contact from the list.
3. The person you are inviting to participate in the video call must accept the offer (see Figure 10-17). Once the contact has accepted the invitation, he or she will be able to see your video.

FIGURE 10-16   This is one way to start a video call.

If your contact has a web cam and wants to share video with you, you'll see his or her web cam on your netbook after you accept the offer to view the web cam. Figure 10-18 shows what your contact will see if you are the only one with a web cam.

FIGURE 10-17   Your contact must accept your invitation to hold a video conversation.

FIGURE 10-18 Your contact will be able to see your web cam after accepting the offer to view it.

Receive Live Video from Others

There are multiple ways to receive live video from others. You can ask a contact to send you his or her web cam video, if he or she has a web cam installed. In Windows Live Messenger, to request to view another's video camera feed, you'll choose Actions, Video, then View the contact's web cam. The contact will have to agree to let you view it after you ask.

Alternately, your contact can work through the steps to send video himself or herself. Again, there are several options for doing this, but generally, he or she will look for the option to start a video conversation or share the web cam. Figure 10-19 shows a video call in progress, with both parties participating.

Be Safe While Using a Web Cam

As with any online activity, it's important to be vigilant regarding your personal safety as well as your computer's overall health. Be aware that people you do not know may try to contact you through your messaging program. You should not accept any invitations from people you don't know; that's first and foremost. Also, it's important to note that people can record video chats. The option is not available inside the major messaging programs (Yahoo! Messenger, Windows Live Messenger, and so on), but it is feasible with third-party software.

FIGURE 10-19 Some web cams are better than others, as you can see in this video conversation.

Here are some additional safeguards:

- Never give out your credit card numbers, cell phone number, social security number, or any other personal information.
- Don't give your mailing address to strangers; in fact, don't talk to strangers!
- Don't accept any files or open anything that's sent to you unless you are positive the file is safe, trusted, and virus-free.
- Consider a gender-neutral ID. This will keep predators away if they aren't sure that you're of a specific gender.
- Block unwanted requests.
- If you're in a chat and you feel uncomfortable, leave the chat. The contact may believe you simply lost your Internet connection.
- Monitor your children at all times when they are on the computer, especially if you allow them to use an instant messaging program and video camera.
- Be careful about posting pictures or personal information about yourself in a public online place without also placing restrictions on who can see the data.
- Always run anti-virus and anti-malware software.

11

Expand Your Netbook with Accessories

- Add RAM for ReadyBoost
- Add hard drive space with a USB drive
- Get an all-in-one AC adapter
- Use a Wi-Fi finder
- Install a GPS receiver
- Purchase an extra battery
- Use an external mouse or keyboard
- Connect a mobile printer

Netbooks are small and portable, which is probably one of the main reasons you purchased your netbook. Thus, it may seem counterintuitive to think about purchasing additional equipment that you'll ultimately end up packing when you're on the go. However, there are a few items that are must-haves that won't take up too much space, such as ReadyBoost-compatible USB RAM, a keychain Wi-Fi finder, and an all-in-one AC adapter (so you can get rid of the myriad adapters you carry for cell phones, personal digital assistants [PDAs], and of course, your netbook).

There are additional accessories you might want that take up more space, though; these accessories can be packed on longer trips or left at home on shorter ones. You may be interested in an external drive for backing up your netbook (see Chapter 8), a GPS receiver, an external mouse or keyboard, a mobile printer, or an extra battery backup. The latter comes in handy on long plane trips, as the netbook's battery generally lasts for only three to four hours.

Small and Portable Everyday Devices

Many devices designed for netbooks are small and portable. Manufacturers know that's important to you. These smaller devices are easy to take with you in a purse, a pocket, or even on a keychain and can really enhance your netbook experience.

Add RAM for ReadyBoost

ReadyBoost is a technology available in Windows Vista and higher that allows you to connect a USB flash drive and use it as RAM. RAM (random access memory) is what your netbook uses to store temporary data for fast retrieval. The more RAM you have, the faster your computer should perform—theoretically, at least.

Earlier netbooks came with only 1MB of RAM. RAM is an internal computer part, so adding more RAM is a task you may not want to pursue for fear of voiding the warranty. Additionally, it may be impossible to add more RAM to your netbook, even if you dared to open the netbook up to try. However, if your netbook runs Windows Vista or Windows 7, it's easy to add RAM externally, using a compatible USB flash drive and ReadyBoost technology.

 ReadyBoost-compatible flash drives can be attached to a keychain, stored in a pocket of a bag, or simply carried in your pocket.

To add a flash drive to act as RAM:

1. Purchase a ReadyBoost-compatible USB flash drive. It should say it's compatible on the box.
2. Plug in the flash drive to an available USB port.
3. When prompted, click Speed up my system using Windows ReadyBoost (see Figure 11-1).

FIGURE 11-1   Connect a ReadyBoost-compatible USB flash drive and choose to speed up your system using ReadyBoost.

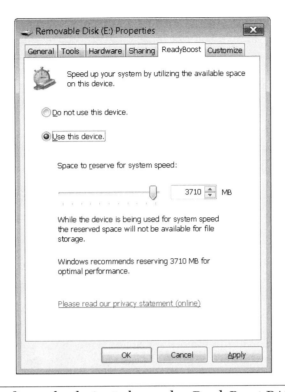

FIGURE 11-2   Configure the device to be used as ReadyBoost RAM.

4. If the device is compatible, you'll see the options shown in Figure 11-2. (If the device is not compatible, you'll be informed.) Choose Use this device and accept the recommended settings.

5. Click OK to apply the settings and close the Properties dialog box.

 Unplug the flash drive before packing the laptop or traveling with it. It's easy to snag the device on something and break it off at the port.

Add Hard Drive Space with a USB Drive

People often confuse RAM and hard drive technologies. RAM, discussed in the previous section, is temporary storage. The computer uses RAM to store instructions and data it thinks it will need right away. The more RAM that's available, the more instructions the computer can store and the faster your computer can access that data. A hard drive, in contrast, is permanent storage. The computer uses a hard drive to store the operating system, your files and folders, your personal settings, and similar data. It takes longer for a computer to pull information off of a hard drive than it does to pull information out of RAM, which is why the computer needs RAM as well as a hard drive.

Most netbooks come with 1 to 2MB of RAM. Most netbooks come with an 80GB hard drive (or larger). You use those 80 + GB to store your personal data. If there ever comes a time when you start to run out of hard drive space, you'll either need to move some of the data you no longer need off of your netbook and onto a CD, DVD, or network or external drive or add more hard drive space. The easiest way to add hard drive space is to use a USB flash drive.

 The main problem with using a USB drive for additional hard drive space is that the USB device is easy to misplace. For security's sake, I suggest you try to free up space on your netbook rather than creating additional space using a USB drive.

To add a USB drive as additional hard drive space (or to use it as a backup device):

1. Connect the USB drive to an available USB port.

 When purchasing a USB flash drive, take into consideration how close your netbook's USB ports are positioned. Avoid purchasing a USB drive whose body is wider than the port itself; otherwise, the device will hang over the port next to it and you won't be able to plug anything into that port.

2. If you're running Windows Vista or Windows 7, you'll see the prompt shown earlier in Figure 11-1. If that's the case, choose Open the folder to view files. The device is ready to use as external storage.
3. If you're running Windows XP, you may or may not be prompted, depending on what's on the USB drive already and how your computer is configured. If you aren't prompted, a window will likely open that shows what's currently on the drive. If you are prompted, it may look something like what's shown in Figure 11-3.
4. Make the appropriate selection and click OK.

FIGURE 11-3 On Windows XP, you're often prompted regarding what you'd like to do with the drive.

If you want to use the flash drive as external storage, simply click Cancel in any dialog box that appears.

Get an All-in-One AC Adapter

All-in-one adapters allow you to connect multiple devices to power outlets using a single device. This means if you purchase an adapter that's right for you, you can leave your cell phone, PDA, netbook, and similar adapters at home. This allows you to carry only one adapter instead of several. Figure 11-4 shows a Lenovo all-in-one laptop and mobile device charger. There are several things to look for in an all-in-one adapter. When you shop, look for the following features:

- It supports and is compatible with your cell phone or PDA, as well as your netbook.
- It works in both standard AC outlets and car chargers.
- It supports or can be upgraded to work in other countries.
- It comes with its own travel case.
- It covers over-current and short circuit protection and works in all temperatures.
- It preferably supports and charges USB devices, such as digital cameras.

FIGURE 11-4   Many manufacturers offer all-in-one adapters to power your mobile devices. Just make sure the one you buy is compatible with your hardware.

Use a Wi-Fi Finder

Unless there's a sign on the door, there's no way to know if there's a wireless connection inside the coffee shop or hotel you're standing in front of. Similarly, unless you're aware of a hotspot inside a hotel lobby, bar and grill, or library, the only way to find out if Wi-Fi is available is to pull out your netbook, turn it on, and wait to see if a connection is available. With a Wi-Fi finder, you don't have to do that. A Wi-Fi finder is a small device you can attach to your keychain that can tell you if there's a hotspot nearby. All you have to do is press the button on the Wi-Fi finder and if the light turns a certain color, you're within range of a hotspot. The Kensington Wi-Fi Finder Plus, shown in Figure 11-5, even offers a signal strength indicator. The more lights, the stronger the signal.

 Just because a Wi-Fi finder locates a wireless hotspot does not mean the connection is free or is open to you. However, in most cases, especially in hotels, libraries, and coffee shops, the connection is made available to you at no cost.

When shopping for a Wi-Fi finder, look for the following features:

- It supports all network types, including 802.11 b and b/g, as well as Bluetooth.
- It offers a way to attach it to a laptop bag or keychain.
- It filters out signals from cell phones, microwave ovens, and similar frequencies.
- It offers a warranty.
- It preferably offers a signal strength indicator.

FIGURE 11-5 Wi-Fi finders allow you to check for Wi-Fi without turning on your netbook.

Install a GPS Receiver

A GPS (global positioning system) receiver knows where it is in the world all of the time. It calculates its own position (and thus your position) using satellites that are in the sky above the earth. Accessing these satellites is free, provided you have the required hardware and software installed on your netbook. You can use a GPS receiver to get directions from one place to another, to show your position in real time on a street map, or to learn your exact location using longitude and latitude data.

When you purchase and install a GPS receiver, you should make sure it offers the following features:

- It is small and connects to an available USB port on your netbook.
- It comes with software that contains the street and topological maps you'll need to obtain directions and locate your position.
- The software offers turn-by-turn directions.
- It gets its power from your USB port and is designed to draw as little power as possible.
- It comes with a long cable.
- It is preferably waterproof and can withstand high or low temperatures.

Devices for Travel

While some devices are small enough to take with you on every excursion, others are larger and more difficult to carry or simply not necessary for every outing. For instance, while you may need an extra battery for long trips on airplanes, you won't need it for a short trip to the local coffeehouse. And while you may want to bring along an external mouse and full-sized keyboard for an extended stay in a hotel, you probably won't need either for a weekend getaway at a beach resort.

Purchase an Extra or Extended-Life Battery

Most computer manufacturers will try to sell you an extra battery during the checkout process. That's because a netbook's battery generally lasts only two to four hours and you'll probably need more battery life than that. If you're going to use the netbook on a long plane ride, in an all-day conference, or for a day at the beach, you're going to want an extra battery.

What's even better than an extra backup battery, though, is an extended-life battery. These newer extended-life batteries often offer 10 to 15 hours of battery power. When shopping for a new battery, look for the following features:

- It is compatible with your netbook.
- It has a warranty.
- It offers at least 12 hours of extended battery life.
- It has gotten good reviews on web sites such as Amazon.com.

Use an External Mouse or Keyboard

You can only type for so long on a small keyboard before your hands start to feel the pain, and there's only so much you can do with a touchpad. Tasks you take for granted with a mouse can really slow you down with a touchpad, especially if the touchpad isn't set to the right sensitivity for you or it is dirty or old. And although netbook keyboards have come a long way, if you need to do a lot of typing, you're going to be better off with an external, regular-sized keyboard. These are two must-haves for long trips if you're only taking a netbook (and not a full-sized laptop).

Using an external keyboard and mouse is easy. You simply plug in the hardware, and if it's Bluetooth, make the connection as instructed in the product documentation. Once connected, using the keyboard and mouse is just like using them on a desktop PC. To install and use an external keyboard and mouse:

1. Connect the keyboard using a USB cable or connect the keyboard's Bluetooth dongle. Wait while the new hardware is installed.
2. If necessary, take the required steps to pair the keyboard and Bluetooth dongle.
3. Open Control Panel and locate Keyboards. You'll see two now, as shown in Figure 11-6.
4. Connect the mouse using a USB cable or connect the required Bluetooth dongle. Wait while the new hardware is installed (see Figure 11-7).
5. If necessary, take the required steps to pair the mouse and Bluetooth dongle.
6. You can now use the mouse and keyboard as desired.

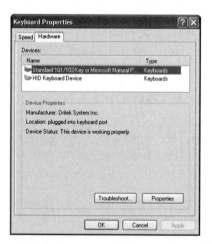

FIGURE 11-6 You can review the properties for your newly installed external keyboard from Control Panel's Keyboard option.

FIGURE 11-7   Mice and keyboards generally install automatically.

Connect a Mobile Printer

You learned how to connect and install a mobile printer in Chapter 8, but you may not know what to look for when shopping for one. Figure 11-8 shows the Canon iP100 Mobile Photo Printer, although you may opt for something smaller, such as a printer that prints only from a media card and only on postcard-size paper or smaller. Either way, here are some guidelines:

- The printer must be compatible with your netbook's operating system and connect via USB or Bluetooth.
- The printer should be the size you want it to be. Remember, you'll be carrying the printer with you on longer excursions.
- The printer shouldn't weigh much. The printer shown in Figure 11-8 weighs only 4.4 pounds.
- The printer should include a warranty.

FIGURE 11-8   You may opt for a mobile printer like this one from Canon.

- The software that comes with the printer should offer a printer driver and printer software (although you may not need the latter).
- The printer should come with starter ink cartridges and paper, and you should be able to easily purchase refills and printer sheets.
- The printer should come with the required USB cables, adapters, a user's guide, and similar items.

PART IV

Online Applications

12

An Introduction to Windows Live Services

HOW TO...

- Download and install Windows Live Essentials
- Know you need web-based services
- Obtain a Windows Live ID
- Send an instant message with Windows Live Messenger
- Set up Windows Live Hotmail with your e-mail address
- Set up Windows Live Mail with your e-mail address
- Create a blog post with Windows Live Writer
- Access Live applications using Windows Live Toolbar
- Upload and e-mail digital camera photos with Windows Live Photo Gallery
- Access SkyDrive
- Get to know other Live products

Windows Live Essentials is a suite of free, web-based applications you can use to do just about anything. With the Live Essentials suite, you can send and receive e-mail, manage digital photos, blog your thoughts and ideas, make movies from your video footage, protect your kids while they're online, and more. Because it's web-based, the programs are ever-changing, always up to date, and allow you to communicate seamlessly with online contacts and interact with others automatically.

The Windows Live Toolbar, a must-have Live Essentials application, puts Live Hotmail, Photos, Calendar, and other Live applications that you use right at your fingertips. From one place, Internet Explorer, you can upload photos to your own personal, and free, Windows Live web site; blog about your vacation; check e-mail; and even share data over the Internet using SkyDrive, another free Windows Live feature.

Don't skip this chapter. You're going to love Windows Live Essentials, and the programs are especially useful for netbook users who are always online. If you work through the chapter sequentially, you'll learn how to set up your own Windows Live Web page, share pictures with others around the world, blog, and more.

 With Windows Live Essentials, you can store data on online servers for free. If you ever lose your netbook, you'll still have access to your pictures and important files the next time you log in to Windows Live Services. You can choose what to store online and protect it with a password.

Get Windows Live Essentials

You'll have to download and install Windows Live Essentials manually because it not installed on your netbook by default. There is a chance that the manufacturer installed it, though, so to be sure, click Start and look through the All Programs list for a Windows Live folder. You'll also need a Windows Live ID, which you'll use to log in to Windows Live applications.

Why You Need Web-Based Services

You may be questioning whether or not to use web-based services such as Live Hotmail, Live Mail, and Live Photo Gallery. If you have Windows XP, you have Outlook Express; if you have Windows Vista, you have Windows Mail. Why opt for something else, then? If you already have the Windows Picture and Fax viewer in Windows XP and Windows Photo Gallery in Windows Vista, why do you also need Windows Live Photo Gallery? These are valid questions and there are several reasons you should still opt for Live services:

 Windows 7 doesn't come with Photo Gallery, Mail, or a messaging program. If you are running Windows 7, you'll need these programs.

- With Live Hotmail, you can retrieve your e-mail from anywhere there's an Internet connection.
- With Live Hotmail, unless you specifically tell Mail to delete items after they're viewed, the default setting is to leave a copy on the Internet server. This means when you get home to your desktop PC, the e-mails you've already viewed on your netbook will still be available. There's no worry that you'll receive and view an e-mail on your netbook and not be able to retrieve it on your desktop computer later. And there's no reason to incorporate syncing software.
- With Windows Live Mail, you can work from your netbook just as you would with Mail or Outlook Express, except you have the added features of the Live applications outlined throughout this chapter.

More About Live Mail

When you access your e-mail from your Windows Live home page, you're using the Windows Live Hotmail interface; it's built into your home page. If you download and install Windows Live Mail, you can use that program from your netbook the same way you'd use Outlook Express, Windows Mail, or Microsoft Outlook, except the application remains web-based, unlike the e-mail program you already have.

- With Windows Live Toolbar, you can easily access your e-mail and publish information to your free Windows Live home page to stay connected 24/7.
- With Windows Live Toolbar, you can add the SkyDrive button and easily back up your files to an Internet server that you can access from your netbook, a laptop, or any desktop PC with an Internet connection. Backing up to an Internet server is much safer than backing up to a USB flash drive. You can't lose an Internet server.
- Windows Live Messenger integrates with other Live services. You can see the online status of your contacts even when you're checking your e-mail. This makes it easy to know when you can and cannot immediately contact them for a quick question or instant message status update.
- With Windows Live Photo Gallery, you can easily upload pictures to your Windows Live home page to share with others or e-mail them with Windows Live Mail. It's all built in. When you e-mail with Windows Live Mail, you can also edit your photos right in the e-mail, including "framing" your photos or adding special effects.
- With Windows Live Writer you can create blog posts and add photos, maps, events, and more, and publish them so your contacts and followers can stay up to date on your activities.

Don't bog down your computer with programs you don't need. Only install the Live services and applications you really want.

Download and Install Windows Live Essentials

As with any download, you must first navigate to the proper download page, click the download button or link, and allow the download and installation to occur by clicking Run.

To download and install Windows Live Essentials:

1. Open Internet Explorer and go to http://download.live.com. You can also go to www.windowslive.com/Get, among other places.

You can use another web browser, but for Windows products, I prefer to use Internet Explorer.

2. Look for the Download button and click it. You'll be prompted to click Download now once more on the next screen. Figure 12-1 shows what you may see.

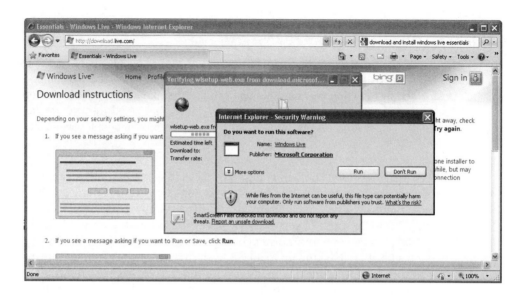

FIGURE 12-1   Click Run to download and install Windows Live Essentials.

3. When prompted, choose the Live applications you want to install (see Figure 12-2). Read the brief descriptions given for each first, though, and install only the applications you think you'll use.
4. Click Install. If prompted to close open programs, do so before continuing.
5. After installation is complete, you'll be asked if you want to make Live Search your default search provider, along with other options. It doesn't matter what you choose here; you can't go wrong. Click Continue.
6. On the last page of the installation wizard, you'll have the option to sign up for a Windows Live ID (see Figure 12-3). Click Sign up if you do not have an e-mail address ending in .Live or .Hotmail, and complete the steps in the next section. If you have an e-mail address such as yourname@hotmail.com or yourname@live.com, click Close.

Obtain a Windows Live ID

To maintain security and protect your personal information on the Internet, you must log in to Windows Live services with a user ID and password. To access all features of all Windows Live programs, you'll want a Windows Live ID that ends in .Live or .Hotmail. Although you can use your own e-mail address as your ID, it's best to obtain a Windows Live ID so that you can access all that Windows Live has to offer.

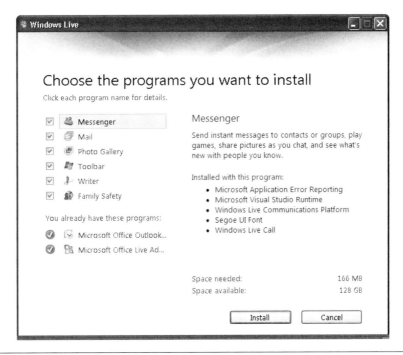

FIGURE 12-2 Download only the programs you think you'll use; you can always repeat these steps to obtain additional programs later.

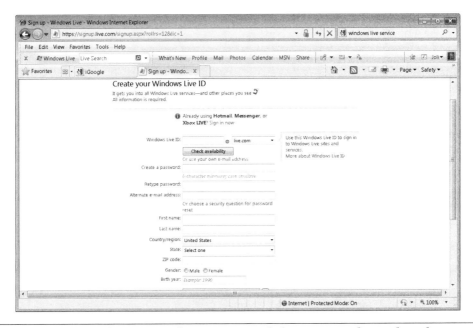

FIGURE 12-3 To obtain a Windows Live ID, click Sign up and complete the next section.

To obtain a Windows Live ID:

1. If you did not click sign up in step 6 of the previous set of instructions, go to https://signup.live.com. Do not opt to input your own e-mail address; choose to create a new e-mail address that ends in .Live or .Hotmail.

Click Check availability after inputting your desired Windows Live ID to see if it's available.

2. Input the required information, answering truthfully, and when complete, click I Accept to accept the terms of service and create your ID.
3. You'll immediately be redirected to your new Windows Live home page at http://home.live.com. You can always browse to this site and log in to view your page, change preferences, and communicate with others via e-mail, through your online profile, and more (see Figure 12-4).

Don't panic! Your Windows Live home page knows your zip code; that's how it knows the weather in your area!

For the rest of this chapter, you should remain logged in to Windows Live services. Additionally, in the sections that follow, I'll only briefly introduce each of the Live applications, offering instructions on completing a single task (such as sending an instant message with Windows Live Messenger or setting up Windows Live Hotmail with additional e-mail addresses you use). It'll be up to you to explore additional features after that.

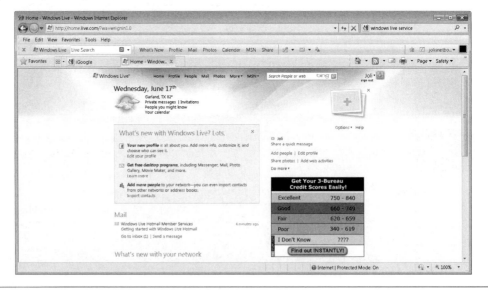

FIGURE 12-4   Once you've created your Windows Live ID, you can access your new, free, personalized web page.

Communicate with Windows Live Applications

The nicest thing about owning a netbook, keeping it with you all the time, and paying for an always-on connection to the Internet is that you can stay in touch with others 24 hours a day. You can check e-mail without worrying about syncing your netbook with your desktop when you get home; you can instant message online contacts; you can publish your status to your home page, to Facebook, to Twitter, or any other social networking site; and you can even take pictures or video with your web cam and post them on your home page with a click of a mouse, er, touchpad.

In the following few sections, you'll learn how to achieve a single task with a specific Windows Live Application. That little bit of knowledge should be enough to propel you to do more. For instance, after you learn how to send an instant message with Windows Live Messenger, it won't be hard to figure out how to play an online game with your contact as well. (There's a Game button.) And, after you learn how to add your personal e-mail address to Windows Live Hotmail (that's the application you use to access your e-mail from your Windows Live home page), it won't take a giant leap to learn how to send and receive an e-mail using that interface. And, after you create your first blog post with Windows Live Writer, it'll be easy to add a picture or hyperlink to your next post. Ultimately, you'll learn just enough here to be dangerous!

Send an Instant Message with Windows Live Messenger

When you first open Windows Live Messenger, you'll be prompted to log in. Log in with the Windows Live ID and password you created earlier in this chapter. Once logged in, you'll see what's shown in Figure 12-5. Before you can have any instant message conversations, you'll need to add a contact. You can add a contact manually (and one at a time) by clicking Add a contact; if you're new to Windows Live applications, this is the best option.

After you've sent the invitation, the person you asked to be your contact will have to accept the invitation, as shown in Figure 12-6. Once your contacts have accepted the invitation, their names will appear in Windows Live Messenger and you can have a conversation with them.

 Tip   Using a web cam with Windows Live Messenger was covered in depth in Chapter 10.

You can now send an instant message to your new contact:

1. Open and sign in to Windows Live Messenger. You'll find the program in the System Tray of the Taskbar and in the Start | All Programs | Windows Live folder.
2. Double-click the name of the available contact (see Figure 12-7).

FIGURE 12-5 You have to add a contact you'd like to communicate with.

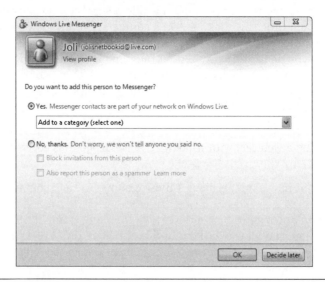

FIGURE 12-6 To add a contact to Windows Live Messenger, you have to send an invitation, and the user on the other end has to accept it.

FIGURE 12-7   Once you see the contacts in your contacts list and they are classified as available, you can send them an instant message.

 You can't have an instant messaging conversation with a contact who is offline, but you can send that user a message that will appear once he or she logs in to Windows Live Messenger.

3. Type the message in the message window, and press Enter on the keyboard when you're ready to send it (see Figure 12-8).
4. Your contact will receive the message and has the option to respond. If the contact does, you'll see his or her response in the instant messaging window (see Figure 12-9).

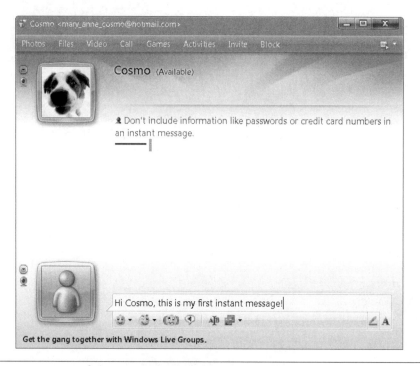

FIGURE 12-8 Type the message in the message window and then click ENTER on the keyboard.

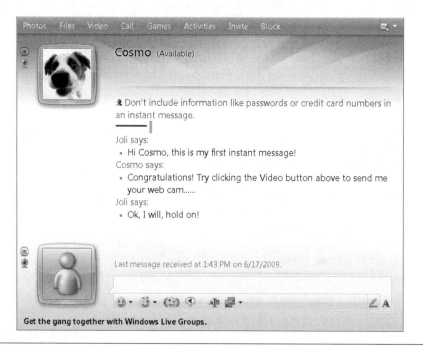

FIGURE 12-9 This is how a conversation in progress looks.

Set Up Windows Live Hotmail with Your E-mail Address

You can use Windows Live Hotmail to check your e-mail from any web browser after logging in to your home page at http://home.live.com. The Mail icon is at the top of your home page. When you click Mail, you'll see at least one e-mail from Windows Live Hotmail Member Services, as shown in Figure 12-10. You can click this e-mail to read it, delete it, move it to another folder, print it, reply to or forward it, or mark it as junk e-mail.

Your Windows Live ID, which is your new .Hotmail or .Live e-mail address, probably isn't the only e-mail address you have, though. You likely have at least one more from your ISP or from another web site such as Yahoo! You can incorporate these e-mail addresses into Windows Live Hotmail to have access to them from the Windows Live Hotmail interface. There is often no need to visit your Windows Live home page to access your .Live mail and then access your ISP's home page to access another e-mail account, when you can access them all from one place.

 Caution   Not all web-based e-mail services play well together. You may have to pay a fee to forward e-mail to another e-mail account.

Using another e-mail account inside Windows Live Hotmail involves two steps. First, you have to add your e-mail account as one you can send from in the Windows Live Hotmail interface. Once that's set up, you'll have to forward your third-party e-mail account to your Live ID account using that account's properties and forwarding options, and only then can you also receive e-mail from other accounts.

To configure a third-party e-mail address as an address you can send from in Windows Live Hotmail:

1. Log on to your Windows Live home page. You can access the page from http://home.live.com.
2. Click Options, then click More options, as shown in Figure 12-11.

FIGURE 12-10   You'll see at least one e-mail when you access Mail; it will be from the Windows Live Hotmail Member Services.

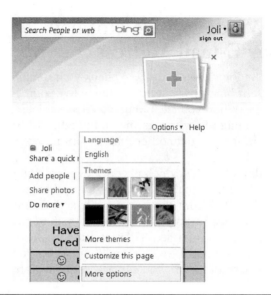

FIGURE 12-11 There are plenty of options to choose from, including the option to add additional e-mail accounts for sending mail.

3. Click Mail on the left side, and then select Send and receive mail from other e-mail accounts.
4. Click Add another account to send mail from, near the bottom of the page. Type the e-mail address and click Send verification e-mail (see Figure 12-12).

To send mail from the newly added account, click Mail to return to the Windows Live Hotmail page, and in the From line, click the down arrow and select the account you wish to use.

FIGURE 12-12 Add an account you'd like to send from.

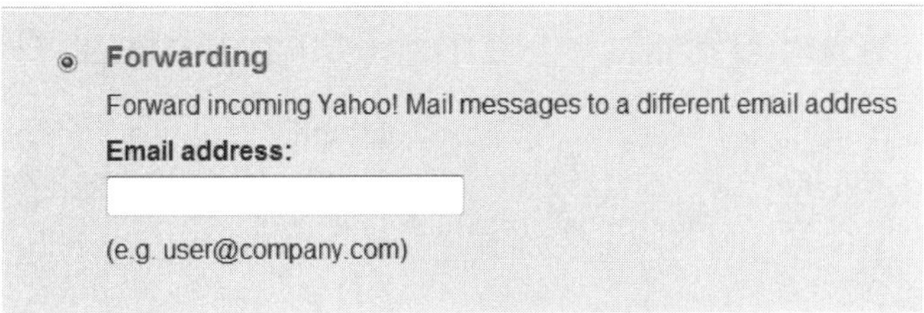

Forwarding
Forward incoming Yahoo! Mail messages to a different email address
Email address:

(e.g. user@company.com)

FIGURE 12-13   To forward e-mail from another account, look for the forwarding option on the ISP's or the e-mail provider's web site.

To receive e-mail from another account, you have to set up e-mail forwarding for the account using the tools available to you. To configure mail forwarding in a web-based application such as Yahoo!, you'll generally click Options and then choose something like Set up Mail Forwarding. Figure 12-13 shows the option to forward a Yahoo! e-mail account to a different e-mail address. Other web sites offer a similar option. In Google's Gmail, click Settings at the top of the Mail page, and then open the Forwarding and POP/IMAP tab.

Set Up Windows Live Mail with Your E-mail Address

As noted earlier, when you use Internet Explorer to visit your Windows Live home page at http://home.live.com, there's a Mail icon at the top of the page. That Mail icon takes you to Windows Live Hotmail, an online, web-based e-mail application. This is a great application for accessing your e-mail from any computer in the world with Internet access.

Windows Live Mail, on the other hand, while still a "live" application, is installed on your netbook and you use it like you would any computer-based application (Outlook Express or Windows Mail). With Live Mail, though, you get some additional features, such as Photo e-mail, RSS data in your inbox, and new and improved search features. Windows Live Mail also offers multiple e-mail support, so you can add e-mail accounts from Yahoo! Mail Plus and Gmail. Of course, you can add your Hotmail or Live e-mail addresses too, allowing you to manage several accounts from a single interface.

You set up Windows Live Mail the same way you set up Outlook Express or Windows Mail: You work through the setup wizard, inputting the required information as prompted. To add an e-mail account in Windows Live Mail:

1. Click Start, click All Programs, and click Windows Live. From the resulting options, click Windows Live Mail.
2. In the left pane of Live Mail, click Add e-mail account.
3. In the first page of the wizard, type your e-mail address, password, and display name.

Did You Know?

Your Display Name Is Anything You Want

Your display name can be anything, and will appear in the From line when people receive your e-mail. Your e-mail address and password must be exactly what your ISP or e-mail provider gave you.

4. If Windows Live can obtain the additional information it needs, the e-mail address will be successfully created and ready to use. If not, you'll be prompted to input the information shown in Figure 12-14.

Tip   To obtain the correct POP3 information, call your ISP or log on to its web site. The settings differ depending on the service provider.

5. Click Finish.

Once Windows Live Mail is configured with the e-mail addresses you use regularly, you can use the program to send and receive e-mail, manage e-mail you want to keep, and maintain a list of contacts.

Tip   Click the arrow next to the New button to create a new e-mail message, a photo e-mail message, or a new event; add a contact; or create a new folder for organizing e-mail.

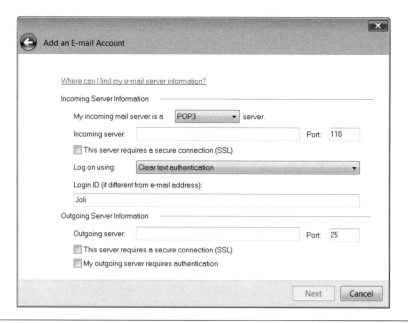

FIGURE 12-14   If Windows Live Mail doesn't know the server names for your e-mail address, you'll be prompted to input them manually.

Create a Blog Post with Windows Live Writer

Windows Live Writer lets you blog about whatever interests you. "Blog" is short for web log, and a web log is a place where you can share your thoughts, ideas, and opinions and discuss your interests. The first time you open Windows Live Writer, you'll need to work through a setup wizard, the first page of which is shown in Figure 12-15.

When you set up Windows Live Writer, you'll be asked where you want to publish your blog and related posts. You can choose among Windows Live (your posts will appear on your Windows Live home page), Windows Live Spaces (another free Windows service you can use to set up your own personal web page), SharePoint blog (another Microsoft service that is related to a larger program, SharePoint), and Other blog service (Blogger, WordPress, TypePad, and all others). Unless you've previously set up a service, you'll want to choose the first option: I don't have a blog; create one on Windows Live for me.

After you've made a selection, you'll need to type in any relevant information about your blog service. If you're using Windows Live, that information consists only of your Windows Live ID and password. Your blog account will be set up for you automatically if you choose this option (see Figure 12-16).

Windows Live Writer will open automatically (or you can open it manually from the Start | All Programs | Windows Live folder) where you can create your blog post (see Figure 12-17). A blog post consists of the following:

- **Post title**   A description of your blog post
- **Blog post**   The post contents
- **Additional features**   Pictures, hyperlinks, maps, tables, and more

FIGURE 12-15   You'll need to work through a setup wizard before you can create your first blog post.

FIGURE 12-16 It's easiest to use Windows Live and let Microsoft set up your blog account automatically.

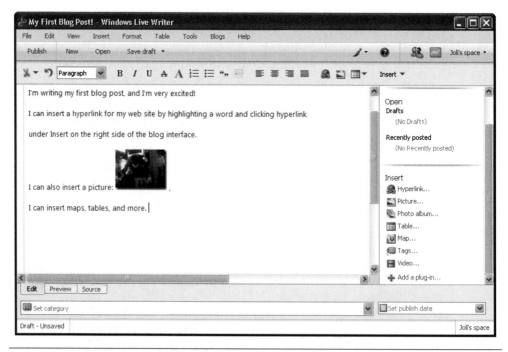

FIGURE 12-17 Create a blog post in Windows Live Writer, and when you're finished, click Publish.

FIGURE 12-18   Access your new blog space from More | Spaces.

After the publishing process has completed, you'll be able to see the post in your new blog space. By default, the blog will open automatically after it's published, but to navigate there yourself, go to your Windows Live home page, click More, and click Spaces, as shown in Figure 12-18. Click View your space to see your new blog entry.

Note   From your Spaces page, you can also edit your profile, share photos, invite friends to view your space, add more blog entries, and more.

Access Live Applications Using Windows Live Toolbar

The Windows Live Toolbar links everything together, and that's why it's a must-have Live application. You can use the toolbar to access your e-mail (shown in Figure 12-19), your profile, photos you and others have recently shared, your personal calendar, the MSN web site, and more. You can add new items to the toolbar too, including options for Wikipedia, MSN Movies, and Office Live, among others.

To use the toolbar, it must be enabled, so if you don't see the toolbar shown in Figure 12-19 (with What's New, Profile, Mail, Photos, Calendar, MSN, and Share), right-click on any toolbar shown and check Windows Live Toolbar (see Figure 12-20).

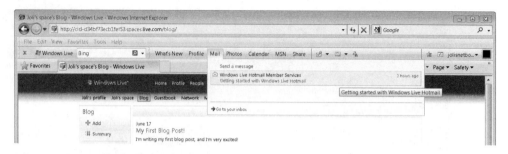

FIGURE 12-19 The Windows Live Toolbar lets you access quick views of personal data such as e-mail, as shown here. Click Go to your inbox to view all your mail.

The icons on the toolbar, in order from left to right, are:

- **Windows Live**   Click this button to go directly to your Windows Live home page.
- **Bing**   Click and type any search words or phrases to locate information on the Internet.
- **What's New**   This shows a preview of your personalized What's New information feed, also shown on your Windows Live home page.
- **Profile**   This displays a preview of your personalized Profile information, also shown on your Windows Live home page.
- **Mail**   This option shows a preview of your personalized Mail information, also shown on your Windows Live home page.
- **Photos**   This presents a preview of your personalized Photos information, also shown on your Windows Live home page.
- **Calendar**   This shows a preview of your personalized Calendar information, also shown on your Windows Live home page.

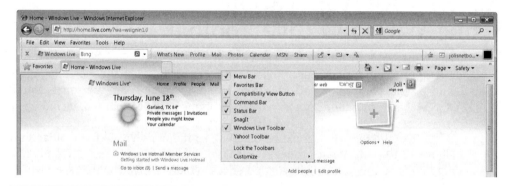

FIGURE 12-20 You can enable or disable the Windows Live Toolbar with a right-click.

FIGURE 12-21   You can translate web pages directly from the Windows Live Toolbar.

- **MSN**   This option displays a preview of your MSNBC news headlines, entertainment news, and sports news, also shown on your Windows Live home page.
- **Share**   This allows you to share favorites on Windows Live with people in your network.
- **Map the addresses on this page**   This option opens the web page www.bing .com/maps/ to map an address on a web page.
- **Get news from MSNBC**   This takes you to the MSNBC home page.
- **Translate this page**   This opens the Bing Translator page, where you can translate any web page into another language (see Figure 12-21).
- **Additional icons**   On the far right of the page are additional icons, including those you add yourself. You can sync favorites across multiple computers; get new toolbar buttons; access options to sign out, change the picture, change the name, view your account, and perform other account-related tasks; and view your profile.

Share with Windows Live Applications

Windows Live Essentials makes it easier than ever to share information over the Internet. You can e-mail photos, store data on password-protected Internet servers, and more, all from the built-in features of the Live applications. That's the reasoning behind having a suite of applications; they all work together!

Upload and E-mail Digital Camera Photos Using Windows Live Photo Gallery

Before you can upload and e-mail digital camera photos using Windows Live Photo Gallery, you need to complete the following tasks:

- Download and install Windows Live Photo Gallery.
- Install your digital camera.
- Take a few pictures with the camera.
- Connect to the Internet.

With that done, connect your camera, turn it on, and follow these steps:

1. If prompted, choose to import with Windows Live Photo Gallery.
2. Type a tag name for the pictures if desired (see Figure 12-22).
3. Click Import.
4. Locate and select the pictures to e-mail.

Hold down the CTRL key to select multiple non-contiguous pictures, or the SHIFT key to select multiple contiguous ones.

5. Click E-mail (see Figure 12-23).
6. Select a picture size when prompted. For e-mail, Small or Medium is best. Click Attach.
7. If you've chosen Windows Live Mail as your default program, it will open. Compose the e-mail and click Send.

To set a default e-mail program, open Internet Explorer, click Tools, then Internet Options, and from the Programs tab, choose the option to select your default e-mail program.

FIGURE 12-22   Type a name to help you organize the pictures you upload.

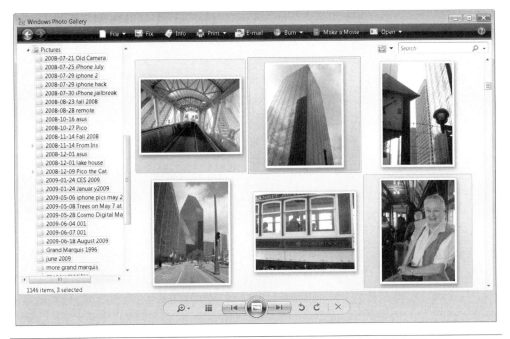

FIGURE 12-23   Select the pictures to send and click E-mail.

Access SkyDrive

SkyDrive allows you to save information and data to an Internet server that you can then access from any other computer that is connected to the Internet. SkyDrive lets you store pictures, files, and even your favorite web sites, and is a great way to back up your data quickly and have access to it from anywhere. You can also add data to the Public folders to share data with your contacts, colleagues, or others.

The best way to get started with SkyDrive is to add a button for it on Windows Live Toolbar and then upload a few files or pictures.

To add a button for SkyDrive:

1. Click the Get new buttons for Windows Live Toolbar button. It's on the far-right side of the toolbar.
2. Click Add next to SkyDrive (see Figure 12-24).
3. Locate the new button on the toolbar. Click the arrow next to the SkyDrive options to see what's available. Click any option to open the related window. For now, click Public documents (see Figure 12-25).
4. When the desired page opens—in this case, the Public SkyDrive folder—you can then click Why not add some files? This will store data on the server.

Note   Adding pictures to SkyDrive works the same way as adding documents.

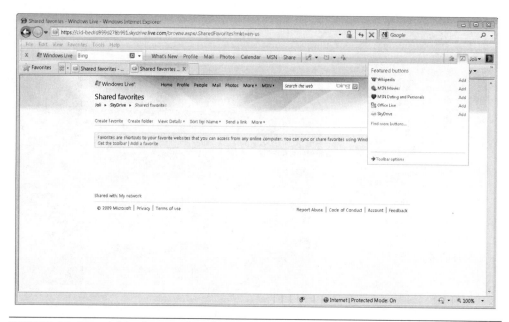

FIGURE 12-24 Add a button for SkyDrive so you can easily access it.

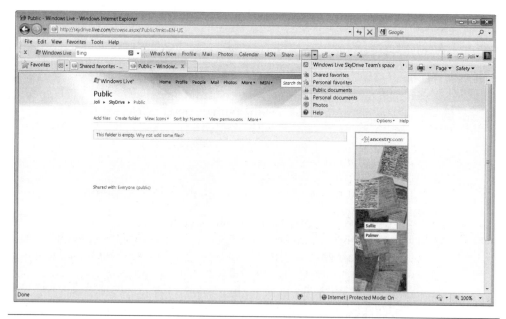

FIGURE 12-25 To add files to SkyDrive, select the appropriate folder.

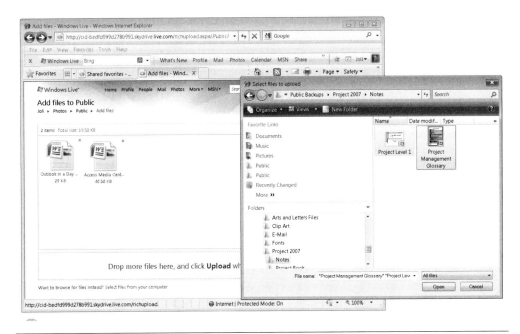

FIGURE 12-26   Drag and drop files from your PC to your SkyDrive space.

5. Although you can drag and drop files (see Figure 12-26), SkyDrive seems to work better if you choose to select files from your computer instead. If you choose the latter, click Open after selecting the files to copy.

6. When you're finished, click Upload.

 You can only copy files, not folders.

7. With the files uploaded, you can now decide who can access the files. For Public folders, the setting is Shared with: Everyone (public) and can't be changed. Permission for private folders can be changed.

Get to Know Other Live Products

There are many other Live products to explore, including Family Safety and Movie Maker, as well as several Microsoft Office–related services. Because it's unlikely you'll be allowing a child to use your netbook or creating resource-intensive movies using it, I won't cover those in depth here. However, if you do have a child who will use your netbook, consider adding and configuring the Family Safety program.

FIGURE 12-27 Windows Live has much more to offer. To find out, visit www .windowslive.com/get.

You can also explore Windows Live programs from www.windowslive.com/get. There you can learn more about online applications, including how to use the Calendar feature, how to create online Groups, and how to best incorporate your Windows Live Space. You can even combine Windows Live with your cell phone by using Windows Live for Mobile. If you're not worn out yet, try it now! It's shown in Figure 12-27.

13

An Introduction to Office Live Workspace

HOW TO...

- Meet the minimum requirements
- Obtain a Live ID
- Get started with Office Live Workspace
- Create lists
- Create notes
- Change sharing options
- Install Office Live Update
- Create a new Word document from inside your workspace
- Open an Excel file saved in your workspace
- Save a PowerPoint presentation to your workspace
- Resolve problems with your workspace
- Visit the Office Live Workspace Community
- Follow on Facebook
- Follow on Twitter

Office Live Workspace is a free online, file sharing, and storage workspace. You can use this workspace to save documents, presentations, spreadsheets, and more, and share them with others. You don't have to share, though; you can use the workspace as a personal, virtual storage area and access your stored data from any computer that has Internet access.

Office Live Workspace is a great application to partner with your netbook. You can use it in place of other collaboration and backup options you may already be using. For instance, with a workspace, you no longer have to save data to a flash drive or e-mail a copy of a file to yourself or others. You simply upload the files to your personal workspace on an Internet server, and they'll be there the next time you log on. You can invite people to your workspace, too, if you want them to have access to your files for collaboration purposes.

Get to Know Office Live Workspace

Office Live Workspace is a must-have addition to your netbook if you regularly work on your netbook or collaborate on projects with others. With your own personal Office Live Workspace, you can save important files to an Internet server using any computer and then access them from anywhere, using your netbook or any other computer that has Internet access.

Once your workspace is set up and your files are stored online, you can then invite others to join you in the workspace. They can view and edit files for collaborative efforts, eliminating the need to e-mail files to colleagues or store them on company servers. You can also take meeting or school notes on your netbook and store them in your workspace, and then access them from your office, home, or dorm room later. You can think of Office Live Workspace as an online 5GB network drive, a drive that you control.

Meet the Minimum Requirements

There aren't too many minimum requirements for running Office Live Workspace, but they are worth listing here:

- You'll need a connection to the Internet to access the files you store online. If you don't have access to the Internet on the computer you're using, you won't be able to access your stored files.
- You need a Windows Live ID with a valid e-mail inbox where you can send and receive e-mail.
- You need a supported web browser:
  - Microsoft Internet Explorer 6, 7, or 8 on Windows XP, Windows Server 2003, Windows Vista, or Windows 7
  - Mozilla Firefox on Windows XP, Windows Server 2003, Windows Vista, Windows 7, or Mac OS X 10.2.x and later
  - Safari on Mac OS 10.2.x and later.

 Mozilla Firefox is listed as a compatible browser for Office Live Workspace, as long as it's running on a Windows computer. Firefox on Linux won't work.

Obtain a Live ID

To maintain security and protect your personal information in a Windows Live Workspace, you must log in to your workspace with a Windows Live ID and password. To access all features of all Windows Live programs, you'll want a Windows Live ID that ends in .Live or .Hotmail. Although you can use your own e-mail address as your ID, it's best to obtain a Windows Live ID so that you can access all that Windows Live has to offer.

To obtain a Windows Live ID:

1. Go to https://signup.live.com. Do not opt to input your own e-mail address; choose to create a new e-mail address that ends in .Live or .Hotmail (see Figure 13-1).

Click Check availability after inputting your desired Windows Live ID to see if it's available.

2. Input the required information, answering truthfully, and when complete, click I Accept to accept the terms of service and create your ID.
3. You'll immediately be redirected to your new Windows Live home page at http://home.live.com. You can always browse to this site and log in to view your page, change preferences, and communicate with others via e-mail, through your online profile, and more.

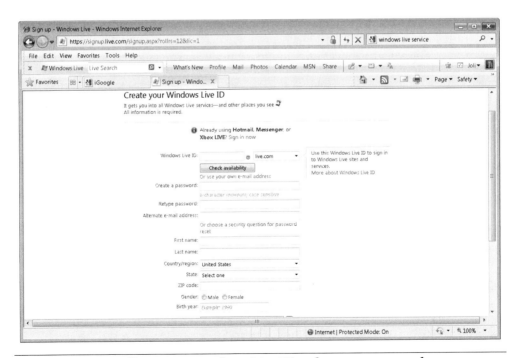

FIGURE 13-1   You'll use your Windows Live ID to log on to your workspace.

Open Your Office Live Workspace

With a Windows Live ID in hand, you can now create and open your own Office Live Workspace. To get started:

 Online applications are changed often during application upgrades and version changes and in response to users' suggestions. Thus, the steps shown here may not be exact, but they'll be close.

1. Using a compatible web browser, go to http://workspace.officelive.com.
2. Click Get Started Now.
3. Type your Windows Live ID to sign in, and click Next (see Figure 13-2).
4. Type your password and click Sign in.
5. Click Create a workspace now, or any related prompt for creating a workspace. (Prompts may change as the Workspace application evolves.)
6. Choose the kind of workspace to create. As shown in Figure 13-3, there are many kinds of workspaces offering options based on the workspace type. If you want to collaborate with others on a project, choose Project Workspace; to manage a business trip or vacation that involves others, consider Travel Workspace; if you're creating a workspace for school, consider Class Workspace, Essay Workspace, or Study Group Workspace.
7. Name your workspace. I'm creating a Household Workspace in Figure 13-4. Note the preconfigured items already in the workspace: Announcement Board, Emergency Contact List, Grocery List, Household Event List, and more.
8. If you'd like to add files to your workspace, click the Add documents now button, also shown in Figure 13-4. Repeat as necessary.

 You can upload multiple files to your workspace by holding down the CTRL key while clicking the files to add.

FIGURE 13-2 To get started with Live Workspace, log in using your Windows Live ID.

FIGURE 13-3   Create a workspace that's right for you. You can have multiple workspaces.

9. Browse to a file to upload, click it, and click Open. The file will appear in your workspace, under the last preconfigured item in the list.

10. If you want to share the workspace with others, click Share this workspace now.

11. Add the e-mail addresses of the people you want to invite. You can invite people as "editors," who can view and change data, or you can invite them as "viewers," who can only view data (see Figure 13-5).

If you've used your Windows Live ID for a while, you may have contacts in your Windows Live address book. Click the book icon next to Editors and Viewers to choose people from your address book.

12. Type a personal message if desired, also shown in Figure 13-5.

13. Configure any other options, such as letting people view this message without signing in, or sending yourself a copy of the invitation. Click Send.

14. Your workspace is complete. Explore your workspace, review your uploaded files, and review preconfigured documents and files. Figure 13-6 shows the Emergency Contact List, already provided for you, where you can easily and quickly add contacts and their e-mail address, name, phone, and more.

Welcome to your new workspace
Each new workspace is a convenient place to store documents and share them with others.

Create	Add	Share
STEP 1: To create another workspace, click ✦ **New Workspace** on the left navigation bar.	**STEP 2:** Add documents you want to store and share. ⊙ Add documents now	**STEP 3:** Share your workspace so friends and colleagues can view or edit its contents.

FIGURE 13-4   Name your workspace and note the items already created for you.

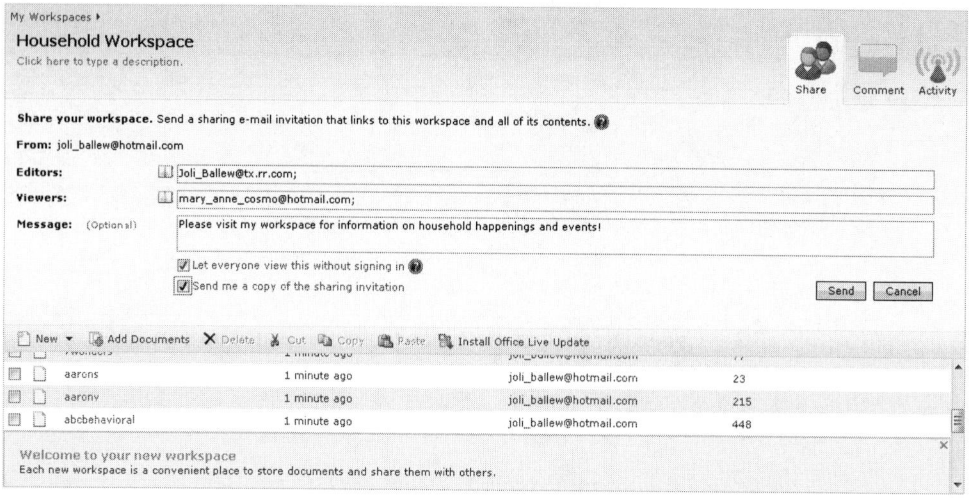

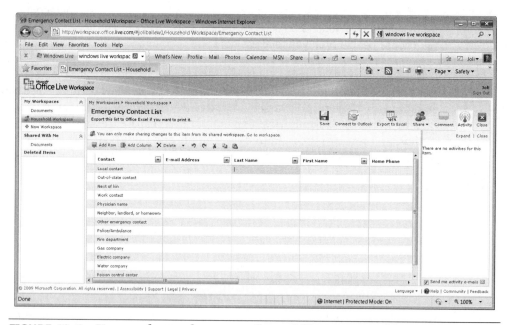

FIGURE 13-5 Invite people to join your workspace by sending them an invitation. You can always click Share later if you want to add more people.

FIGURE 13-6 Your workspace has preconfigured files you can add to. Click Save to save changes.

Utilize Your Live Workspace

Once your workspace is set up, you can begin using it. Beyond sharing files with others, storing your important files online, and inviting others to join you in your workspace as editors or viewers, you can also create lists and notes, share even more files, and more. In this section, you'll learn how to do all three of these things, and perhaps you'll see even more you'd like to do!

Create Lists

You can create a list of items using the New menu options inside your workspace. First, log in to your workspace (go to http://workspace.office.live.com), choose the workspace to work in if you have more than one, and click the New button. Here are the exact steps:

1. Log in to your workspace.
2. Under My Workspaces, verify that the workspace you want to use is selected. You may have more than one or you may have navigated to another window, so it's always best to check. You can see this later in Figure 13-7.
3. Click New. Notice the options, shown in Figure 13-7.
4. Click inside the single column/row entry and type a column title (see Figure 13-8).
5. Click Add Row, Add Column, or Delete to edit the list.
6. Click Save when finished (see Figure 13-8).

 Click the title of the list, currently List 1, to change the title of the list. Note that you can click below it to add a description.

7. Click the down arrow next to Column 1 to view sorting options.

 To make changes to the sharing options for this list, you'll have to go to your workspace. You can do that by clicking the workspace in the left pane.

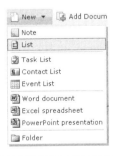

FIGURE 13-7   The New button lets you create notes, lists, documents, and more.

FIGURE 13-8   Create your list and save it with list options.

Create Notes

You can create a note using the New menu options inside your workspace. First, log in to your workspace (go to http://workspace.office.live.com), choose the workspace to work in if you have more than one, then click the New button. Here are the exact steps:

1. Log in to your workspace.
2. Under My Workspaces, verify the workspace you want to use is selected. You may have more than one or you may have navigated to another window, so it's always best to check. You saw this earlier in Figure 13-6.
3. Click New and choose Note.

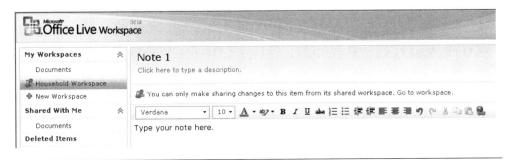

FIGURE 13-9   Add notes if desired, using New | Note.

4. Click the title Note 1, to change the name of the note if desired.
5. Type the note, then apply fonts and more using the editing options (see Figure 13-9).

Change Sharing Options

After creating notes and lists, or after uploading additional files, you may find you need to change your sharing options or what you're sharing. You do this inside your workspace. To change the sharing options for a file:

1. Log in to your workspace.
2. Under My Workspaces, verify that the workspace you want to use is selected. You may have more than one or you may have navigated to another window, so it's always best to check.
3. Click View sharing details.
4. To remove a person from your sharing list, click the X next to the user's name.
5. Choose Share with more and add additional people to share with, or choose Stop sharing to stop sharing files with others (see Figure 13-10).

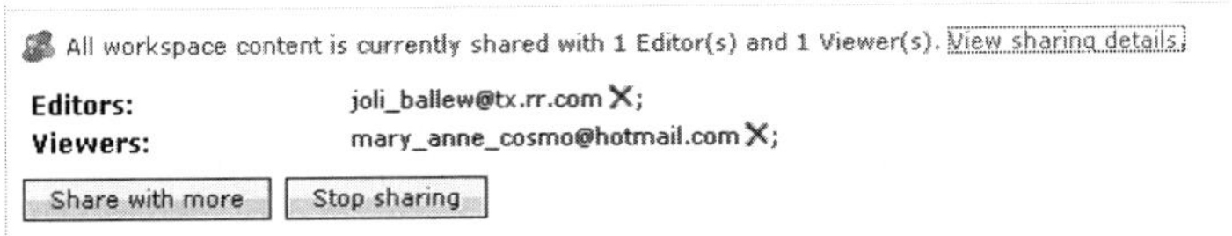

All workspace content is currently shared with 1 Editor(s) and 1 Viewer(s). View sharing details.

Editors: joli_ballew@tx.rr.com X;
Viewers: mary_anne_cosmo@hotmail.com X;

Share with more   Stop sharing

FIGURE 13-10   Change sharing options using the sharing details settings.

Access Your Workspace from Word, Excel, or PowerPoint

You may have noticed earlier when you clicked New in your workspace that Word document, Excel spreadsheet, and PowerPoint presentation were available. This is shown in Figure 13-11, in case you missed it. You can use these programs to create these types of files from inside your workspace. When you make one of these selections, the corresponding Microsoft Office application that is installed on your netbook will open.

To get the most out of this feature, you'll need to install the Office Live Update. You'll be prompted to do this the first time you click New Word document, New Excel spreadsheet, or New PowerPoint presentation (see Figure 13-11).

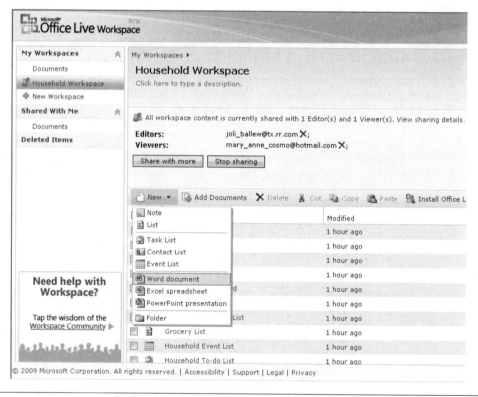

FIGURE 13-11 Word, Excel, and PowerPoint can be accessed through your workspace, and your changes can be automatically saved back to the workspace when you're finished.

Install Office Live Update

Using the Office Live Update in conjunction with Office Live Workspace allows you to configure the documents, spreadsheets, and presentations you create in Microsoft Office to save directly back to your workspace. You won't even have to save the data to your netbook if you don't want to.

It's safer to save data to an online Internet server. If your netbook is stolen, your documents and data won't be.

As noted earlier, in order to make all of this work to its potential, the first time you choose to create a new Word, Excel, or PowerPoint file from inside your workspace, you'll be prompted to install the Office Live Update. When prompted, click Continue, and let the add-in install (see Figure 13-12).

This Office Live Add-in may require you to install other updates, so be prepared to work through additional installations and possibly reboot your netbook.

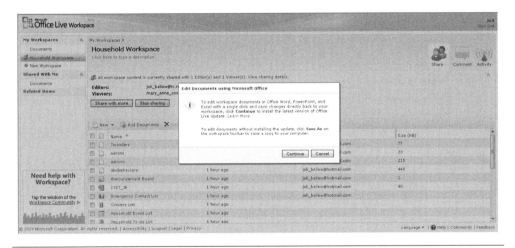

FIGURE 13-12 When prompted to install Office Live Update, do so. Click Run to add the update and follow the prompts to install.

Create a New Word Document from Inside Your Workspace

When you're working online, you can choose to create a new Word document using tools inside your workspace. To create a new Word document in this manner:

1. Sign in to your workspace.
2. Click your workspace in the left pane.
3. Click the New button.
4. Choose Word document, as shown in Figure 13-11 earlier.
5. Your version of Microsoft Word will open where you can create the new document (see Figure 13-13).
6. When you click Save or Save As, the document will save back to your workspace by default, not to your netbook (see Figure 13-14). You can change this by selecting a different place to save the file, perhaps on your netbook or a network drive, if you desire.

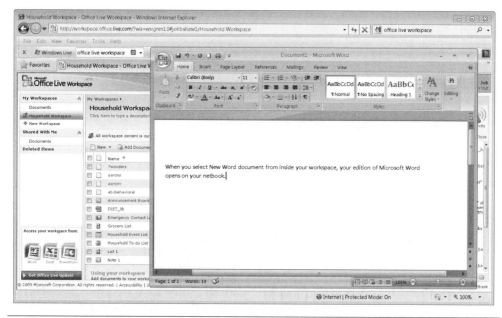

FIGURE 13-13   When Microsoft Word opens, work as usual.

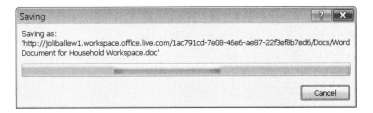

FIGURE 13-14   By default, the new Word document will save to your workspace, not to your netbook.

With Word documents in your workspace, you can now open and view those documents online and from anywhere. This means you can view your document from any computer that has Internet access, simply by logging in to your workspace. You can also click Edit to make changes to the document using the Office edition installed on your netbook. Figure 13-15 shows Chapter 8 of this book, accessed from my workspace.

Online applications of Word, Excel, and PowerPoint are coming soon. This means you'll be able to edit these kinds of files online, using online tools and applications. There's more information at the end of this chapter.

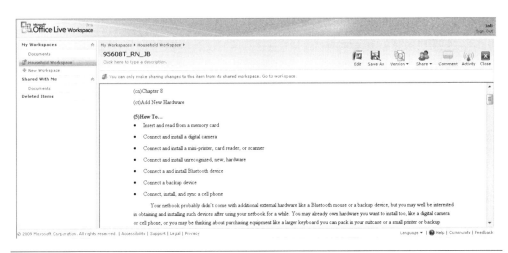

FIGURE 13-15   You can read documents online once you've uploaded them.

Open an Excel File Saved in Your Workspace

Just as you can open Word files inside your workspace for viewing as shown in Figure 13-15, you can also open Excel files (as well as myriad other file types). To view an Excel file online:

1. Log in to your workspace and verify there's an Excel file in your file list. If not, you'll have to upload an Excel file to continue.
2. Double-click the Excel file to open it.
3. View the Excel file in your web browser and click Edit to edit the file (see Figure 13-16).

Save a PowerPoint Presentation to Your Workspace

As with Word and Excel, after installing the Office Live Update you have the option to save any new file, spreadsheet, or presentation to your workspace. To save a presentation to a workspace:

1. Open Microsoft PowerPoint on your netbook.
2. Open or create a PowerPoint presentation.
3. Click the Office button and point to Save to Office Live.
4. Choose the workspace to save to (see Figure 13-17).

Aug Sept Oct

	A	B	C	D	E	F	G	H	J	L	M	N	O	P
1	Date	Breakfast	Lunch	Dinner	Additional	Snacks (or total)	Total	Work Out Yes/No (Yes=1 HR+)	Weight After WO (Start 166)	WEEKLY AVERAGE Goal	Blood Sugar	Time of Day	Blood Pressure + where taken	Obstacles/Notes
2	20-Aug	300	440	300		330	1063.18966		164	164				
3	21-Aug	250	390	600		200	1440	y	162					
4	22-Aug	300	300	200	300	500	1600	y	162					Pat's Party
5	23-Aug	300	350	500	640		1790	y	161					
6	24-Aug	300	220	600	160	220	1500	Yard						
7	25-Aug	500	380	400	300	100	1680	N	162					Didn't sleep well
8	26-Aug	300	200	450	400	200	1550	y	163	MET: 163				
9	27-Aug	225	420	500	160	250	1555	y	162					
10	28-Aug	350	250	400	500	250	1750	y	161					

FIGURE 13-16 You can view almost any type of file inside your workspace, including Excel files, as shown here.

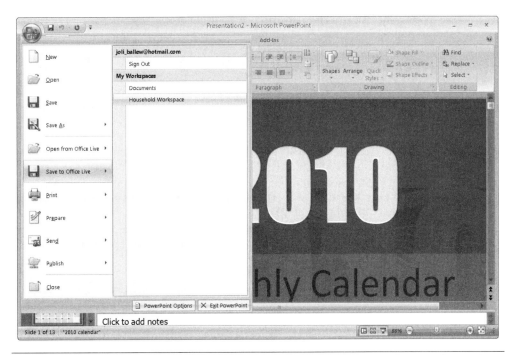

FIGURE 13-17   You can save the presentation directly to your workspace, bypassing the uploading process after file creation.

Resolve Problems with Your Workspace

There are a few problems you may run across when working in your new workspace. Certain files may not open, for instance, or you may get errors when trying to work in your workspace. Listed here are the most common problems and their solutions:

- **You receive a script error when working in your workspace.**   Click the F5 key on the keyboard to remove the error and continue working.
- **A document won't open in the workspace.**   You'll have to click Save As to download the document to your computer because the document is either:
  - Not a document with a supported file type. Office Live Workspace supports .doc, .docx, .dot, .dotx.
  - Too large to render in the workspace.
  - Contains images too difficult to render in the workspace.
- **You can't see everything in a column, pane, or view.**   Click and drag the pane itself to resize it.

- **You can't open a document.** It is either not a supported file type or it has been blocked automatically. Some file types that are blocked automatically for your security include:
  - **.asp** Active Server Page
  - **.bat** Batch file
  - **.com** Microsoft MS-DOS program
  - **.csh** Script file
  - **.lnk** Shortcut link
  - **.msi** Microsoft Windows Installer package
  - **.url** Uniform Resource Locator or Internet shortcut link
  - **.ws** Windows Script file
- **You receive a warning in Internet Explorer regarding Microsoft ActiveX controls.** Enable the controls to resolve the issue:
  1. Click Tools, and click Internet Options. (Don't see Tools? Click the ALT key on the keyboard.)
  2. Click the Security tab.
  3. Click Internet, then click Custom Level.
  4. In Settings, click Enable under Active scripting and Scripting of Java applets (see Figure 13-18).
  5. Click OK, then click OK again.

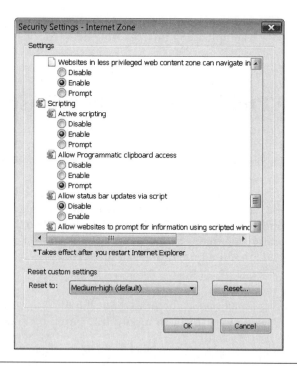

FIGURE 13-18 You'll have to enable Active scripting to resolve ActiveX error messages.

Learn More About Office Live Workspace

There are many ways to learn more about Office Live Workspace, especially knowing that it will evolve as it matures. That's the great thing about online applications and spaces such as this one: The creators of the application can easily apply changes without having to send out CDs or new editions. If you have decided you like Office Live Workspace, there are several ways to stay on top of the changes and learn more about its features.

Visit the Office Live Workspace Community

Currently, at the bottom of your workspace home page, there's a link to Community. Click it to access the Office Live Workspace Community, where you can register and join the community, and then use the site to get information and connect with others who also use Live Workspace. When you have a problem, it can be an invaluable resource.

To get started with the community:

1. Click Community at the bottom of your workspace. Note that as things evolve, the link may move to the top or sides of the window.
2. Register and join (see Figure 13-19).

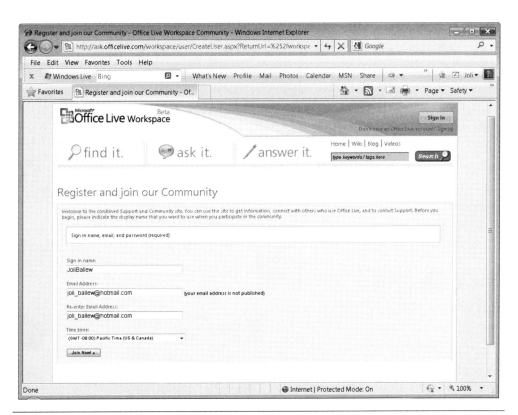

FIGURE 13-19   You'll have to register to join the Office Live Workspace Community.

3. Under the Find it tab, you can type keywords to search for answers to questions that have already been answered.
4. Under the Ask it tab, you can ask a question by composing a post to publish to the community.
5. Under the Answer it tab, you can review questions others have asked and answer them, if you desire.

Follow on Facebook

You can get information about Windows Live Office and related workspaces from Facebook. The link to visit is www.facebook.com/office live. If you like what you see in Figure 13-20, click Become a Fan.

Follow on Twitter

You can get information about Windows Live Office and related workspaces on Twitter. The link to visit is http://twitter.com/office_live. Click Join today if you like what you see in Figure 13-21.

FIGURE 13-20 Facebook offers lots of Office Live Workspace groups, some public and some private. This is the official site.

FIGURE 13-21   Learn more about Office Live on Twitter.

Coming Soon!

As you saw earlier in this chapter, when you open a compatible Microsoft Office document inside your workspace, you can view it in its online setting. For now, though, when you click Edit to work with the file, the full version of the Microsoft Office program installed on your computer opens. It is there you perform the editing tasks.

Soon there will be new Microsoft applications that allow you to view, edit, and share Word, Excel, PowerPoint, and OneNote files online, from any computer that connects to the Internet. These will be aptly named and are shown in Figure 13-22:

- Word Web
- Excel Web
- PowerPoint Web
- OneNote Web

Word Web application

Excel Web application

PowerPoint Web application

OneNote Web application

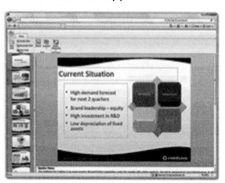

FIGURE 13-22 New web applications will allow you to edit online, a feature not available in current Microsoft workspaces.

Office Live Web applications are lightweight versions of the Office programs you know, can be used in conjunction with Live Workspace, and are delivered right through your browser. With these Live Web applications, you can view and edit Word, Excel, PowerPoint, and OneNote files online. You'll be able to work from anywhere, collaborate easily, and extend your Microsoft Office experience on the Web.

14

An Introduction to Google Apps

HOW TO...

- Sign up for a Google ID
- Install the Google Toolbar
- Send and receive e-mail with Gmail
- Send and receive instant messages with Google Talk
- Create an event in Google Calendar
- Configure notifications to go to a cellular phone
- Share online documents with Google Docs
- Create a web site with Google Sites
- Use Google products on your cellular phone
- View maps with Google Maps
- Explore the world with Google Earth

Google Apps, available at www.google.com/apps, are free applications you can use to enhance your netbook experience. Like Windows Live applications, Google applications offer web-based programs you can use to send, receive, and manage your e-mail, instant message with friends and family, stay organized with an online calendar, share documents and files in an online workspace, and more. With Google products, you can even create your own web site, add Google features to your mobile phone, get directions with Google Maps, and explore the world with Google Earth.

Although there seem to be more Google applications than there are Windows Live applications, the basic applications offer just about the same thing that Windows Live do (e-mail, instant messaging, sharing documents and files). There are a few differences in function, but not many. The online applications you choose mostly have to do with preference, not features.

Set Up Google Apps

As with any web-based application, you first need to obtain the proper ID and log in to the web site. That's what you'll do with Gmail and the Google Calendar; both are completely web-based and don't have to be downloaded. You can then download and install any applications you want to try that do require a download, such as Google Talk, Google Earth, or the Google Toolbar.

When choosing what to download, you should start with the applications you think you'll use the most. For instance, if you don't like your current e-mail program, you may want to give Gmail a try. However, if you're happy with Windows Live Messenger, there's no reason to download and install Google Talk. I will suggest you get the Google Toolbar, though. The Google Toolbar brings all of the Google apps together and will help introduce you to Google apps. It's easy to disable or uninstall if you decide you don't like it.

It may be best to skim the chapter and look at the screen shots before you commit to anything that has to be downloaded.

Sign Up for a Google ID

The first step in doing anything at all with Google apps is to get a Google account (Google ID). With a Google account, you can customize your Google Home page, view recommendations, get more relevant search results, set up a new e-mail and instant messaging address, and more. With your account set up, you can then access any of your web-based Google applications from any computer that is connected to the Internet.

To get a Google ID that you can use with all of the available Google applications:

1. Navigate to www.google.com/gmail.
2. Click Create an account.

You don't have to use your Gmail account or read the e-mail that arrives at that address. The purpose at this time for obtaining a Gmail account is to access all of Google's services easily.

3. Fill in the required information, including your current e-mail address, and a password for signing in (see Figure 14-1).
4. Navigate to www.google.com. You should be automatically logged in. If not, log in with your new Google ID and password.
5. If desired, set up your home page. You can do this now or later. Or never.
6. Click My Account in the top-right corner.

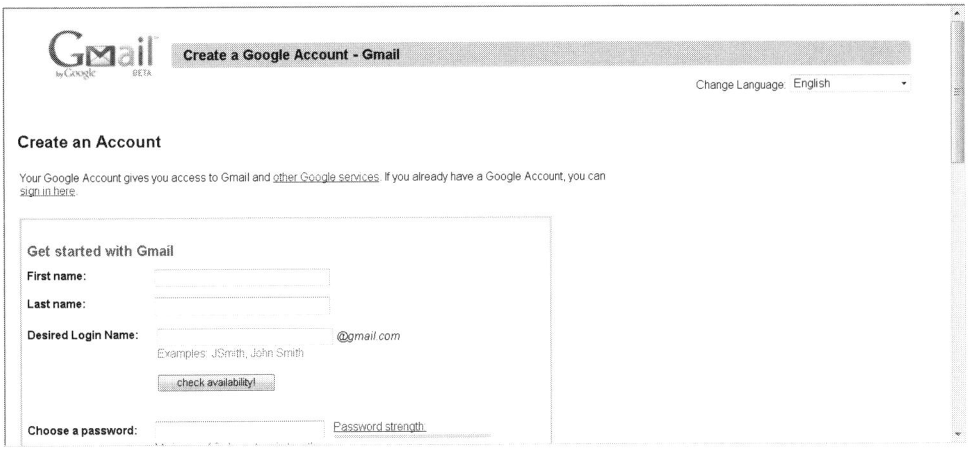

FIGURE 14-1   Create a Google account to customize your Google applications experience.

7. Your Google Accounts page will look something like the page shown in Figure 14-2. If desired:
    a. Create a personal profile with information about yourself.
    b. Edit your personal information without creating a public profile.
    c. Change settings related to e-mail, passwords, or password recovery options.
    d. Try new products, such as Gmail, Alerts, iGoogle, Groups, and more.
8. At the top of your Google Accounts page, click Google Home to return to your home page.

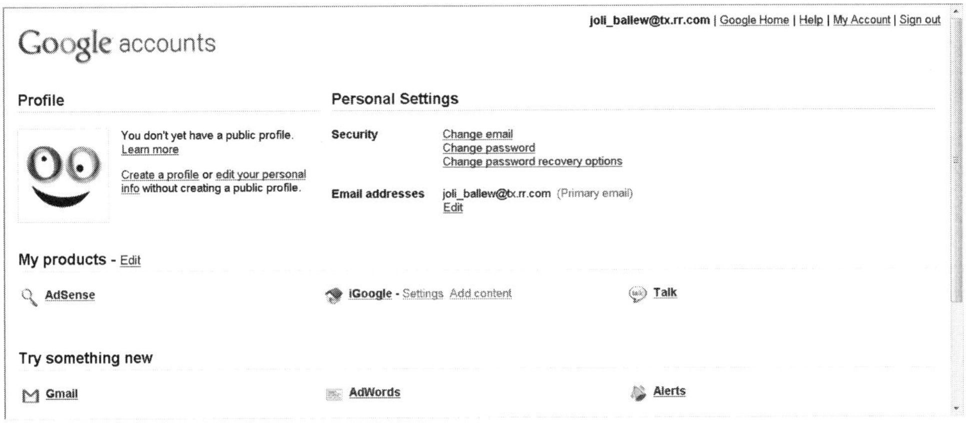

FIGURE 14-2   Your Google Accounts page allows you to personalize your preferences.

Install the Google Toolbar

If you think you'll like using Google Apps, you will want to install the Google Toolbar. Although it's best not to bog down your netbook with applications and toolbars you won't use, a few applications, such as the Google Toolbar, can enhance your netbook experience.

The Google Toolbar offers the following features:

- **Enhanced Search Box** When you type information into the search box, you'll see a list of useful suggestions. For instance, if you type **Google**, you'll see Google-related results in a drop-down list. In Figure 14-3, google maps is highlighted. Clicking that will take you directly to Google Maps, removing the step of looking through a list of search results on a second page.
- **Custom Buttons** Easily add custom buttons to the toolbar for items you use often. Consider adding Google Calendar, Google Documents, or Web History (see Figure 14-4).
- **Mobile Toolbar Settings** Your toolbar settings, bookmarks, and custom buttons will appear on any computer that you use to log in to Google, whether it's from your netbook or your desktop PC.
- **Automatic Suggestions** If you mistype a URL, Google will offer suggestions for what it thinks you're looking for. If you see it, simply click it to go there.

To download and install the Google Toolbar:

1. Navigate to http://toolbar.google.com.
2. Click Install Google Toolbar. You may also see a version number.
3. Review the Terms of Service and set preferences as desired (see Figure 14-5).
4. Click Accept and Download.
5. In Internet Explorer, click Run, Run, and Run again. Take similar actions in other web browsers.
6. A new instance of your web browser may open. If that happens, close this one. The new window will have the toolbar installed and a page related to the Google Toolbar will open.

FIGURE 14-3 The Enhanced Search Box makes locating items on the Internet faster.

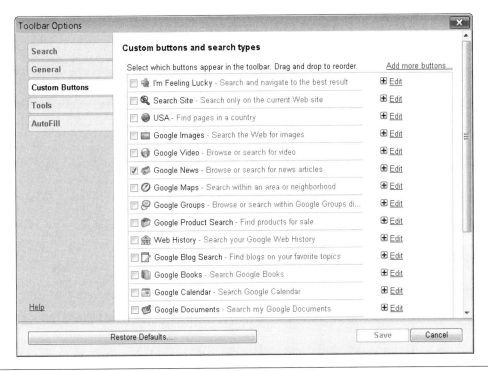

FIGURE 14-4   Add the buttons you use most for quick access to your favorite Google applications.

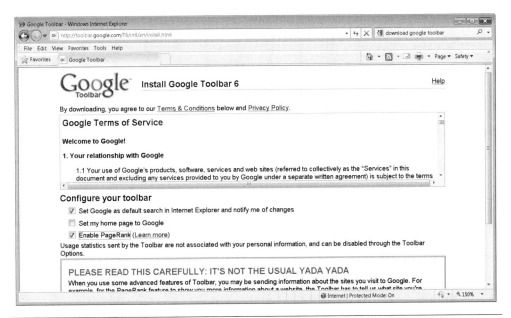

FIGURE 14-5   Read the Google Toolbar information and click Accept and Download.

E-mail and Instant Messaging

E-Mail and instant messaging are at the heart of any web-based application, and Google offers Gmail and Google Talk in their suite of applications. To use these applications, you'll need an e-mail account that ends in @gmail.com. The first time you click Mail on your Google home page, you'll be prompted to create it. If you worked through the first section, you already have a Gmail account. If you don't, return to the section "Sign Up for a Google ID" to get one now.

Send and Receive E-mail with Gmail

With a Gmail account (or a Google ID, whatever you prefer to call it), you can access and use Gmail with no download, no installation, and no setup. Simply click Mail or Gmail at the top of your Google home page, sign in if prompted, and you will have access.

 If you have a Gmail ID, you have e-mail in your Inbox from Google.

To access Gmail, receive e-mail, and send an e-mail:

1. Go to www.google.com and log in. You may be logged in automatically.
2. Click Gmail, shown in Figure 14-6. (You may see Mail.)
3. If prompted to run any ActiveX controls, do so. You may see a yellow bar across the top of the web browser window. Click it to run the control.
4. New e-mail appears in your Inbox. You should have at least one e-mail from the Gmail Team (see Figure 14-7). Click any e-mail to read it.
5. To reply to any e-mail, click Reply. You can also click Forward to send the e-mail to someone else.
6. Type your message and click Send. If you clicked Forward, you'll also need to type an e-mail address (see Figure 14-8).

 Look for a link to Google Home at the top or bottom of any Google web page. Click Google Home to return to your home page quickly.

FIGURE 14-6 Look for Gmail and click it to go to your Gmail Inbox.

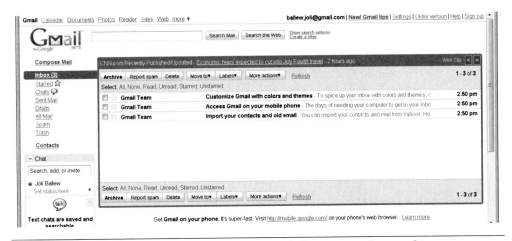

FIGURE 14-7   E-mail appears in your Inbox. Click any e-mail to read it.

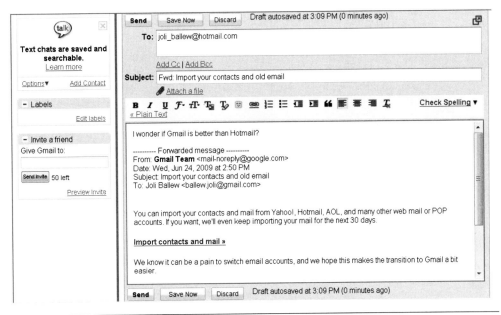

FIGURE 14-8   Gmail is web-based. You do everything inside your browser, thus there's no need to download the application.

Did You Know?

Chat

On the left side of the Gmail interface is Chat. You can use Chat to send and receive instant messages with online contacts. To use this, click Add Contact, wait for the contact to accept your invitation, and then click the name to initiate a chat inside the Gmail window.

Send and Receive Instant Messages with Google Talk

Although you can send and receive instant messages from inside your Gmail home page, there are other options. An older application, Google Talk, offers many more features, and is a better instant messaging solution.

To download Google Talk:

1. Navigate to www.google.com/talk.
2. Click Download Google Talk.
3. As prompted, click Run, and Run again.
4. Accept the terms of service, and click Finish.
5. From the Google Talk home page, click Add Google Talk to your iGoogle page.
6. You can now access Google Talk from your Google home page as well as from the Google Talk application on your desktop. Figure 14-9 shows the Desktop application.

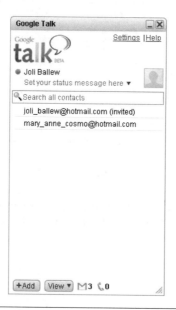

FIGURE 14-9 Google Talk will open as a separate application on your desktop.

In the next two examples, I'll be using the Google Talk application that sits on the desktop.

To add a contact in Google Talk:

1. After logging in to Google Talk, click +Add (see Figure 14-10).
2. As shown in Figure 14-10, type the name of the contact to add. You can also click Choose from my contacts if you have contacts in your Gmail address book.
3. Click Next, then Finish.

Your contact will have the word "invited" in parentheses beside his or her name in your contact list until he or she has accepted your Google Talk invitation.

To send an instant message in Google Talk:

1. Add contacts as detailed in the previous section. Wait until you see that one of your contacts is online. There will be a green dot by their name (see Figure 14-11).
2. Click the contact's name to open the conversation window.
3. Type your message and press Enter. Figure 14-12 shows how an ongoing chat looks onscreen.

You can click Send Files to send the contact a file, such as a document, song, or picture.

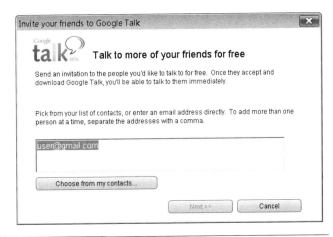

FIGURE 14-10   Click +Add to add a contact. You have to have at least one contact if you want to have an instant messaging conversation.

FIGURE 14-11 Online contacts, those you can chat with, have a green dot by their name.

FIGURE 14-12 A chat between two people looks like this.

Using Calendar, Google Docs, and Google Sites

In addition to the basic applications, Gmail and Google Talk, there are many more Google applications to explore. In fact, there are too many to detail here. However, in the interest of introducing the applications you may be most interested in for your netbook, I'll introduce Calendar, Google Docs, and Google Sites.

Create an Event in Google Calendar

Google Calendar is another web-based application, which means you don't have to download or install anything to use it. You only need a Google ID. You can access the Google Calendar application from the More link at the top of your Google home page, as shown in Figure 14-13.

When you open the Calendar application the first time, you'll be prompted to verify your name and time zone. Make changes as desired and click Continue. Then, magically, the Google Calendar appears, complete with today's activities (see Figure 14-14).

To add an event to Google Calendar:

1. Go to www.google.com and log in.
2. Click More, and then click Calendar.
3. If necessary, type your name and choose your time zone. You only have to do this the first time you use the calendar.
4. To add an event, use the arrows to navigate to the day of the appointment.
5. Click inside the hour and day you wish to create the event.
6. Type the name of the event and click Create Event.

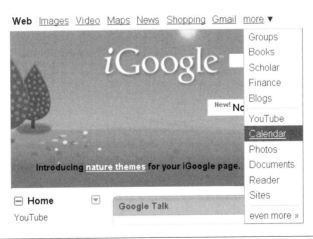

FIGURE 14-13   Google Calendar can be accessed from the More link at the top of your Google home page.

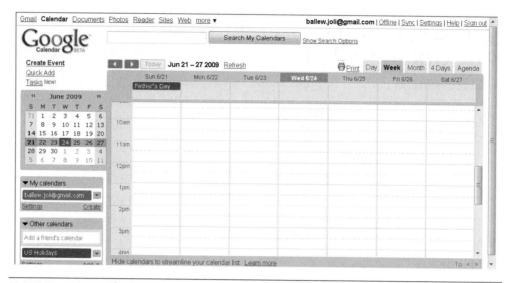

FIGURE 14-14 The Google Calendar is a full-fledged calendar application.

7. The new event will appear in your calendar (see Figure 14-15).
8. Click the event to set a reminder, invite guests, add a description, and more (see Figure 14-16).
9. Click Save.

Tip A reminder will, by default, consist of both a pop-up and e-mail that will appear ten minutes prior to the event. You can change this setting and others as detailed next.

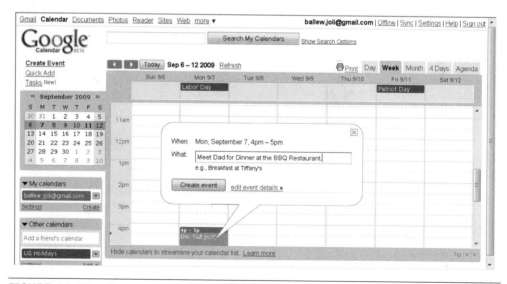

FIGURE 14-15 Create an event in Calendar.

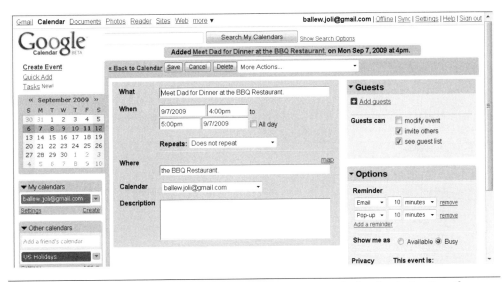

FIGURE 14-16   After adding an event, you can set a reminder for it, invite others, and more.

Configure Notifications to Go to a Cellular Phone

By default, event reminders are sent to you via e-mail on your computer and any other mobile device you have configured to receive e-mail ten minutes prior to each event. You'll also get a pop-up on your computer at that time. You can change this behavior if desired.

   To change the way notifications are sent by default in Google Calendar:

1. With Windows Calendar open, locate Settings. It's likely at the bottom of the Calendar window, on the left side. Click Settings. This is shown in Figure 14-17.
2. Under Calendar, click Notifications. This is also shown in Figure 14-17.
3. To change the number ten to something else, highlight it and type a new number; then, from the drop-down list, choose minutes, hours, days, or weeks.
4. You can also change how your receive invitations from others by selecting Email or SMS. SMS messages can be configured to go to your cell phone. SMS stands for Short Message Service and allows short text messages to be sent between two SMS-capable devices.
5. If you choose to receive notifications via SMS, click Set up your mobile phone to receive notifications, then follow the prompts to input your cell phone number.

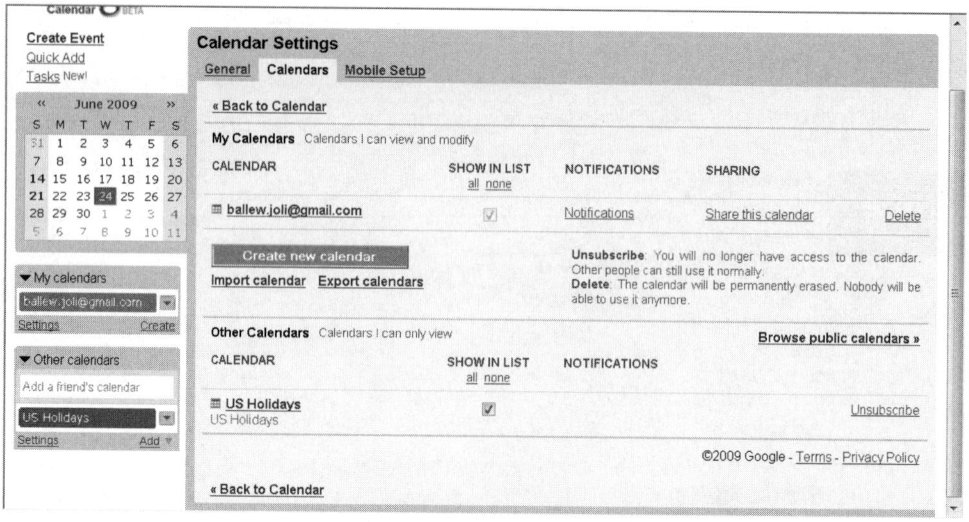

FIGURE 14-17 To change how you are notified by Google Calendar when a reminder has been set, configure notification settings.

Share Online Documents with Google Docs

As with Google Calendar and Google's Gmail, Google Docs is an online web-based application and thus requires no download or installation on your part. Simply navigate to www.google.com/docs and start working with the program.

The features of Google Docs include the ability to:

- Create, share, and edit documents online, from anywhere you can connect to the Internet.
- Upload and work with all kinds of data, including Microsoft Word documents, presentations, and worksheets; OpenOffice data, HTML, and text files; and more.
- Create spreadsheets, documents, and presentations online without having to open an associated program on your netbook.
- Edit documents online simultaneously with anyone you choose, a feature not currently available in Windows Live Workspace.
- Keep track of changes, and who made them, and revert to a previous version easily.
- Publish documents online and share those finalized documents with anyone you choose.
- E-mail your documents as attachments.
- Organize your documents list by creating folders and moving data into them.
- Access and use templates, tools, and display features.
- Stay secure with online security features. Robots and web spiders can't get to your data and your documents won't appear in any web search indexes.

To share a document, presentation, or spreadsheet online:

1. Navigate to www.docs.google.com. If prompted, log in.
2. Click the Upload button.

Click the New button to create a new document, spreadsheet, presentation, form, or folder.

3. Click Browse to locate the file on your computer you'd like to upload.
4. Locate the file and click Open.
5. Click Upload File, shown in Figure 14-18.
6. The uploaded file will appear in the Google Docs window. To return to the Google Docs home page, click Google Docs at the top of the page.
7. To create a folder for the file and move it there:
   a. Click New, and click Folder.
   b. Name the folder and add a description.
   c. Click Save.
   d. Click All Items, locate the file to move, and drag it to the new folder (see Figure 14-19).

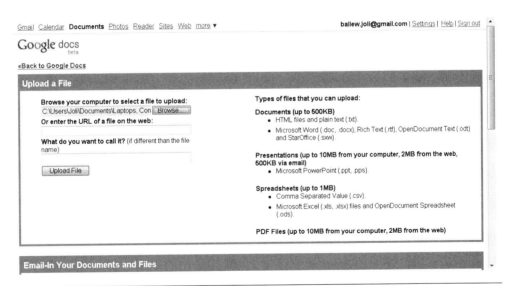

FIGURE 14-18   To upload a file from your netbook, click Browse, locate the file, and click Upload File.

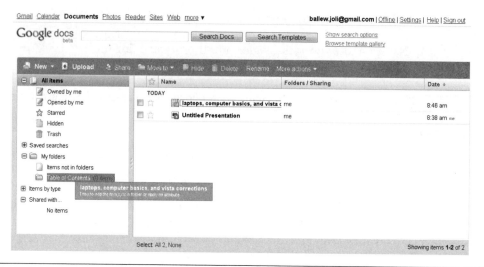

FIGURE 14-19 Google Docs makes it easy to create organizational folders and move files into them.

Create a Web Site with Google Sites

Google Sites is another free service. It enables you to create web pages easily, control who can visit and/or edit your web site, and allows you to keep data in a single place. You can create a web site just for your family, your colleagues, or even your sports team.

To create a basic web page in Google Sites:

1. Navigate to www.google.com/sites.
2. Log in if prompted.
3. Click Create Site.
4. Type a name for your site and a description (see Figure 14-20).
5. Decide if everyone can view the site or only people you specify.
6. Select a site theme.
7. When prompted, type the code shown. It'll appear at the bottom of the Web page and is not shown here.
8. Click Create Site.

From your new web page, explore the options. Note that you can:

- **Attach files** Click Attachments, click Browse, and locate the file to upload.
- **Add comments** Click Comments to add a comment to the site.
- **Edit the sidebar** Click Edit Sidebar to change or add sidebar items. You can add a countdown to a specific date, for example.
- **Edit the page** Click Edit Page to add text to the page, add links, change the background color, insert images, and more.

Figure 14-21 shows these options.

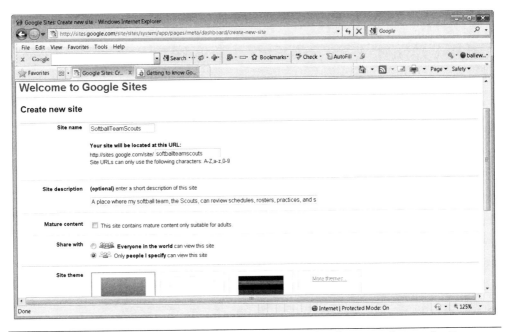

FIGURE 14-20   It's easy to create your own personal web site with Google Sites.

FIGURE 14-21   It's easy to personalize your Google Site.

Expand Your Reach with Other Google Products

Google offers so many products it's hard to decide which ones to try first. Without naming all of the available products, here are a few of my favorites, which you can find at www.google.com/options:

- **Alerts**   Get e-mail alerts and updates on any topic you want.
- **Book Search**   Search the full text of online books.
- **Checkout**   Enter your credit card and mailing address information to get through the checkout process more quickly when making online purchases.
- **iGoogle**   Personalize your Google home page with news, games, and more.
- **Patent Search**   Search the full text of U.S. patents.
- **Blogger**   Create your own blog.
- **Groups**   Create mailing lists and discussion groups.
- **Picasa**   Edit and share your favorite photos.
- **Translate**   View web pages in other languages.

A few items not listed are Google Maps and Google Earth and applications you can install to your cell phone. These are my favorites and are detailed in more depth next.

Use Google Products on Your Cellular Phone

Google Mobile, www.google.com/mobile, lets you search, use Gmail, access YouTube, and access other Google products directly from your cell phone. As shown in Figure 14-22, you start by selecting your phone from a list of compatible devices. From there, you can

FIGURE 14-22   Choose your phone to begin.

view the applications available for your phone, view "getting started" files and videos, and have a link sent to your phone to begin.

On cell phones with web browsers, you can also visit m.google.com from your phone to get started.

Some of the most useful mobile applications for cell phones include:

- **Mobile App**   Allows you to search web content faster and launch other Google products more easily.
- **Maps**   Makes it easy to search for local business and get driving directions.
- **Gmail**   Lets you stay connected to Gmail and stay in touch right from your mobile phone.
- **Sync**   Allows you to synchronize your mobile phone's calendar and contacts with Google.
- **Reader**   Lets you read your favorite blogs and newsfeeds and share content with friends.
- **Docs**   Lets you view documents, spreadsheets, and presentations from your mobile phone.
- **Google Earth**   Lets you view a satellite image of the earth, type addresses and locations, and zoom in on any part of earth that a satellite can reach.

View Maps with Google Maps

Google Maps is a nice application bookmark on your netbook's web browser because you can use it to find just about any address in the world. Beyond that though, many addresses you'll look up also come with a picture of the home, business, or intersection. In Figure 14-23, I've searched for the Houston Texas Space Center, selected Space Center Houston, and clicked Street view. The figure thus shows the entrance to the Space Center.

To use Google Maps:

1. Go to www.google.com/maps.
2. Type in your home address or another place you will recognize if a picture is available. Make sure to add a city and state.
3. You'll see something similar to what's shown in Figure 14-24. If available, click Street view. You'll see the image; an example is shown in Figure 14-25.

You can click and drag inside any photo to move around the photo and see different views.

FIGURE 14-23 Google Maps not only offers directions to a business, residence, or place of interest, but it also offers Street view, allowing you to see where to turn or what the address looks like.

FIGURE 14-24 Google Maps shows you where an address or place of interest is, and offers the option to Get directions.

FIGURE 14-25   Many homes, businesses, and places of interest also offer a photo.

Explore the World with Google Earth

Google Earth is another free application that allows you to view any part of earth via satellite imagery. You can view maps, terrain, and even galaxies in space. You can view the ocean floor, take 3-D tours of buildings in the Google Earth Gallery, and even listen to audio and voice recordings when "visiting" certain places.

Unlike many of the other Google applications, you have to download and install Google Earth. You can get it from http://earth.google.com. Click Download Google Earth to get started.

Once Google Earth is installed, it's best to read the tips available. They'll help introduce you to Google Earth.

To locate an address on Google Earth, under the Fly To tab, type the address, including the city and state; then press Enter. Double-click the image to zoom in. To locate a business, under the Find Businesses tab, type a business type, such as museum, library, restaurant, or bank. Type a city and state. Press Enter to search.

During your searches, you may find more than one result. In the left pane, select the result you want. In Figure 14-26, I've selected the Dallas Museum of Art. Notice there's an aerial view that I can zoom in on, various tools, and even a review of the business.

Note there is also a directions tab and lots of tools to explore. There's also a Help menu, where you can get more information. You can also view tours, view the sky, see Mars, and more. Figure 14-27 shows part of a Sightseeing tour. You can see that Sightseeing is selected in the left pane.

Type in your own address to see if you can view your own home in Google Earth.

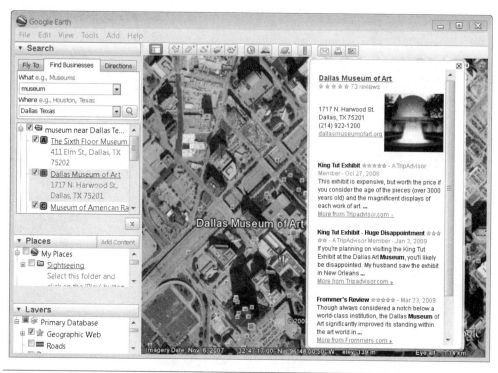

FIGURE 14-26   Search for and locate any business you desire.

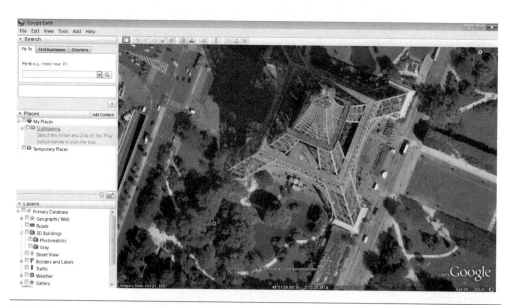

FIGURE 14-27   Take a sightseeing tour to experience Google Earth.

15

An Introduction to OpenOffice.org

HOW TO...

- Know what Open Office applications you need
- Download and install Open Office applications
- Explore available Open Office Extensions
- Explore Writer
- Export a text file as a PDF file
- Explore Calc
- Open a Microsoft Office Excel file in Calc
- Explore Impress
- Start building a new presentation from a template
- Explore Draw
- Get Open Office Support

OpenOffice.org is a free suite of applications you can use to create text documents, presentations, and spreadsheets, and to draw images or create databases. If you're not in the market for an expensive office suite of applications such as Microsoft Office, OpenOffice.org (from here on referred to as Open Office) may be right for you. Open Office is compatible with most other office applications too, including programs offered by Microsoft. This means you can use Open Office Writer to create a text document, and a person using Microsoft Office Word can open it.

Open Office programs install on your netbook, and thus aren't web-based like Google Apps are. Because they must be installed, they require the use of your netbook's precious few system resources. However, Open Office products offer much more functionality than Google Apps, and may be what you need if you need more than Google Apps can give.

 Installing applications on a netbook requires the netbook to offer up resources to it, so make sure you install only the programs you need and want.

Get to Know Open Office

Open Office is an open source office software suite. Open source means that its source code is open to developers and users, and can thus be modified to suit the needs and desires of anyone. It also means that anyone can make changes to the software and redistribute it to others, and allows for modifications and derived works without regard to licensing or royalties. Finally, it means that anyone can report bugs, request features, or enhance the software in any way.

 Linux is an open source operating system, which explains the great number of derivations of the product.

Open Office is available in many languages and works on most computers, even Linux. Because Open Office is free of any licensing fees, you can use Open Office at home, at work, or throughout an entire enterprise, even in state or government offices. It also means you can install it on as many computers as you like, with no need to purchase additional licenses or bother with licensing at all.

Know What Open Office Applications You Need

You can download any or all of the five Open Office applications. They are:

- **Writer** A word-processing program, similar to Microsoft Office Word, that offers familiar word-processing features such as AutoCorrect, AutoComplete, AutoFormat, Styles and Formatting, Text Frames and Linking, Indexing, Tables, and more. You can use Writer to create simple memos or large publications, including magazines and newsletters.
- **Calc** A spreadsheet program similar to Microsoft Office Excel. It has all of the number-crunching features you'd expect, from creating your own formulas to DataPilot technology.
- **Impress** A presentation program similar to Microsoft Office PowerPoint. Impress includes 2-D and 3-D clip art, special effects, animations, and drawing tools. You can save your work as a PDF file or as HTML, among other formats. Figure 15-1 shows Impress open on a Linux netbook.
- **Draw** A program similar to Microsoft Paint, a program included with all editions of Microsoft operating systems, but with much more depth. With Draw, you can create quick sketches or complex graphics and diagrams. You can create flowcharts, network diagrams, and organizational charts too.
- **Base** A database program similar to Microsoft Office Access. With Base, you can create and modify tables, forms, queries, and reports, and choose from a variety of templates and wizards to get you started. Because it's highly unlikely you'll be doing any of that on a small netbook, Base won't be covered here. You may, however, want to view a database on your netbook. To view a database, click File | Open.

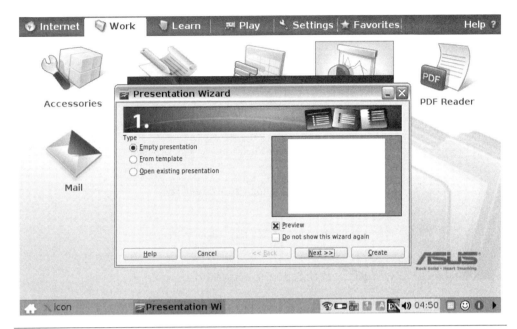

FIGURE 15-1   Open Office is an excellent addition to any Linux netbook and often comes preinstalled.

Download and Install Open Office Applications

Open Office is easy to download and install on a Windows computer, and if you know how, you can install it on Linux running Firefox. As shown in Figure 15-2, you need only click the link to start the installation on a Linux machine and the download process starts automatically. Once the download is complete, for Linux anyway, you'll need to visit the Help pages at OpenOffice.org for further instructions on how to install the applications. Installation is simple on Windows.

Installing Open Office on a Windows-based netbook is done the usual way:

1. Visit www.openoffice.org.
2. Click the link to download the product.
3. Click Run, Run, and possibly Run again.
4. Follow the instructions for installation. During installation, when prompted, do not choose Complete. Choose Custom.
5. By default, all applications will install. Click any feature you do not want to install (see Figure 15-3).
6. Continue to work through the wizard until the installation is complete.
7. Double-click the OpenOffice icon on your desktop to open the application. Click Next to start the setup process (see Figure 15-4).

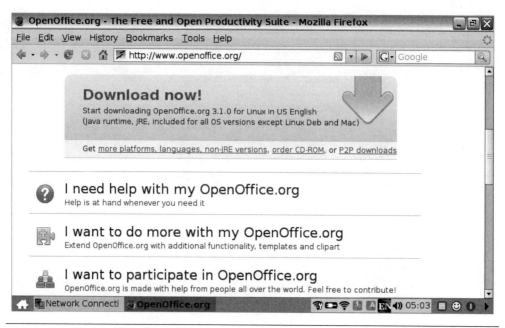

FIGURE 15-2   Open Office is easy to download on Linux, but you'll still have to follow the steps in the Open Office Help files to complete the installation.

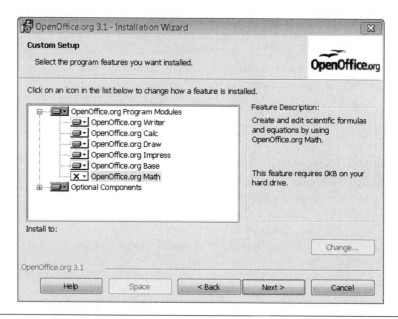

FIGURE 15-3   Click to choose programs you do not want to install.

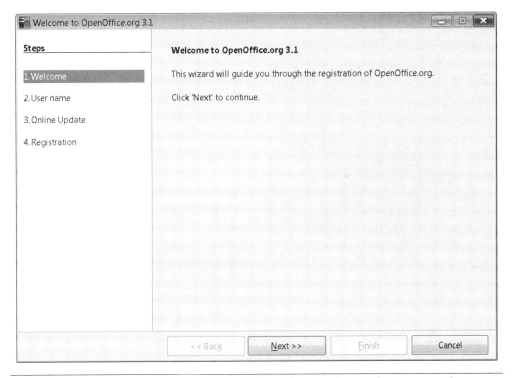

FIGURE 15-4   After installation, you'll still need to perform a few setup tasks.

8. During setup, you'll be prompted:
   a. To add your name and initials.
   b. To elect to check for updates automatically.
   c. To register the product.
9. Open Office will open where you can begin using the program (see Figure 15-5).

Explore Available Open Office Extensions

Extensions are add-ons for Open Office applications. They help you extend Open Office by opening up new features to you. For instance, you can download and install various extensions that will help you work better, including these most popular extensions:

- **Sun Presenter Console**   This extension provides more control over your slide show presentations, including the ability for you to see the upcoming slide, slide notes, and a timer. While you can see these things, your audience can see only the slide.
- **Professional Template Pack**   A group of professionally designed templates for Writer, Calc, and Impress. You can use these templates to spice up any document, spreadsheet, or presentation.

FIGURE 15-5 After installation and setup is complete, Open Office will be ready to use.

- **Dictionaries** Extensions exist for dictionaries in just about any language imaginable, including Swedish, Russian, Norwegian, German, and Danish, among many others.
- **Kaleidoscope** An extension for Draw that allows you to create patterns of shapes, object, and pictures, and allows you to rotate and scale them, among other things.
- **Calendar Collections** Currently, a 2009 Yearly Calendar Collection is available and quite popular.

To view these extensions and others:

1. Navigate to http://extensions.services.openoffice.org.
2. Under Extensions, click any option to sort what's available. Try Most Popular (see Figure 15-6).
3. To download any extension, click its title, and on the resulting page, click Get It.
4. Follow the prompts to download the extension. The process differs based on your web browser.

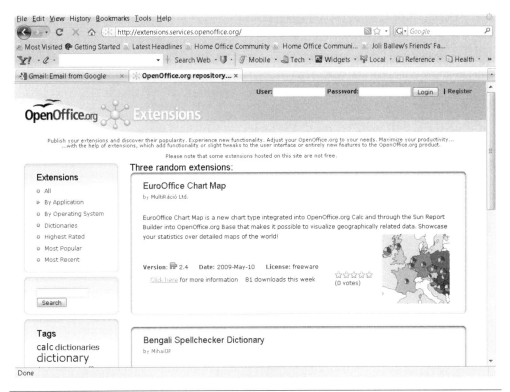

FIGURE 15-6   There are many types of extensions you can download to enhance Open Office applications.

Explore Writer

To get started with Writer, double-click the OpenOffice.org icon on your desktop on Windows, or if you're using Linux, locate the Writer application. The Writer application will open, and will look a bit like earlier versions of programs you may be familiar with, such as Photoshop or Word. The best way to get to know Writer is to type a few words, highlight them, and click icons on the formatting toolbar (see Figure 15-7).

Here are a few things to try on the formatting toolbar from left to right:

- **Styles and Formatting**   Click this small button on the far left of the formatting toolbar to open the Styles and Formatting window. From there you can choose from a variety of headings, indents, character styles, pages styles, and more.
- **Apply Styles drop-down list**   The first drop-down list on the left offers a list of formatting styles, including Heading 1, Text body, and more.

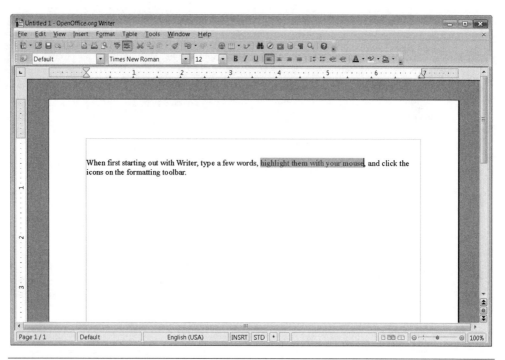

FIGURE 15-7 Writer doesn't look that special, but there are a lot of features available in the toolbars.

- **Font drop-down list** Click the arrow to access this drop-down list and choose a desired font (see Figure 15-8). Highlight text before selecting a font to apply the font to the selected text only. To set the font for text you intend to type next, simply select a font.
- **Font Size** Click this drop-down list to change the font size. As with fonts, you can select the text first or apply the font size to future text.
- **Bold, Italic, and Underline** Click these icons to change the way the font looks.
- **Align Left, Centered, Right, Justified** Click these icons to change where selected text appears on the page. Click Center to move text to the center position of the line.
- **Numbering, Bullets** Click these toggle icons to turn on and off numbering and bullets.
- **Decrease Indent, Increase Indent** Click these icons to move text left or right on indention.
- **Font Color, Highlighting, Background Color** Click these icons and related drop-down lists to apply color and highlighting to fonts.

Right-click any toolbar to customize it. You can add or remove commands, rename commands, or even create your own toolbar.

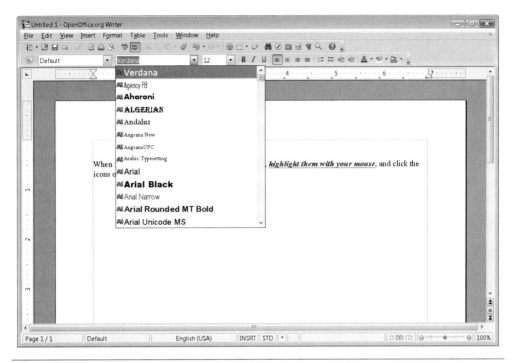

FIGURE 15-8   You'll use the Font drop-down list quite often.

The Standard toolbar sits above the formatting toolbar in OpenOffice.org 3.0 (see Figure 15-9). Hover your mouse over each icon to see what it offers. From this toolbar, you can create new documents, open existing ones, send the document in an e-mail, export the document as a PDF, print it, check spelling, undo, and much more.

Finally, click each menu title, File, Edit, View, Insert, and so on, to see what these menus offer. For more information about Writer, click Help and OpenOffice.org Help, or press F1.

Export a Text File as a PDF

One of the features I enjoy most about Open Office Writer is the ability to easily export a file to PDF. PDF stands for Portable Document Format and was created by Adobe. Anyone can open a PDF file using Adobe Reader, another free application. PDF files can be read online or offline, and they appear exactly as they do in printed form. With a PDF file, you never have to worry if the font you choose for your file is what's seen by the recipient, which can be a problem in other text file formats.

To export a text file as a PDF file:

1. Create a text file in Writer.
2. Click File, and click Export as PDF (see Figure 15-10).

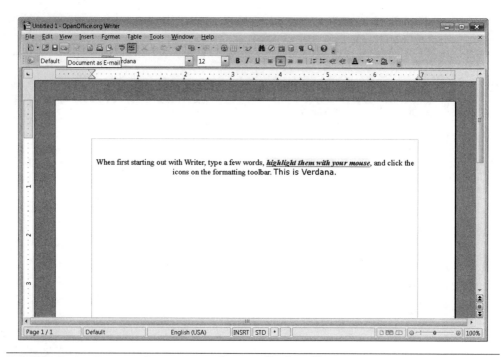

FIGURE 15-9   Review the icons on the Standard toolbar.

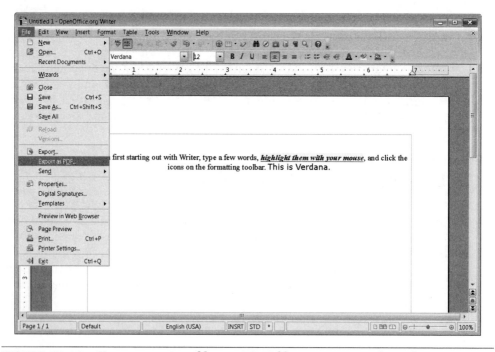

FIGURE 15-10   Export your text file as a PDF file to guarantee that others can open it and it retains its attributes.

3. Configure settings if you like; however, the default settings are most often fine.
4. Click Export.
5. Type a name for the file and click Save. Note the file will be saved by default in your Documents folder unless you've changed that default setting.
6. When you reopen the file from the Documents folder, or when someone else opens the file, it will open in Adobe Reader, as shown in Figure 15-11, unless other programs (such as Photoshop) have been configured to open these types of files.

 You can e-mail a file easily. Click File, Send, Document as E-mail, E-mail as Microsoft Word, E-mail as PDF, and more.

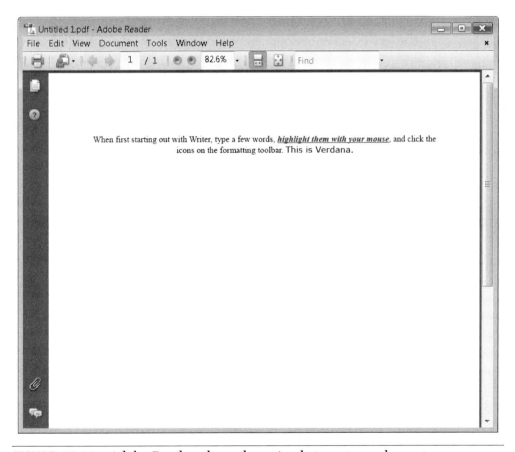

FIGURE 15-11   Adobe Reader, shown here, is what most people use to open PDF files.

Explore Calc

Calc is the Open Office spreadsheet program. It looks like older versions of Microsoft Excel and offers similar functionality. Like Writer, there's a Formatting toolbar, Standard toolbar, and Menu bar with familiar menus like File, Edit, and View. You can see the name of each icon by hovering your mouse over it (see Figure 15-12). If you're not familiar with spreadsheet programs, most of this will look a bit foreign to you; however, if you've used Microsoft Excel or something similar, you'll feel right at home with icons including (but not limited to):

- On the Formatting toolbar:
  - **Number Format options** As shown in Figure 15-11, there are multiple number format icons, including Currency, Percent, Standard, Add Decimal Place, and Delete Decimal Place. These options help you quickly apply numbering attributes to selected data.
  - **Borders** Click to see options for formatting your spreadsheet's data cells with borders.
- On the Standard toolbar:
  - **Document as E-Mail** Click to send the current spreadsheet in an e-mail.
  - **Export directly as PDF** Click to export the spreadsheet as a PDF document.
  - **Spelling and AutoSpellcheck** Click either to use and configure spell check.
  - **Hyperlink** Click to add a hyperlink to selected text.
  - **Sort Ascending and Sort Descending** Click to sort data as desired.
  - **Find and Replace** Click to find data and replace it with something else.

Font, font size, Bold, Italic, and so on work the same way in Calc and other Open Office programs as they do in Writer, introduced in the preceding section.

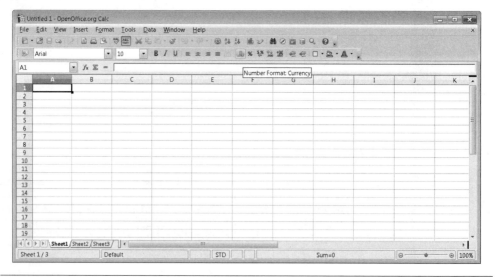

FIGURE 15-12 Hover the mouse over toolbar icons to see what they offer.

- From the Menu bar:
  - **Edit | Delete Cells**   Among other options from the Edit menu, select this to delete cells in a spreadsheet.
  - **View | Toolbars**   Click to view the available toolbars. You may want to add the Form Controls toolbar or the Insert toolbar, among others.
  - **Insert | Cells**   From the Insert menu you can insert cells columns, rows, breaks, and more.

Open a Microsoft Office Excel File in Calc

If you have an Excel file on your computer, you can open it in Calc. You may have an Excel file from a tax accountant, a previous project, or from a project file. You can find out if you have any Excel files by searching for *xls* or *xlsx*.

To open any Excel file in Calc:

1. Locate the file to open. You may find it in search results, on your desktop, or in your Documents folder.
2. Right-click the file and click Open With.
3. Choose scalc.exe (see Figure 15-13).

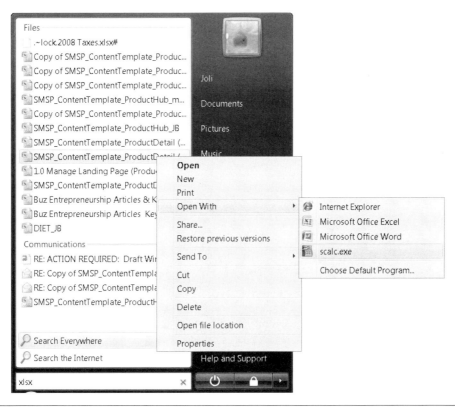

FIGURE 15-13   You can open Microsoft Excel documents in Calc.

Did You Know?

Use Keyboard Shortcuts

Listed next to many of the Menu bar's drop-down list options are keyboard shortcuts. For instance, File | Open offers the keyboard shortcut CTRL + o. Sometimes it's easier to use a keyboard shortcut than it is to use the netbook's touchpad.

Explore Impress

The first time you open Impress, Open Office's presentation program, you'll be prompted to choose what type of presentation to create. If you've never used a presentation program (such as Microsoft PowerPoint) before, it's best to start with a template. If you have presentations on your netbook you created, click Open existing presentation and browse to it. Once you have a presentation open, you can review the options. The Impress interface is shown in Figure 15-14.

Start Building a New Presentation from a Template

Impress's presentation template and presentation wizard pages are quite, well, impressive. You can get a good start on a professional-looking presentation by working through the pages and typing information at the prompts. To start building a new presentation using one of Impress's templates:

1. Open OpenOffice.org and click the icon next to Presentation.
2. From the first Presentation Wizard page, click From Template.

FIGURE 15-14 Impress is a presentation program that looks like earlier versions of Microsoft PowerPoint.

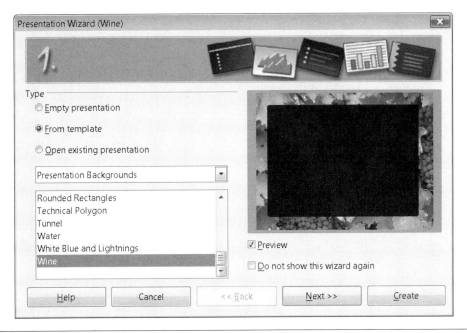

FIGURE 15-15   Choose from any of several presentation backgrounds.

3. Verify Presentation Backgrounds is selected and select any template underneath (see Figure 15-15). Click Next.
4. Select a slide design. You'll most likely want to accept the default, Original. You can go back later and explore the other options. Click Next.
5. Select a slide transition (how each slide moves from one to the next) and the presentation type. You many only want to change Effect here until you have more experience with the product. Click Next.
6. Type the answers to the questions shown in the next screen regarding your company name, subject, and your idea (see Figure 15-16). Click Next.
7. Click Create.

With the basic presentation created, you can now begin editing the slides. There are several menus and toolbars to explore, as there were in Writer and Calc. Some will look familiar, including File, Edit, View, Insert, Format, and Tools. A new menu option, Slide Show, lets you play the slide show, change slide show settings, or even rehearse with your slide show.

To edit your first slide, double-click inside the slide in the center pane. Text will appear based on your answers in the Presentation Wizard (see Figure 15-17). You can insert additional slides from the toolbar's Slide option, change the slide design, and perform other related presentation tasks. For more help on Impress, click the Help menu.

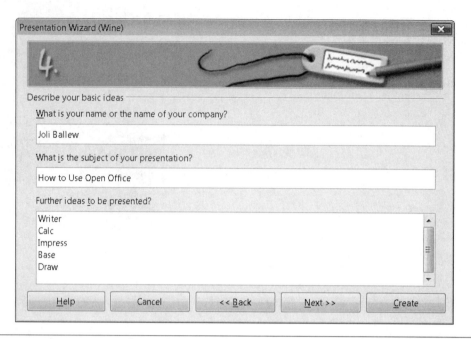

FIGURE 15-16 Type information related to your presentation when prompted.

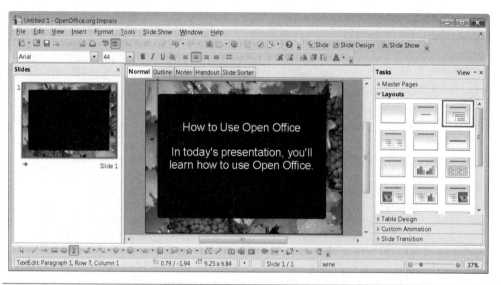

FIGURE 15-17 Impress is an easy program to get started with, but there are so many options it can become overwhelming to a new user. You can get help from the Help menu.

Explore Draw

Draw is the Open Office image drawing program. It's much more functional and offers many more features than Microsoft Paint, and offers features (for free) you'd find in extremely expensive programs such as Photoshop, CorelDraw, and similar programs. However, it can drain your netbook's resources, be hard to work with using a touchpad and small keyboard, and in the end, you'll probably find you'd rather do graphics work on a desktop PC anyway, due to the nature of the work. However, for the sake of completeness, an introduction to Draw is in order.

With Draw, you can create the following on a desktop PC (although you probably will not be able to do so on a netbook due to its limited resources):

- **Animated GIFs**   These are drawings that "move" or are animated. Animated GIFs can be used on web pages or presentations.
- **3-D Objects**   These are 3-D objects or representations of objects, such as buildings or products.
- **Animation Effects**   These are effects you can apply to your animations.
- **Charts**   These are charts with 3-D views.
- **Flash versions**   You can create Flash versions of your work.
- **Flowcharts, graphs, and illustrations**   Create complex flowcharts and organizational charts for presentations or web pages.

However, if you're looking for a simple use for Draw, to learn a little about the program, you can open a photo in Draw and add text. To add text, click the *T* at the bottom of the Draw interface. As with other programs, you can set the font, font size, font color, and more (see Figure 15-18).

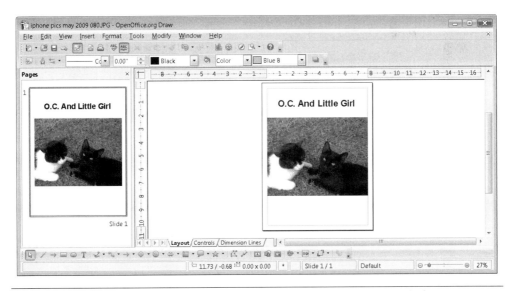

FIGURE 15-18   Draw is a comprehensive drawing program, but it likely requires too many resources to be used effectively on your netbook.

Get Open Office Support

If you have decided you like Open Office and plan to use it as your main office suite, you'll need support options for resolving problems, learning how to use the intricate features, and getting help quickly with you need it. You can do all of this and more from www.openoffice.org. From the home page, simply click I need help with my OpenOffice.org.

There are lots of ways to get help:

- **Free community support**   You can get free community support in various categories, including a community forum, mail list, tutorials, FAQs, and more. From http://support.openoffice.org, select the option desired (see Figure 15-19).
- **Commercial support and training**   There are many professional organizations that will help you learn more about Open Office, including Sun Microsystems.
- **OpenOffice.org books**   There are many books on Open Office. Start at Amazon .com and search Open Office for ideas.
- **General community resources**   You may be able to find community resources in the form of user groups, templates, samples, macros, or other contributor-based options.

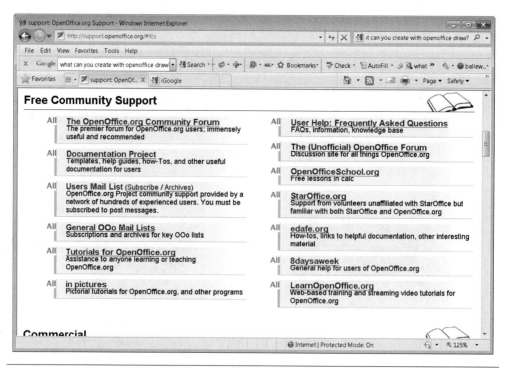

FIGURE 15-19   Free community support is a good option when you need an answer fast.

16

Additional Web-Based Applications to Try

HOW TO...

- Play a game using Kongregate
- View a video on YouTube
- Watch TV with Hulu
- Stay in touch with friends using Facebook
- Upload and share photos on Flickr
- Explore the applications of Zoho
- Explore Zimbra Desktop
- Create a schedule using Yahoo! Calendar
- Store data online with Box.net
- Find more web-based applications

Because netbooks are small and have limited resources, if you have a fairly fast always-on Internet connection, it's often best to work with web-based applications. When you use a web-based application, you don't have to download and install anything, which saves hard drive space in the short run. In the long run, using applications you don't have to download helps keep applications off your netbook that may run in the background without your knowledge, tying up system resources and slowing down your computer.

Hard drive space is especially valuable when you have a netbook that has a solid-state hard drive, because these types of drives are quite smaller than traditional hard drives. In the earliest netbooks with solid-state drives, the capacity was only 4 to 8GB, whereas traditional drives offered 160GB or more. With regard to your computer's resources, the earliest netbooks came with only 1GB of RAM and your new netbook may not have much more, which is a very small amount for managing multiple programs running at the same time.

You've learned about several web-based applications already. In Chapter 12, you learned about Windows Live Essentials; in Chapter 13, you discovered Office Live Workspace; and in Chapter 14, you looked at Google Apps. While not every application in these suites is web-based, they do offer a starting point and lots of neat online features.

As you probably surmised by the chapter title, there are lots more web-based applications out there, by companies that aren't as well known as Microsoft or Google. You may find that these applications suit you better than the ones you've learned about thus far. You may also find online games you'd like to explore, as well as popular web sites such as YouTube. In this chapter, you'll learn about some of these applications and where to look for more.

Fun and Games

We've focused a lot in this book on how to set up your netbook, install programs, add hardware, and get online. We haven't focused much on fun and games. While you'll start out with several games from the Games folder (from the Start menu), there are other ways to have fun using your netbook. In this section, you'll learn a little about some free online applications and web sites you can interact with when you're looking for a little rest and relaxation.

Play a Game Using Kongregate

Kongregate is a community-centered gaming web site that lets its visitors play thousands of user-submitted online games for free. Those interested in creating games can upload them to the site to share them with others, and those interested in only playing the games can earn badges, level up, and create their own user profile for chatting with other players in chat rooms, via private messages, and in forums, after registering (registration is free). You can find Kongregate at www.kongregate.com. Figure 16-1 shows the Kongregate web site and a game in progress called Learn to Fly.

There are several categories of games, including but not limited to:

- **New**   Browse the newest and most recently uploaded games.
- **Top Rated**   View the highest rated games on the site. You'll be able to view when the game was uploaded, how many instances of the games have been played (gameplays), the average rating, among other information.
- **Strategy/Defense**   View a list of games that are defined as strategy games or defense games.
- **Adventure/RPG**   Browse games of adventure.
- **Shooter**   Browse games that require you to shoot at things, like bubbles, monsters, zombies, and more.
- **Puzzle**   View puzzle games that require thought, strategy, and skill.
- **Action**   Browse action games.
- **Sports**   Browse sports games.
- **Multiplayer**   View a list of multiplayer games.

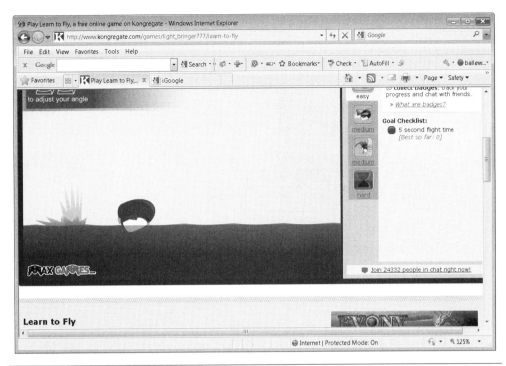

FIGURE 16-1   You don't have to register and log in to play the free games, but if you want to collect badges, track your progress, and chat with friends, you'll need to work through the short registration process.

View a Video on YouTube

Some laptops come with a YouTube icon right on the desktop. Whether you have an icon depends on the netbook manufacturer. You can click this icon to access YouTube, or you can visit www.youtube.com. There are several tabs at the top of the web page, including Videos. The Videos page offers a list of categories, shows, movies, and more that you can browse. You can also type anything in the Search box or review the most-viewed video list.

To locate and view a video on YouTube:

1. Visit www.youtube.com.
2. Click the Videos tab.
3. From the left pane, under categories, click a category that you like. Figure 16-2 shows Pets & Animals.
4. Click any video to watch it.

Generally, videos with the most views are the funniest videos on YouTube, the most informative, or the most disturbing.

FIGURE 16-2 Browse YouTube videos for information or a laugh.

Watch TV with Hulu

Hulu is a free web site that lets you watch some TV shows or show excerpts online. You may not get the best performance from a wireless Internet connection as you would with a faster, wired connection, but it's worth a try, especially if you're stuck in an airport on a layover with nothing to do!

You must meet a few requirements prior to viewing Hulu videos. To enjoy videos at Hulu, you will need the following software installed on your computer:

- Internet Explorer 6.0 or above, Firefox 1.5 or above, or Safari 2.0 or above
- JavaScript and Cookies must also be enabled
- Adobe Flash Player 9.0.115 or above
- Microsoft Windows XP SP2, Microsoft Windows Vista, Windows 7, Macintosh OS X, or Linux

To access Hulu and browse the available shows:

1. Visit www.hulu.com.

Tip You may be prompted to download Adobe Flash Player so you can view the videos on Hulu. This is mandatory. However, Flash Player is software you should have anyway, so it's okay to download it.

2. Browse the web site. Try Most Popular, shown in Figure 16-3.
3. Click any video to play it.

Stay in Touch with Friends Using Facebook

Facebook is a very popular social networking site where you can create a personal profile, invite others to view your profile, and then update your profile as often as you like. You can search for and add friends, upload photos and videos, and join groups. With Facebook, you can remain in touch with your friends even when you're logged off of the site or when you're not connected to the Internet (such as when your netbook is turned off). You can easily change your profile prior to shutting down your netbook, to say where you are now and where you're going or where you can be reached. With Facebook Mobile, you can keep in touch via your cell phone too.

You are in charge of your Facebook page, and you get a specific web page just for yourself. You can find me at www.facebook.com/joli.ballew. If you aren't my friend, you'll see what's shown in Figure 16-4. If you are my friend, you'll see what's shown in Figure 16-5.

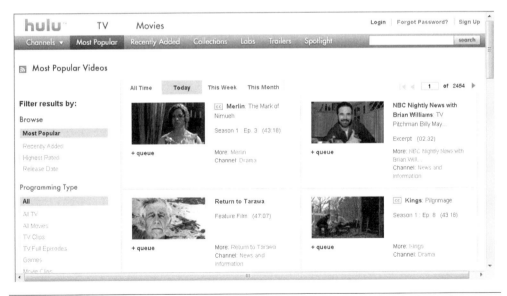

FIGURE 16-3   Browse Hulu and locate a video you'd like to watch. Click it to begin playback.

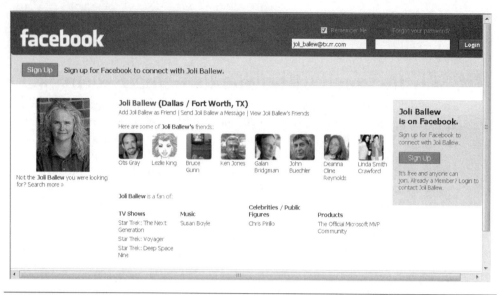

FIGURE 16-4 How a Facebook profile page looks to strangers.

It's very easy to get started with Facebook:

1. Go to www.facebook.com.
2. Fill in the information required: full name, e-mail, password, sex, and birthday, as shown in Figure 16-6.
3. Click Sign Up.

FIGURE 16-5 How the same Facebook profile page looks to friends.

FIGURE 16-6   Create a basic profile with your name, e-mail address, sex, and birthday.

4. Type the text shown in the box and click Sign Up once more.
5. When you receive the Welcome e-mail, click the link to verify the e-mail address. Your new Facebook page will open.
6. Facebook may add the names of friends it thinks you may know. You can click Confirm or Ignore, or scroll to the bottom of the page and click Skip this step.
7. If desired, click Find Friends. Otherwise, click Skip this step (see Figure 16-7).
8. Complete your profile information by adding the name of your high school and college and the related class years and the company you work for.
9. Click Save and Continue.
10. Select friends or additional friends you know from a list of suggested friends, and then click Save and Continue.
11. Select a network to join or click Skip this step.
12. Click View and Edit Your Profile to view your page.
13. Click Wall to see your new Facebook page.

As you add information to Facebook, you'll begin to see additional options such as add a profile picture, upload videos or pictures, add suggested friends, and take quizzes.

Ignore If You Want

If you click Ignore to ignore a friend request, the person requesting the friendship will not be informed. He or she will be informed only if you accept the request.

FIGURE 16-7 You can let Facebook search your address book or contact list to locate friends on Facebook already.

Upload and Share Photos on Flickr

Flickr, at www.flickr.com, is an online tool that allows you to share photos with anyone you like. A "basic account" is free and it's easy to set up. You simply fill out the registration pages and you're ready to upload and share photos. As with other online sites, you can create a personalized page with your profile, upload photos, and find friends who also use Flickr. You can view and manage your Flickr contacts, explore Flickr groups, and even read a Flickr Blog.

Once you're logged in, work through the three steps shown in Figure 16-8 to set up your personal Flickr page. First, you'll personalize your profile; next, upload your first photos; and last, find friends.

When you're ready, look for the Upload button to get started uploading your own photos:

- With registration and your profile completed, click Upload. If you're lost, look for "your photostream."
- Click Choose photos and videos.
- Select the pictures to upload and click Open (see Figure 16-9).
- Select your privacy options, and click Upload Photos and Videos.

 Flickr offers various upload tools if you find that the basic uploader introduced here isn't enough for you.

- Click Home. Your home page will show the pictures just uploaded.

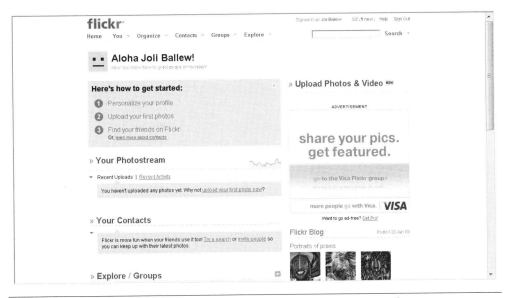

FIGURE 16-8   Flickr is social networking and photo sharing wrapped up into one site.

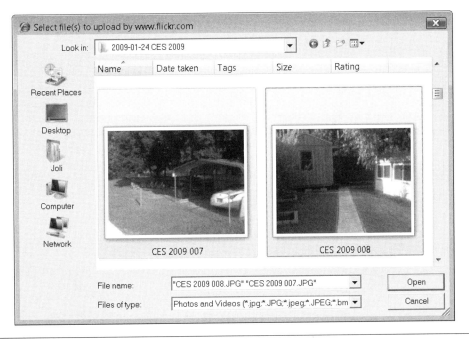

FIGURE 16-9   Select the pictures to upload.

Work and Scheduling

Life is not all fun and games. Sometimes you have to work too. There are lots of tools available for working online—in fact, way too many to introduce here. However, there are a few that stand out, including Zoho, Zimbra, and Yahoo! Calendar.

Explore the Applications of Zoho

The Zoho web site at www.zoho.com looks quite a bit like Google's application page. As with Google, you'll need to register for access, and most of the applications are free. The Zoho web site is shown in Figure 16-10.

Some of the Zoho applications you may want to try include:

- **Zoho Mail**   This web-based e-mail service provides an online interface that allows you to send and receive e-mail and manage the e-mail you want to keep. One of the best things about Zoho Mail is that there are no advertisements, not even in the free version. You also get spam protection, a personalized e-mail address, and plenty of storage.
- **Zoho Writer**   Zoho Writer allows you to share and collaborate with others online, import and export documents, edit your documents with online tools, post what you write to a blog, and choose from a variety of templates.

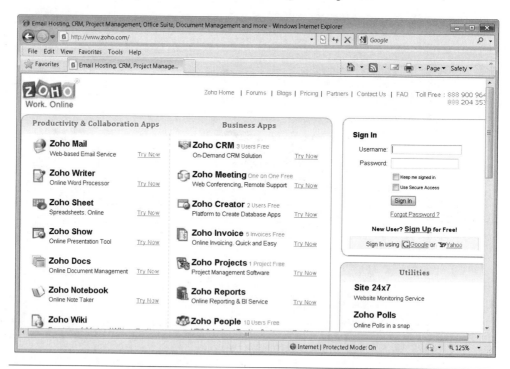

FIGURE 16-10   Zoho offers productivity and collaboration applications that are mostly free.

Zoho Sheet is Zoho's spreadsheet program; Zoho Show is the presentation program.

- **Zoho Share**   This is an online repository where you can upload data for the purpose of sharing it with others.
- **Zoho Planner**   Zoho Planner is an online organizer that enables you to make to-do lists, set reminders, upload files and images you can access from any computer with an Internet connection, and keep notes.

Explore the Yahoo! Zimbra Desktop

Zimbra is an open source collaboration suite of applications that makes e-mail manageable; claims to change the way you work with others; and works anyplace, on any machine, including Linux. There's also Zimbra mobile for Blackberry, iPhone, and others, and instant messaging (IM) software, calendar tools, and syncing software. Zimbra has a Linux look, with tabs and a brown background, and is well suited for a netbook.

From a single interface, you can access the features, such as Mail, Calendar, Tasks, IM, Documents, Briefcase, and Preferences. You can view a video of Zimbra features at www.zimbra.com/demos/zimbra_tour.

You should start by downloading and installing the application called Yahoo! Zimbra Desktop. You perform the download and installation as you would with any application suite. When you first open Zimbra Desktop, you'll be prompted to configure an e-mail account with it. Click Add New Account and follow the prompts. Zimbra Desktop is shown in Figure 16-11.

 When installing Zimbra Desktop, accept the defaults when you don't know what to select. You may be prompted about ports or other items you don't understand.

As you can see in Figure 16-11, there are several tabs that run across the top of the interface. As you click the tabs, the interface changes. Having these tabs at your fingertips makes incorporating the features simple and intuitive.

 To learn more, click Help.

Here are a few features available from the Zimbra Desktop interface:

- **Search the Web**   Type anything here to search for the item on the Internet or locally.
- **Mail**   Receive and read e-mail here, and use the Reply, Spam, and other tools to manage the e-mail you receive.
- **Calendar**   Click the Calendar tab to add events and appointments, set reminders, repeat the event, and more.

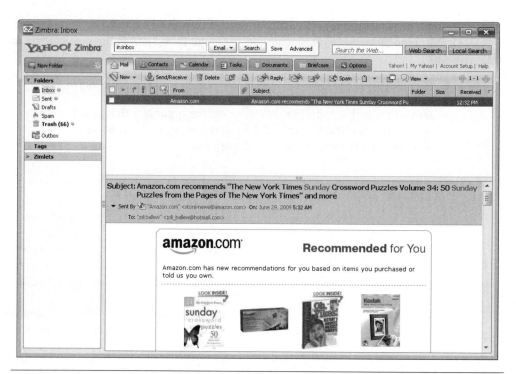

FIGURE 16-11 Zimbra Desktop is an all-in-one web-based e-mail and application suite.

- **Tasks** Click here to add a task. All data is fused together in one interface, making viewing tasks simple.
- **Documents** Click this tab to work with documents. There's also a New menu where you can create a new e-mail, enter a new contact, set an appointment, perform tasks, and upload files.

Create a Schedule Using Yahoo! Calendar

If you use Zimbra or Zoho, introduced in this chapter, or if you use another application introduced in this book such as Google Apps or Windows Live Essentials, you probably already have a calendar application. There's another calendar option, though: Yahoo! Calendar. You can access your personal calendar at http://calendar.yahoo.com. If you aren't already logged in to Yahoo!, you'll be prompted to log in.

Yahoo! Calendar offers sharing, syncing, and other options you'd expect, such as the ability to create appointments and events. You can also view the calendar by day, week, month, or year. Because the calendar is web-based and is provided by Yahoo!, it has built-in tabs for checking your e-mail, accessing contacts, and even taking notes. If you're a fan of Yahoo! and have a Yahoo! account, you may like this calendar better than any of the others (see Figure 16-12).

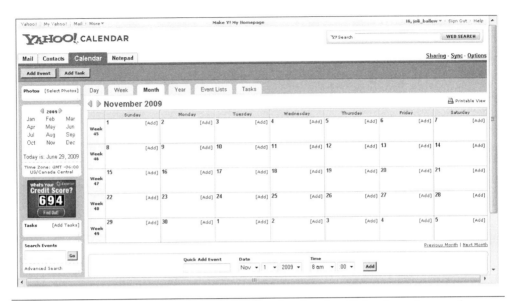

FIGURE 16-12   Yahoo! Calendar is integrated with other Yahoo! services such as Mail, Contacts, and Notepad.

Store Data Online with Box.net

As you may recall, many of the available, free, web-based software suites offer a free place to upload and store data. Office Live Workspace offers free Internet server space, as do Google Docs and Google Sites. You can upload pictures to Flickr and Facebook, and Zoho and Zimbra offer storing and sharing options too. So why would you want to look at additional online storage options?

Web sites that are dedicated to providing a safe place to store and share data offer many more features than web sites that offer multiple types of applications do. And you'll find that dedicated storage, sharing, and collaboration web sites have plenty of users to back up their claims as "easy to use" and offering "full-featured collaboration." One favorite, Box.net, claims that over 50,000 businesses use its product.

At Box.net (www.box.net), there are three plans: Lite, Individual, and Business. The Lite plan is free. With the Lite version you get:

- Five collaboration folders
- 1GB of storage
- 25MB file uploads

This isn't actually that impressive, though. Office Live Workspace offers 5GB of online storage, and Google Docs places limits on what you can save by counting your files. You can have a total of 5,000 documents and presentations and 5,000 images. With both, you can create your own collaboration folders and upload large files. Even lesser known web sites offer more than this; DropBox offers a 2GB storage area, larger than the 1GB available here.

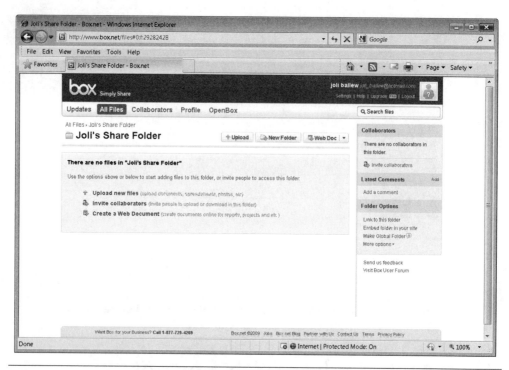

FIGURE 16-13   Box.net is intuitive and easy to use. If you need more features than a free web storage site can give you, consider upgrading to something like this.

So why use Box.net or anything like it? The answer is simple. Either your colleagues are using it or you need a lot more storage space than a free web site can give you, and you're willing to pay for it. Figure 16-13 shows Box.net. Note that it's easy to upload new files, invite collaborators, and create web documents.

Where to Find More Web-Based Applications

As netbooks become more and more popular, web-based applications created for them will become more and more commonplace. To stay on top of the latest netbook news, you can subscribe to or visit web sites dedicated to netbooks. There are several that offer RSS feeds you can subscribe to:

- **www.netbookupdates.com**   This web site posts daily news and in-house articles regarding netbook technology, and is growing rapidly. By clicking the orange RSS button on the Internet Explorer toolbar, you can easily subscribe to Netbook Updates web site. Figure 16-14 shows a new article on Windows 7 upgrades to Asus EeePC models.

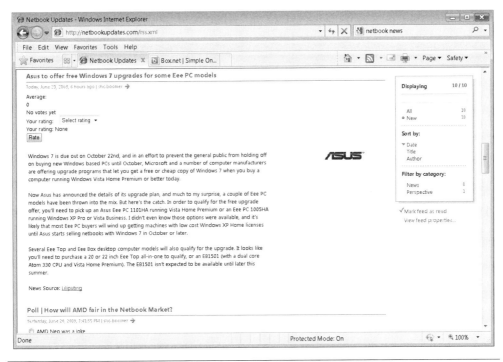

FIGURE 16-14   Subscribe to your favorite netbook web site's RSS feed and get the latest news about netbooks easily.

- **www.netbooknews.com**   This web site posts blogs, podcasts, articles, and other content about netbooks. As with most netbook sites, you can subscribe using the RSS button in Internet Explorer or other web browsers.
- **www.allabouteeepc.com**   This web site offers netbook news, hacks, and how-to articles. As with other netbook sites, you can subscribe using the RSS button in Internet Explorer or other web browsers.
- **www.netbookchoice.com**   This web site offers information on netbook manufacturers, where to buy, shopping options, labs, forums, and more. As with other netbook sites, you can subscribe to an RSS feed.
- **www.netbookreviews.net**   This web site offers reviews of netbooks and the reviews are categorized by manufacturer. An RSS feed is available.

What Is RSS?

RSS feed is a format for delivering web content that changes often. RSS stands for Rich Site Summary, although sometimes you'll see it as Really Simple Syndication.

17

An Introduction to Windows 7

HOW TO...

- Use the new Start menu
- Use the new Taskbar
- Navigate with Windows Explorer
- Move windows in new ways
- Change the view of Control Panel
- Use Gadgets
- Apply a new theme or background
- Create a personalized screen saver
- Watch Internet TV
- View connected devices using Device Stage
- Connect to a wireless network
- Troubleshoot network connections with the Network and Sharing Center
- Resolve problems with the Action Center
- Find and fix other problems

The newest netbooks now come preinstalled with Windows 7. Windows 7 is a better choice than previous operating systems, for many reasons. Windows 7 manages resources more efficiently and offers enhanced battery life when compared to Windows Vista; it offers dozens, if not hundreds more features than Windows XP; and it's compatible with hardware and software, and is much easier to use than Linux when performing downloads and working through installations. Windows 7 is a great option for your netbook.

This chapter offers a crash course on Windows 7. You won't learn everything or be introduced to every new element, but you will learn how to navigate the file system, use new desktop enhancements and interface features, and find and fix problems with networks, hardware, software, and even the operating system itself. You won't learn about using Windows Live Photo Gallery, Media Player, Internet Explorer, and the like, because using these features hasn't changed much; you will learn about the major changes, though, and you'll be up and running with Windows 7 in no time.

 It's very important to know what features are missing from Windows 7. You won't find Outlook Express or Windows Mail; in fact, you won't find any e-mail program at all. You won't find a messaging program or Windows Photo Gallery. You'll need to get your own. We suggest Windows Live Essentials, detailed in Chapter 12.

Should You Install Windows 7?

Even if your netbook came with Windows XP or Vista, the manufacturer may have offered you a free copy of Windows 7 to entice you to go ahead and make your purchase instead of waiting until Windows 7's release. If Windows 7 is an option for installation, consider it. Windows 7 has a ton of new features and has gotten rave reviews. Most reviewers prefer it over Windows Vista.

 If you are considering installing Windows 7, check with the manufacturer to make sure your netbook supports it before purchasing the program.

There are pros and cons to installing Windows 7. Windows 7 is much different from Windows XP, and at first it may be confusing and hard to get used to, so before you commit, make sure you're ready to spend some time learning its features. Its interface is so completely revamped that even those familiar with Windows Vista will find themselves scratching their heads.

Windows 7 does not include familiar features like Outlook Express or Windows Mail and has no messaging program, so you'll have to download this yourself. This is easy to do, though, and the options provide you flexibility in choosing a program. You may opt for Google Mail, Windows Live Mail, or something else, for instance.

Beyond the cons, though, once you've gotten used to the Windows 7 interface and learned about the changes to the operating and file system, you'll find you probably really like the changes to the Taskbar, Search menu, Control Panel, and the Network and Sharing Center and enjoy using the hundreds of other enhancements and new features available.

Here are some more reasons to make the move:

- The Desktop Gadget Gallery lets you add gadgets to your desktop to stay up to date on the news, weather, stocks, and more.
- The new desktop enhancements let you "shake" windows to minimize them, "snap" them to the sides of the desktop, and even "peek" at the desktop through open windows by making them transparent.
- The Homegroup feature allows you to share data easily with other Windows 7 computers on your network.

- Windows Live Essentials, a free program and a single simple download, offers Mail, Messenger, Photo Gallery, Writer, Movie Maker, Toolbar, and Family Safety. Because these are web-based, they are much more flexible than the programs you're used to. These applications aren't part of Windows-based operating systems, but any Windows user can download and install them.
- There are a lot of desktop backgrounds to choose from, even regional ones. You'll enjoy browsing through the new desktop options.
- There are lists everywhere. You can access "jump lists" and get where you need to go quickly, or use pop-outs from the Start menu.

Use the New Start Menu, Taskbar, and Windows Explorer Interfaces

The first few things you'll notice when you turn on your Windows 7 netbook or install Windows 7 on an existing one are the changes to the Taskbar and Start menu. The Taskbar is now one long bar instead of the more familiar sectioned one, and it seems larger and roomier than in the past. The Start menu offers a window for searching, and offers recently modified data in pop-out lists. As you can see in Figure 17-1, the pop-out list for Windows Media Center shows recently recorded TV shows.

FIGURE 17-1   The Start menu's pop-out lists offer quick access to recently modified data.

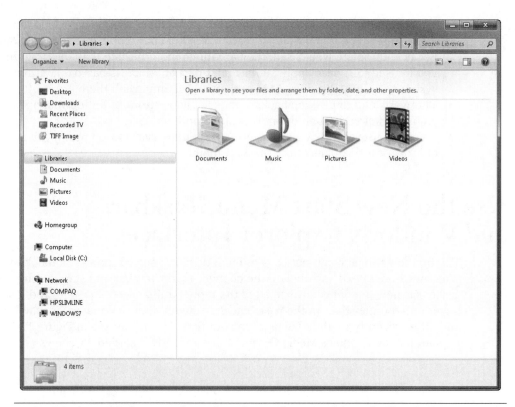

FIGURE 17-2 Windows Explorer has changed quite a bit and offers links to areas of the operating system you access often.

If you're a fan of Windows Explorer, you'll notice lots of changes there too (see Figure 17-2). On the left side of the window, you have easy access to Favorite places like the Desktop, Downloads, Recorded TV, or whatever else you use often. You'll see Libraries, the part of the operating system that holds your personal data, such as Documents, Music, Pictures, and Videos. There are also links to your Homegroup (more on that later), Computer, and Network.

Use the New Start Menu

The Windows 7 Start menu works the same as the Start menu you're used to. You can select any item from the Start menu to open the item; you can click All Programs to access a list of programs, accessories, and system tools and open them; and you can use pop-out lists to access recently modified data. If you've never used Windows Vista, though, you'll notice a feature that really stands out: the Search window.

The Start Search window is one of the greatest features of Windows 7. With it, you can start typing the name of anything you'd like to access, and live search results will appear in the Start menu's left pane. You can then click the item to open it. The more you type, the more you limit the results. Figure 17-3 shows an example. By typing

FIGURE 17-3   The Start Search window lets you easily search for and access data, programs, and accessories.

Disk, you can access Disk Cleanup or Disk Defragmenter without having to click through various lists to get to it (Start | All Programs | Accessories | System Tools). You can also access files that contain the word *disk*, as well as other disk-related programs and features.

You can also see in Figure 17-3 that there's an option to shut down the computer with a single click. With Windows XP and Windows Vista, you had to click an arrow first and then choose Shut down. You can change what this button shows by editing the properties for the Start menu, as shown in Figure 17-4. (Just right-click the Start button and choose Properties.)

To get acquainted with the Search menu:

1. Click the Start button.
2. Locate your name in the top-right of the Start menu and click it to open your personal folder.
3. Click the Start button again.
4. In the Start Search window, type **Internet**. Note the results. A sample is shown in Figure 17-5.

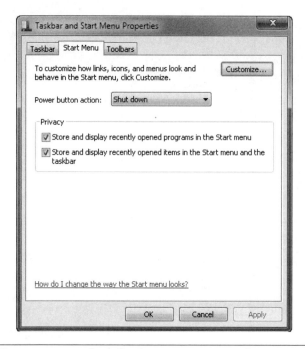

FIGURE 17-4 You can personalize the Start menu using the Properties dialog box.

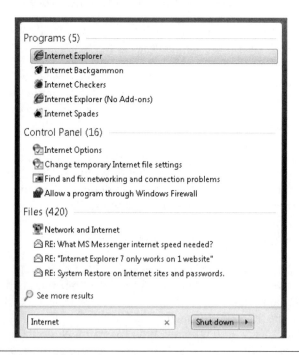

FIGURE 17-5 Type a word into the Start Search window to see results related to that word.

5. Click Start again. Click All Programs.
6. Note the programs in the list and click Back.
7. Continue exploring as desired.

Tip   Right-click the Start button and click Properties to change how the Start menu looks.

You can also "pin" program, folders, and other data to the Start menu if you use them often and want easy access. To do this, browse to the item to pin, right-click the item name, and select Pin to Start Menu. Note you can also pin items to the Taskbar. Figure 17-6 shows an example.

Use the New Taskbar

The first thing you'll notice about the Taskbar is that it's no longer in sections. The Quick Launch area is gone and the Notification Area blends in nicely with the rest of the Taskbar. When you open a program, its icon still resides in the Taskbar, but you can hover the mouse over any icon to see a small thumbnail of any open window or program, as shown in Figure 17-7.

FIGURE 17-6   You may want to pin items to the Start menu if you use them frequently.

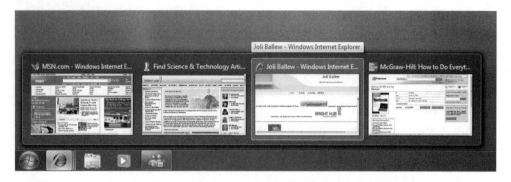

FIGURE 17-7 The Taskbar is improved in Windows 7. You can easily view thumbnails of open windows.

You can still personalize the Taskbar by right-clicking and choosing Properties, and you can still lock or hide the Taskbar easily (see Figure 17-8).

To familiarize yourself with the Taskbar:

1. Open several windows or programs.
2. Hover your mouse over any icon on the Taskbar to view its thumbnail (see Figure 17-9).
3. Click any icon on the Taskbar to bring it to the front of other programs and windows.

FIGURE 17-8 Right-click the Taskbar and choose Properties to make changes to the Taskbar.

If you hover your mouse over an
icon, you can view its thumbnail.

FIGURE 17-9   You can view thumbnails of open windows.

Left-click and "shake" any open window to minimize all of the other windows.
Left-click and shake again to bring the windows back to the desktop. To shake a
window, click its title bar with the mouse, and while holding down the left mouse
button, move the mouse left and right.

4. Click the folder icon to open your personal folder.

Right-click any icon on the Taskbar to open a jump list. Jump lists offer quick and
easy access to things you'll do most.

5. Hover your mouse over the small rectangle at end of the Taskbar. It's the last
   item on the right. This will show the desktop.

Navigate with Windows Explorer

If your experience with computers has been mostly with Windows XP and earlier, you
may not have used Windows Explorer very much. If you've used Windows Vista, you
have a little more experience, but for the most part, it seems Windows Explorer was
something to be avoided. With Windows 7, Windows Explorer has become an integral
part of navigating your computer, and it's important to understand how it's laid out.

Did You Know? Aero Peek

Hovering the mouse over the Show Desktop icon only temporarily shows the
desktop. When you move your mouse away, the windows open on the desktop
reappear.

You'll run into the Explorer window anytime you open your personal folder; that's the folder with your name on it you access from the Start menu. You'll also find it when you click other Start menu items—Documents, Pictures, Music, or Computer. You can access Windows Explorer by right-clicking the Start button too. Figure 17-10 shows Windows Explorer.

As you can see in Figure 7-10, when you hover the mouse over the folders in the left (navigation) pane, arrows appear. You use these arrows to expand or collapse subfolders. Here, Pictures has been expanded to show two subfolders: My Pictures and Public Pictures. My Pictures is selected. In the right pane, the pictures (and their respective subfolders) stored on my netbook are shown.

To familiarize yourself with Windows Explorer:

1. Click Start, and click your personal folder. Your personal folder is the one with your name on it.
2. Click Favorites in the Navigation pane if it isn't already selected. Notice what's shown. You can probably access your desktop, Downloads, My Documents, My Pictures, and more.

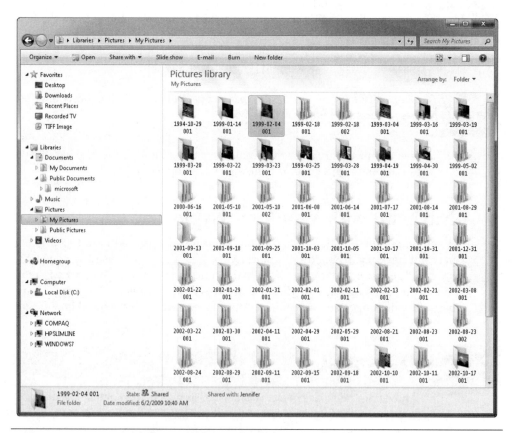

FIGURE 17-10 In Windows Explorer, the left pane allows you to navigate the data on your computer; the right pane is generally used to access it.

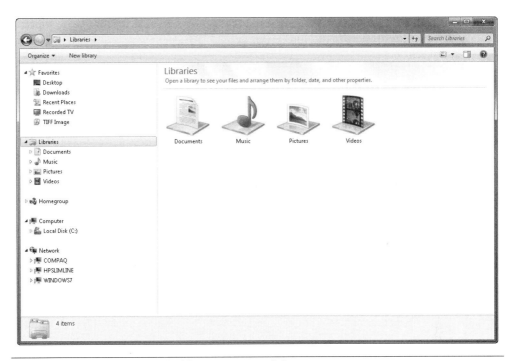

FIGURE 17-11   Libraries hold your personal data.

3. In the Navigation pane, click Libraries. You'll see Documents, Music, Pictures, and Videos, as shown in Figure 17-11. Double-click any folder in the right pane to open the library and see what's stored there.

4. Click Homegroup. If you've set up a homegroup to share data with other computers on your local network that also run Windows 7, you'll see information related to that. If you have not set up a homegroup, you'll see information on how to do that.

 Tip   Click Computer to see the drives and devices connected to your computer. You probably won't see too much there because you're using a netbook.

5. Click Network. If you are connected to a network, you'll see network devices there.

Personalization and Little-Known Features

Windows 7 has lots of tricks up its sleeves. There are new ways to move, minimize, size, and maximize windows; new icons for changing the view of windows; gadgets you can add to your desktop to help you stay abreast of the weather, news, stocks, and other ever-changing data; and plenty of ways to personalize Windows 7 using backgrounds, screen savers, and themes. You can also watch TV if you have a TV tuner, but it's likely you don't have such hardware on a netbook. However, it is possible to watch Internet TV from Media Center or from web sites such as Hulu.com if you get bored.

Move Windows in New Ways

There are lots of features in Windows 7 that you'd never know about if someone didn't tell you about them. For instance, you can drag icons on the Taskbar to put icons in a different order on it. You can "shake" a window to minimize all the other windows on the desktop. And you can drag and drop a window to one side of the desktop to have it automatically resized to half of the screen.

Here's a complete list of things you should try while you have several windows and programs open:

- **Drag a window upward** Click and drag any window to the top of the desktop to have it maximized to take up the entire screen.
- **Drag a maximized window downward** Click and drag any maximized window downward to restore it from its maximized state.
- **Drag a window to the side** Click and drag a window to the left or right side of the screen to resize it to take up exactly half the screen. Drag it away from the side to restore it.
- **Minimize other windows** Click and shake the top of any window to minimize all of the other open windows. Repeat to restore them.
- **Touch the screen** If you have a compatible touch screen monitor, you can touch the monitor to move windows, browse pictures, or perform other tasks.
- **Drag Taskbar icons** Drag any Taskbar icon to move it to another area of the Taskbar.

Change the View of Control Panel

Control Panel is where you make changes to your netbook's features. As with the Control Panel in Windows XP or Windows Vista, you can configure security options, install hardware, uninstall programs, configure user accounts, change the appearance, and more. However, the Windows 7 Control Panel looks quite a bit different from what you're used to, as shown in Figure 17-12.

If you prefer something a little more familiar, or if you work better with lists than with categories, try Small icons or Large icons:

1. Click Start, then click Control Panel.
2. In Control Panel, click Category.
3. Select Small icons or Large icons. Figure 17-13 shows small icons.

Tip Explore each of the Control Panel icons in any view to familiarize yourself with the Control Panel options.

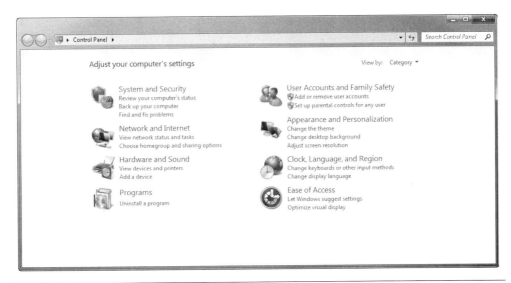

FIGURE 17-12   Control Panel now has a Search window and a new look. This is Category view.

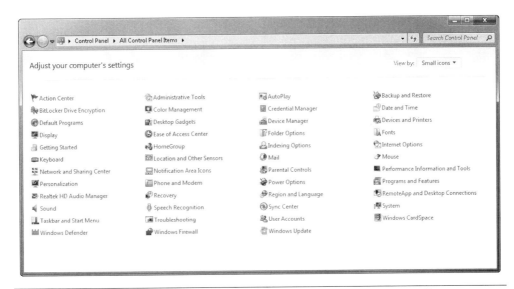

FIGURE 17-13   Choose Small icons (or Large icons) if you prefer a different Control Panel view.

Use Gadgets

Gadgets are single-service applications that sit on your desktop. Their purpose is to offer updated information on things like the weather, news, stocks, or the time. Some gadgets are created by or specific to third parties, such as Google's Facebook Gadget, which allows you to get Facebook notifications right on your desktop, while other gadgets ship with Windows 7 and are used for more generic applications such as having easy access to the weather.

Windows Vista had a Sidebar that held gadgets. Windows 7 offers the Desktop Gadget Gallery, where you can pick and choose what gadgets you'd like to appear on your desktop and place them wherever you like. You can move the gadgets anywhere on the desktop that suits you. You can access the Desktop Gadget Gallery from Start | All Programs. Figure 17-14 shows the Gadget Gallery.

To add and configure a gadget:

1. Click Start, and in the Start Search window, type Gadget.
2. From the results under Programs, click Desktop Gadget Gallery.

 Tip   You can also click Start | All Programs | Desktop Gadget Gallery.

3. Select any gadget and drag it to your desktop. You may want to select several: Feed Headlines, Weather, and Clock.
4. To configure a gadget or to personalize it:
   a. Hover the mouse over the gadget until the wrench appears (see Figure 17-15).
   b. Click the wrench to access the configuration options.
   c. Make the desired changes.
   d. Click OK.

FIGURE 17-14   The Desktop Gadget Gallery lets you drag and drop gadgets to your Desktop.

FIGURE 17-15   Click the wrench icon to open the configuration options. (Click the **X** to remove the gadget from the desktop.)

Change Personalization Options

There are lots of new personalization options for backgrounds, including the option to rotate the pictures you like the best on a schedule you choose. You can also use the pictures you've added to Windows Live Photo Gallery as a screen saver. You can even change the size of the text and other items on your desktop with a single click, among other options.

To access the personalization options, simply right-click an empty area of the desktop and choose Personalize. You can also access the Personalization window from Control Panel. Once in the Personalization window, you can select a theme, change the background, apply a screen saver, and more.

To familiarize yourself with the new Personalization window and apply a new theme or background:

1. Right-click an empty area of the desktop and choose Personalize.

 You can access all of the personalization options from Control Panel.

2. Click any theme under Aero Themes to apply it. Note that you can also choose to get themes online if you don't see anything you like here (see Figure 17-16).
3. Hover your mouse over the Show Desktop area of the Taskbar so you can see the desktop. (Show Desktop is at the very end of the right side of the Taskbar.)

Did You Know?

Themes

A *theme* is a group of settings applied together. Some themes change the background as well as sounds, screen savers, and mouse pointers. The most elaborate themes may also change desktop icons.

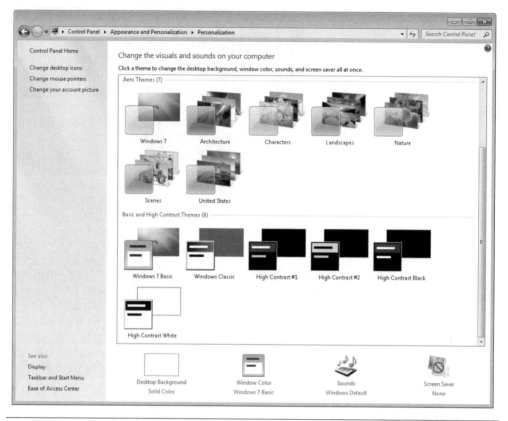

FIGURE 17-16 Browse the available themes and click to select and apply.

4. Repeat steps 2 and 3 as desired.
5. Click Desktop Background.
6. In the Picture Location drop-down list, verify that Windows Desktop Backgrounds is selected (see Figure 17-17).
7. Click Clear all.
8. Hover your mouse over a picture to use as the background and place a checkmark in the resulting square on the picture. If you select only one picture, you will not have the option to rotate, or change, the picture on a schedule.
9. Select as many other pictures as you like. If you select multiple pictures, the option to Change picture every will become available.
10. Choose how often to change the pictures. To show the pictures in random order, check Shuffle.
11. Click Save Changes.

 Picture location options include more than Windows Desktop Backgrounds. You can also choose from Pictures Library (your own pictures), Top Rated Photos, and Solid Colors.

FIGURE 17-17   There are lots of new backgrounds to choose from; you can select as many or as few as you like, and you can rotate them on a schedule.

To create a personalized screen saver:

1. Right-click an empty area of the desktop and click Personalize.
2. Click Screen Saver.
3. From the Screen saver drop-down list, select any screen saver to apply it (see Figure 17-18). Click Settings to personalize it. Not all screen savers have settings options.
4. From the Screen saver drop-down list, select Photos.
5. Click Settings.
6. Click Browse and locate the folder that contains the pictures to use as a screen saver. Click OK.
7. Select a slide show speed (Slow, Medium, or Fast), and click Shuffle pictures if desired.
8. Click Save.

Tip For the best slide show screen saver, create a subfolder in the My Pictures folder, copy or move pictures to it, and then select that folder in step 6.

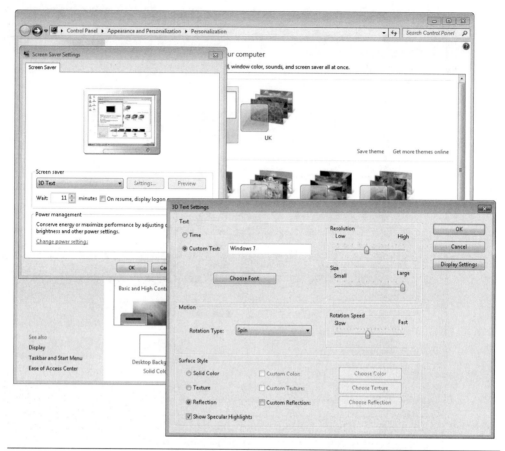

FIGURE 17-18 Some screen savers, such as 3D Text, have settings options.

Watch Internet TV

If you have Windows 7 Home Premium, Professional, or Ultimate installed on your netbook, you'll have access to Media Center, where you can watch Internet TV. Internet TV is an option under Extras. If you don't have one of these Windows editions, or you can't find what you're looking for from the Internet TV option, you can visit a web site such as www.hulu.com and get your TV fix there.

To watch Internet TV from Media Center:

1. Click Start, then click Media Center. You can also find it in the All Programs list.
2. Scroll down the Tasks drop-down list and click Internet TV, as shown in Figure 17-19. It may or may not be "beta," depending on how new or old your netbook is.
3. Click the channel, show, or category to browse, and locate the show or preview you'd like to watch (see Figure 17-20).
4. Click any show to watch it.
5. If you don't find what you want in Media Center, try navigating to www.hulu.com.

FIGURE 17-19   Locate some form of Internet TV. Options will change as the operating system is updated.

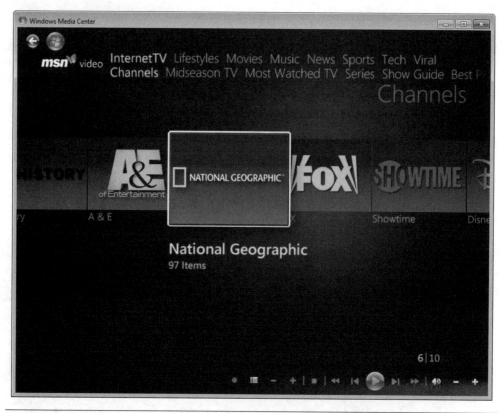

FIGURE 17-20   There are lots of options in Internet TV, but in its current release, many are simply previews.

Internet TV has a long way to go in Media Center before it's a viable option for viewing TV on your netbook. However, there are web sites that offer free programming, such as Hulu.com. From Hulu, you can watch entire episodes of your favorite TV shows from *The Office* to *Family Guy* to *Grey's Anatomy* to *The Tonight Show* (see Figure 17-21).

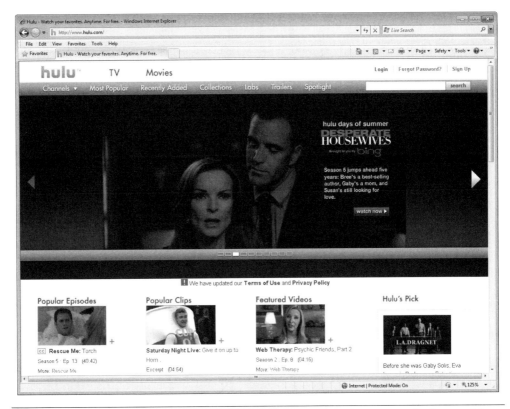

FIGURE 17-21   Hulu.com offers entire TV shows and you're sure to find something you'd like to watch there.

Making Connections

You'll find that making connections with other computers, shared or connected hardware, the Internet, and public and private networks is easier with Windows 7 than any other operating system before it. Device Stage lets you view and manage your connected devices intuitively, and pop-ups from the Taskbar's Notification Area allow you to connect to networks on the fly. When applicable, you can use the Network and Sharing Center to view, manage, and troubleshoot network connections.

View Connected Devices Using Device Stage

You probably won't have too many things connected to your netbook, but on occasion you may connect a full-sized keyboard or mouse, a digital camera, a monitor, or even speakers. You might also connect an external drive for backing up data or a printer, among other things.

Beyond what you connect physically, you may "connect" to hardware via a network. You might have permission to access a shared printer, or connect to a computer that offers shared media. You'll see all of this in Device Stage, a new feature in Windows 7.

To see what's connected to and/or available to you from your netbook and to manage the devices:

1. Click Start.
2. Click Devices and Printers.
3. Right-click any item to view and manage its properties (see Figure 17-22).

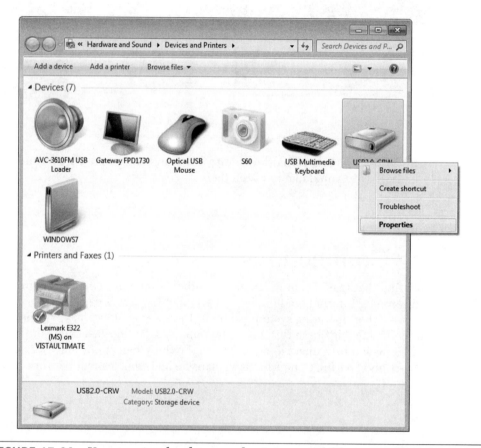

FIGURE 17-22   You can view hardware and printers available to you from your netbook from the Start menu's Devices and Printers option.

Connect to a Wireless Network

If there's a wireless network within range of your netbook, and if your wireless LAN adapter is enabled, you'll be notified. You won't be notified if the wireless functionality is disabled. You can click the pop-up notification to join the network, or if you miss the notification, you can click the network icon in the Taskbar's Notification Area to view available networks and select the one to connect to.

 To increase battery life, disable the wireless LAN feature when you aren't actively seeking out or connecting to wireless networks.

To connect to a wireless network:

1. Turn on your wireless laptop and get within range of a free Wi-Fi hotspot.
2. Make sure the wireless LAN feature is enabled. There may be a button on the side or front of the netbook or a function key to press.
3. Wait a few seconds to see if you are prompted that wireless networks are available.
4. If the pop-up menu lists the wireless network you want to connect to, click it.
5. If you do not see the wireless network you want to connect to, if you miss the pop-up menu, or if you want to view all wireless networks, click the network icon in the Notification Area of the Taskbar (see Figure 17-23).

Network icon

FIGURE 17-23   Click the Network icon to view available wireless networks.

FIGURE 17-24 You will have to type a network key to gain access to a secure network.

6. Click the network to connect to. If the network is a free Wi-Fi hotspot, you may be connected automatically.
7. If prompted, type the network security key (see Figure 17-24).
8. Click the Network icon again if you want to verify that you are connected (see Figure 17-25).

FIGURE 17-25 Clicking the Network icon offers information about your connected network, including the signal strength.

Troubleshooting

Windows 7 offers several troubleshooting tools you've likely never seen before. The Network and Sharing Center offers wizards for troubleshooting network and Internet connections, whereas the Action Center helps you resolve problems involving security and maintenance. There is also a generic Troubleshooting option, where you can get help with problems related to the installing and running of older programs in Windows 7, hardware and sound, networks and the Internet, appearance and personalization, and system and security.

Troubleshoot Network Connections with the Network and Sharing Center

The Network and Sharing Center is a one-stop shop for setting up, managing, and troubleshooting your networks. From here, you can view a network map, view your active networks, set up networks, and even set up a homegroup. There are many ways to open the Network and Sharing Center, but the easiest is to click the Network icon on the Taskbar's Notification Area and select Network and Sharing Center (see Figure 17-26).

 You can type **Network** in the Start Search window to locate and open the Network and Sharing Center.

Because this section is dedicated to troubleshooting, we'll focus on the two ways to troubleshoot network-related problems. The first is to click the X in the network map (the X represents a connectivity problem), and the second is to work through a more complete troubleshooting exercise to locate and resolve problems with network adapters, shared folders, incoming connections, and similar associations.

To resolve problems related to an Internet connection:

1. Open the Network and Sharing Center by clicking the Network icon in the Notification Area of the Taskbar.
2. Click the red X in the network map, shown in Figure 17-27.

FIGURE 17-26 It's easy to open the Network and Sharing Center from the Notification Area.

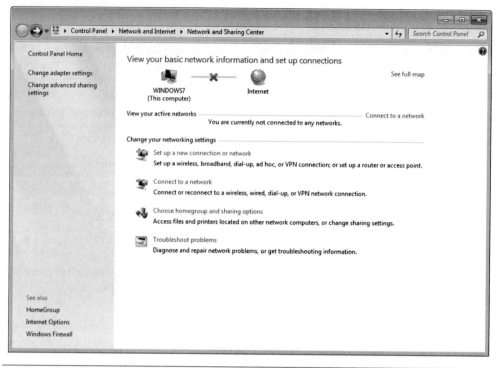

FIGURE 17-27   A red **X** indicates a connectivity problem.

3. Perform the resolutions in order as presented. This may include:
   - Enabling the wireless LAN hardware.
   - Connecting an Ethernet cable.
4. Click Check to see if the problem is fixed.

If the basic troubleshooter does not resolve your problem, or you believe you have a different type of network-related problem (like one related to your network adapter or with accessing shared folders):

1. Open the Network and Sharing Center.
2. Click Troubleshoot problems.
3. Select the option that best describes the problem you're having. In Figure 17-28, Shared Folders is selected.
4. Click Next to begin the troubleshooting wizard, and follow the steps to resolve the problem.

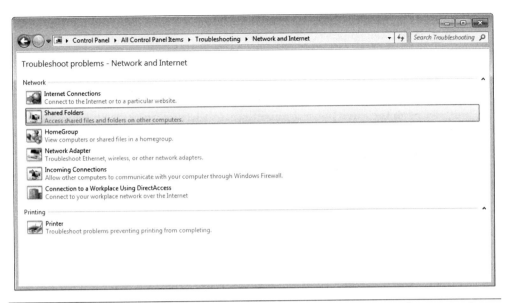

FIGURE 17-28   To troubleshoot more complex network issues, use the Network and Internet troubleshooting wizards.

Resolve Problems with the Action Center

The Action Center is where you'll go to resolve security and maintenance-related problems. The easiest way to open the Action Center is to click the Action Center icon in the Taskbar's Notification Area (see Figure 17-29).

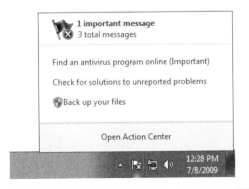

FIGURE 17-29   Access the Action Center from the Notification Area of the Taskbar.

Once you've opened the Action Center, you can resolve any issues that have been discovered. Common problems include:

- **No anti-virus software installed** Windows 7 does not come with anti-virus software; you have to purchase, download, and install it yourself. Click Find a program online if you see this message (see Figure 17-30).
- **Problems have been detected and solutions may exist** Windows 7 watches for and records information about problems you encounter on your netbook. You can see if any of these problems have been resolved by clicking Check for solutions.
- **Failure to create regular backups of your data** Windows 7 keeps track of when you perform backups using the Backup and Restore Center. If there was a problem with your last backup or if you've yet to create a backup, click Run backup now (see Figure 17-30).

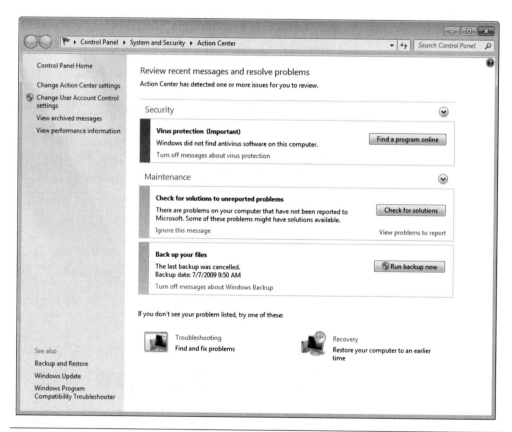

FIGURE 17-30 The Action Center enables you to resolve problems related to security and maintenance.

Find and Fix Other Problems

The Action Center offers wizards to help you resolve other problems you encounter. To select from a variety of troubleshooting options, click Troubleshooting. Figure 17-30 shows a "clean" Action Center and the Troubleshooting option. Clean means that nothing is wrong, nothing needs updating, and everything is the way it's supposed to be.

There are currently five troubleshooting options, all shown in Figure 17-31:

- **Programs**   Choose this option if you are having problems with a particular program, especially an older one. You may be able to run the program in Compatibility Mode, which will allow it to run in its native operating system environment.
- **Hardware and Sound**   Choose this option if you're having problem with a hardware device or the sounds on your netbook. You can troubleshoot audio recording and playback from here too.

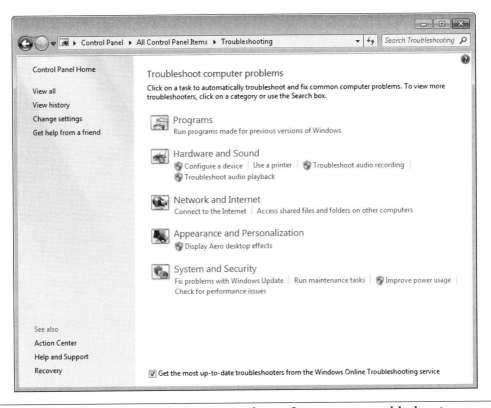

FIGURE 17-31   Click Troubleshooting to choose from various troubleshooting wizards.

- **Network and Internet**   Although you'll likely use the Network and Sharing Center to resolve connectivity problems, you can also access some of those features here.
- **Appearance and Personalization**   Choose this to troubleshoot display properties, including those related to Aero desktop effects.
- **System and Security**   Although you'll likely use the Action Center to resolve problems related to system and security, you can access basic features here, such as fixing problems with Windows Update, running maintenance tasks, improving power usage, and checking for performance issues.

Index

Internet tab for Linux, 15
Internet TV, 282–285
invitations in Office Live Workspace, 193–194
iPhones, 116
italic fonts
    Calc, 242
    Writer, 238
iTunes, 116

J

jump lists, 267, 273
justified text in Writer, 238

K

Kaleidoscope extension, 236
Kensington Wi-Fi Finder Plus, 158
keyboards, 17
    external, 160–161
    shortcuts, 18, 244
Kongregate site, 250–251

L

large icons, 276–277
Launch Manager, 134
Learn tab for Linux, 16
Learn to Fly game, 250–251
libgphoto2 application, 109
libraries in Windows 7, 275
Licensing Agreement page, 95
Linux
    automatic public network connections, 55
    digital cameras with, 109
    Firefox browser with, 190
    Open Office for, 232–234
    overview, 15–16
    password-protected screen savers, 29
    shared data on, 77–78
    web cams, 135–136
    wireless network connections, 51
lists
    jump, 267, 273
    Office Live Workspace, 195–196
    wireless networks, 55–57
Lite version for Box.net, 261
Live Hotmail, 166
Live Workspace. *See* Office Live Workspace
Local Area Connection Properties dialog box, 65
local area networks, 67–68

M

MacBook Air, 16
mail. *See* e-mail
Mail icon, 182
malware, 121

Manage Add-ons window, 91–92
Map the addresses on this page icon, 183
maps
    Google Earth, 229–230
    Google Maps, 227–229
Maps application, 227
media card readers
    for backups, 114
    locating and using, 7
Media Center, 282–285
memory
    vs. hard drives, 155–156
    for ReadyBoost, 154–155
memory cards
    inserting and reading from, 106–108
    media card readers, 7
Menu bar in Calc, 243
messages
    instant. *See* instant messages
    SMS, 221
    video. *See* video messaging programs
    Windows Live Messenger, 171–174
messaging IDs, 142–144
microphones, 6
Microsoft ActiveX controls, 204
Microsoft Scanner and Wizard, 109
mini-printers, 110
minimizing windows, 276
Mobile App application, 227
mobile printers, 161–162
modems, 79
mouse, 160–161
Movie Maker, 187–188
moving windows, 275
MSN icon, 183
Multiplayer game category, 250
Music option, 13–14
My Computer option, 9, 11
My Documents option, 11
My Network Connections window, 63
My Network Places, 11, 63
My Pictures folder, 274
My Pictures option, 11

N

names, display, 178
Network and Internet Connections option, 48, 70
Network and Internet troubleshooting option, 294
Network and Sharing Center
    crossover cables, 74–75
    network connections, 60–61, 63, 285
    private networks, 57–58
    Start menu, 13
    troubleshooting with, 289–291
    Windows Vista, 72, 127
    wireless networks, 55